ALSO BY KATHRYN SHEVELOW

Charlotte

FOR THE LOVE OF ANIMALS

FOR THE LOVE
OF ANIMALS

*The Rise of the Animal
Protection Movement*

Kathryn Shevelow

HENRY HOLT AND COMPANY

NEW YORK

Henry Holt and Company, LLC
Publishers since 1866
175 Fifth Avenue
New York, New York 10010
www.henryholt.com

Henry Holt ® and *® are registered trademarks of Henry Holt and Company, LLC.*

Copyright © 2008 by Kathryn Shevelow
All rights reserved.

Distributed in Canada by H. B. Fenn and Company Ltd.

Library of Congress Cataloging-in-Publication Data

Shevelow, Kathryn, [date]
  For the love of animals: the rise of the animal protection movement / Kathryn Shevelow.—1st ed.
    p. cm.
  Includes bibliographical references and index.
  ISBN-13: 978-0-8050-8090-2
  ISBN-10: 0-8050-8090-2
  1. Animal welfare—Great Britain—History—18th century.   I. Title.
  HV4805.A3S54   2008
  179'.30941—DC22   2007047353

Henry Holt books are available for special promotions and premiums.
For details contact: Director, Special Markets.

First Edition 2008

Designed by Fritz Metsch
Printed in the United States of America
1   3   5   7   9   10   8   6   4   2

For my parents,

JANE AND GEORGE SHEVELOW,

who taught us to love animals

CONTENTS

FOR THE LOVE OF ANIMALS

INTRODUCTION:
SAVED

✳   ✳   ✳

A GRAY TABBY cat with gorgeous green eyes and fuzzy white paws like bedroom slippers sits purring on my lap as I write: a loving creature with a big personality, he likes to watch the cursor scurry around the computer screen. His name is Graham, and my husband and I met him seven years ago at our local humane society shelter here in California, where he had arrived as a kitten, malnourished and sick, his beautiful coat filthy and matted. The police, responding to neighbors' complaints, had investigated a foul-smelling house where they found more than seventy emaciated, flea-ridden cats. Graham's rescuers administered food and antibiotics, cleaned him up, gave him his improbable name (for a cat)—a name that we could not change, for it suits him perfectly—and put him in the kitten adoption room, where he claimed the attention of everyone who entered. We were lucky to arrive shortly thereafter, and he went home with us that day: he was irresistible then, and he remains irresistible now.

Graham shares our home with two other cats. Our calico, Chloe, whom we adopted from the same shelter eighteen years ago, is the undisputed matriarch of us all. She still loves to drape herself over my shoulders and ride regally around the house. Young Maxine, whose lynx-point coloring and stocky, bowlegged body give her the appearance of a Siamese cat crossed with a bulldog, had been found on the street as a sickly stray kitten and taken to our veterinarian. Now sleek and healthy, she requests our attention by tapping us gently with her paw, gazing up at us with her endearingly crossed blue eyes.

My stepdaughter in Washington, D.C., adopted Elsa, a loving brindle pit bull mix, from a local shelter: Elsa had been removed from a backyard littered with feces and broken glass, where she had been tied up, starved, and exposed to the weather; she was restored to health, put up for adoption, and now enjoys watching television on the living room couch. My sister in Ohio has a sweet Labrador retriever, Molly, who was discovered twelve years ago when she was an abandoned puppy, wandering the streets of her town. The animal control officer, a friend, picked her up, took her to a vet, and then called my sister: now Molly enthusiastically dives into the family pool after tennis balls. Another sister and her husband, who live on an Ohio farm, foster horses that the humane society has rescued from their abusive owners. Their current resident, a Thoroughbred named Hank, came to them a living skeleton; only the photograph taken at the time of his arrival makes it possible to connect that frail beast with the chestnut beauty frisking in their pasture today.

Most of us take these kinds of stories for granted. Many of us know someone who has adopted a rescued animal, and quite a few of us have done so ourselves. Sadly, the other side of this coin is that animals so commonly need to be rescued. Whether by running a dogfighting ring or a disease-ridden puppy mill, by leaving horses to starve in a grassless paddock, or by obsessively hoarding and neglecting cats, humans are capable of extraordinary cruelty to the nonhuman animals over whom they have power. Often the stories are simply heartbreaking—sometimes owners are too sick, elderly, or poor to care for their pets, as was probably the case in Graham's original home. Other stories supply horrifying examples of negligence and cruelty. There is nothing new in this.

What *is* new, however—quite new, historically speaking—is that we have laws designed to protect animals from mistreatment. We hold their abusers accountable. Rescues like those that saved Graham, Elsa, and Hank are often the result of investigations conducted by authorities—police, animal control officers, and humane law enforcement agents—who upon receiving reports of suspected animal abuse are empowered to enter private premises, confiscate animals if their condition warrants it, and often make arrests. Abusers may find themselves in court, and if convicted they face penalties ranging from a fine and probation to prison.

It is all too true that our current animal cruelty laws are woefully inadequate, covering too few animals and permitting too many exemptions, inconsistent enforcement, and slap-on-the-wrist punishments. Political progress on animal welfare issues is slow and uneven. Pets may now have protection from abuse, but, like all other beasts, they are still viewed as property. Large categories of animals—most importantly, those in our politically powerful industrial agriculture system—are exempt from most anticruelty laws. Nonetheless, there *is* progress: animal protection laws *do* exist and, however slowly, they are increasing in number and strength.

Furthermore, animal protection and animal advocacy have acknowledged places within our society. The television channel Animal Planet airs several animal protection programs whose online fan sites register thousands of hits every month. Newspapers and television news programs routinely carry exposés about animal abuse. The U.S. government gives official sanction to animal advocacy groups that work against individual and corporate cruelty, and that, through local offices, engage in animal rescue, such as the ASPCA, the Humane Society of the United States (HSUS), People for the Ethical Treatment of Animals (PETA), Farm Sanctuary, the Fund for Animals, and many, many more. Whatever their ideological and practical differences, these organizations are registered charities; our donations to them are tax-deductible. In many cases, particularly as regards our factory food system, such groups have been far more responsible for advances in alleviating animal suffering than our legislatures have been.

Behind our existing animal welfare laws stands another historically new development: a social consensus that the abuse of animals is wrong. Granted, what constitutes "abuse" is still very much debated in our society, even among animal welfare advocates, and many people feel much more affection and compassion for some animals, such as cats, dogs, and horses, than they do for others, such as cows, pigs, and chickens. (Sympathy grows even scarcer when we leave the realm of mammals and birds altogether and begin to consider reptiles and insects.) Many of us might be animal lovers, but that does not necessarily mean we will support animal protection for all animals equally, embrace the concept of animal rights, or avoid eating feedlot-produced beef. The recent prosecution of the highly lucrative dogfighting ring associated with the NFL star Michael Vick and the exposure of the subculture that profits from it have provoked a defensive backlash invoking class, race, and the nature of dogs that is strikingly similar to arguments against animal protection made two centuries ago.

Despite these inconsistencies, however, most of us would probably agree with the general proposition that animals are sentient fellow creatures that deserve protection from cruel treatment (however variously we define that term and however far we believe animals' claims upon us extend). Many of us also believe that the law is a fitting instrument for securing that protection, and want to see the laws extended. Whether we consider animals as pets, as food, or as subjects in scientific experiments, many of us would shrink from arguing that humans have the right to treat all other creatures however we wish, that their fate at our hands is not worth considering, or that our legislatures have no business passing laws to protect at least some of them.

But people did not always see it this way. Quite the contrary: not so long ago, the very concept of animal protection would have seemed preposterous—or simply been unimaginable—to most people. There have always been humans who felt a particular bond with, and compassion for, nonhuman animals. But widespread public concern for the well-being of animals is a historically recent phenomenon, and laws designed to protect them from cruelty came about only after a long, slow process of reform, which is far from over. The world's first national animal protection law did not appear until 1822. Why then? How did it come about? What had begun to change in society's thinking and feeling about animals that made a national legislature, for the first time in history, take this step to protect some "dumb brutes" from some of the suffering humans had for so long inflicted upon them?

The answer to these questions takes us to England—just as it would if we were to search for the origins of other reforms, such as the abolition of slavery and the improvement of conditions in mental hospitals and prisons. For animal welfare was inextricably tied to other humanitarian causes: it was part of a larger wave of reform that swept England in the later eighteenth century and began slowly to achieve results over the subsequent decades. But the seeds of animal protection had begun to germinate much earlier, and had especially begun to grow during the previous one hundred and fifty years, when Britons, both at home and in their American colonies, began, slowly but in increasing numbers, to think differently than they had before both about the nature of animals, and about humans' relationship to, and responsibility for, them.

The abuse of animals had been so common and so widespread that England had gained a reputation as the world's cruelest country, yet it was that country whose parliament passed the first national animal protection law in history. How this came to happen is the story of this book: how concern for animals, once a matter of the individual feelings of a small number of people, came to touch a public and then a political nerve. How citizens began the process of giving animals a status that the laws of our country, incomplete though they still are, have built upon. And how a social and political movement dedicated to protecting animals became possible—a movement that would one day ensure that a gray tabby kitten did not die of hunger and disease, but instead was saved to grow up into the beloved cat named Graham who sits on my lap, purring.

AT THE POINT when animal protection sentiments began to coalesce into something resembling a political movement, there were more sheep in England than people. The country's economy was still predominantly agricultural, with a great many animals, domestic and wild, living in rural villages and the countryside. But for some time, the human population had been moving from the country to the larger cities, particularly to London. During the previous century and a half, that city's population had swelled, and by 1800, more than a million people lived there. London was the world's largest city, the muscular capital of a wealthy country that was rapidly industrializing at home and extending its imperial sway to the far reaches of the globe.

Because London was the seat of national government, it was there that the cause of animal protection was centered: it was primarily the situation of urban beasts that caught the attention of the first reformers. The city was filled with animals, and in conjunction with the human society to which they were intimately connected, animal society had its hierarchies, its specialization of trades, its elites, its downtrodden. Walking along the pedestrian paths that ran along the sides of the city's busy thoroughfares, one encountered many extremes of animal life. Teams of four well-fed and matching horses trotted smartly by, drawing carriages in which wealthy women bedecked in furs and feathers cradled pampered lapdogs. They shared the street with emaciated donkeys panting as they staggered under impossible loads, and exhausted cows stumbling the last few miles of their long journey to market. Pigs roamed the town, rooting through garbage dumps and eating household waste, and milkmaids made their rounds with their cows and she-asses, whom they milked on the spot. In certain neighborhoods, a banging drum and the shouting of boisterous children would alert pedestrians that a bear or bull was being paraded along the street en route to the bear garden.

An aristocratic house might display a beautiful gilt-framed painting of a horse by George Stubbs, while a spaniel in a jeweled collar proudly posed in the lower foreground of a family portrait. Mastiffs lounged in the hall, while outside the town houses, half-starved mongrels fought over scraps of offal, and urchins stoned cats to death for fun. The fashionable set rattled off to Newmarket for the horse races, whose contestants and their aristocratic owners were listed in the London newspapers. Visiting a country estate in the fall, one would hear the gunfire of shooting parties intent upon bringing down grouse, or the cries of the hounds and hunters as they galloped after foxes and hares.

Pets were joining households in unprecedented numbers. Despite the abundance of working animals, as more and more people of all ranks moved from the country into the city, pets became for many of them the most immediate, and often the only, source of regular personal contact with beasts. Then as now, the attachment to companion animals ran deep. Middle-class girls wrote sentimental poems mourning the demise of finches and squirrels; the novelist and clergyman Laurence Sterne tugged the heartstrings of many readers when he wrote of the caged starling that lamented, "I can't get out." Women poets used the idea of the transmigration of souls, borrowed from both the ancient Greeks and the Hindus, to imagine their cats' afterlives in verse; grown men wept when a favorite dog died. Street vendors were trailed by their faithful mongrels, while the proprietors of stalls at Covent Garden market cried, "Buy a fine singing bird!" (Shedding a tear for Sterne's starling did not necessarily preclude keeping one's own caged bird.) Wealthier animal lovers added to their English-born menageries creatures such as macaws and monkeys, tigers and giraffes, for Britain's imperial reach, which brought home silks, brightly colored feathers, and rare skins for the milliners and haberdashers the rich patronized, also created a flourishing trade in live exotic beasts.

Animals featured prominently in the theater, fairs, and street entertainments: horses provided verisimilitude at the opera, performing dogs gave the audience some relief after a few acts of bowdlerized Shakespeare, and white doves were released inside the playhouse to conclude a spectacle. The Giant Hog was a perennial favorite at Bartholomew Fair, while the Learned Pig and his many sagacious barnyard brethren astonished crowds with their ability to solve mathematical problems and read minds.

Cockfighting, dogfighting, and the baiting of bulls, bears, badgers, monkeys, cats, and ducks (and any other animal that could be tied to a stake and attacked by dogs) attracted fervid spectators from across the social spectrum, often women as well as men. Although these sports increasingly came to be seen as disreputable, there were many cockpits and animal-baiting arenas throughout London. Bloody spectacles may have been popular in squalid neighborhoods such as Hockley in the Hole or raffish boroughs such as Southwark, but they were by no means restricted to such places. Cockfighting was a sport of aristocrats: there was a famous cockpit near the Inns of Court and another in Westminster, the seat of Parliament and the Crown. Throwing clubs at tethered roosters was a favorite Shrovetide pastime in much of the country, and entire towns celebrated the annual baiting of a bull.

Most working animals, of course, labored in occupations other than entertainment and sport. Some carters took good care of their horses, but many others, whether from poverty, drunkenness, or simply ignorance and indifference (the latter three traits by no means unknown to their social superiors), did not. It was extremely common to see horses, ribs visible through ragged coats and sores festering under their harnesses, straining to pull overloaded wagons through mired roads as their masters beat them on the head with cudgels.

Visiting in the middle of the sixteenth century, the Mantuan diplomat Annibale Litolfi quipped that England was a paradise for women, a purgatory for servants, and a hell for horses. However debatable with respect to women, his comment about horses was often repeated in following centuries, for it rang all too true. Carriage horses, hunters, and racehorses who could no longer serve their wealthy masters were typically sold to pull hackney coaches and wagons, and when they grew old or sick, their new owners often found it economical to cut back their feed and drive them until they dropped, after which they could be sold to the knackers, where horses awaiting slaughter were not fed, and often died of starvation before they could be killed. The violence perpetrated against cows, pigs, and sheep at Smithfield and the other slaughterhouses made even callous Londoners blanch. At outbreaks of disease such as rabies—a fearsome contagion and poorly understood— the common official response was to order that all dogs and cats on the street be hunted down and killed.

Donna Haraway quite rightly observes in her *Companion Animal Manifesto* that humans' relationship with animals cannot be reduced to issues of compassion and protection. Today, that relationship seems to become more extensive and complex every moment as we learn more about the nature of animals' capacities, further discredit the label of "anthropomorphism" that has too long blocked our recognition of animals' consciousness and feelings, and think more seriously about the ways in which human and animal life are intertwined. But in earlier times, to posit that we have the moral obligation not just to treat animals kindly but also to pass laws that institutionalize protection for animals, and to assert that animals might even have a *right* to that protection, was as significant an advance as it is now to consider, for instance, that our hunting of elephants and caging of chimpanzees have inflicted upon them dysfunctional mental states that, in humans, we would readily call depression, trauma, and even psychosis. To many people not so long ago, the idea that animals are even capable of suffering was an absurdity—and an irrelevance.

THERE HAD ALWAYS been individual Britons who deplored cruelty and indifference to animals, but it was not until the later eighteenth century that enough voices were raised on animals' behalf to prompt parliamentary attempts to protect them, and not until the early nineteenth century that animal protectors won their first victory. Amid a storm of public agitation, vicious name-calling, and heated debates in the legislature, in the newspapers and in the streets, the British Parliament passed the Ill-Treatment of Cattle Act in 1822. (The term "cattle" covered most large working animals, including horses and donkeys.) In the words of Richard Ryder, a present-day animal rights campaigner, the Ill-Treatment of Cattle Act was "the first national law anywhere in the world, passed by a democratically elected legislature which dealt specifically and entirely with cruelty to animals." Prior to this moment, laws that governed the treatment of animals viewed them as property. Injuring another's beast was a crime against the animal's owner, not against the animal; injuring one's own beast was not a crime at all. The Ill-Treatment of Cattle Act was the first national law to give animals some degree of protection for their own sakes.

Richard Martin, member of Parliament for Galway, Ireland, wrote the bill—known popularly as Mr. Martin's Act—and drove it through Parliament. One of Martin's supporters, referring to the Irishman's direct, emphatic political style, compared him to a bullet, an apt metaphor in more ways than one. Stocky and compact, Martin in a surviving portrait looks rather like a bullet (albeit a modern one, the musket balls of his own day being round). He had an intimate acquaintance with actual ammunition, too, for he was a notorious duelist and bore scars on his body from past gunfights, including one to avenge the killing of a dog. To his political and personal enemies, he was an eccentric, unpredictable, even buffoonish troublemaker. To his friends and admirers, however, he was "Humanity Dick."

Two years after the passing of Martin's Act, a clergyman named Arthur Broome called a meeting whose agenda was to discuss the continuing struggle to protect animals from cruelty. More than twenty men responded to his summons, including Richard Martin. A young journalist named Samuel Carter Hall covered the meeting, and later recalled that memorable day. The group was small, but what it lacked in size, it made up in enthusiasm, thanks to Martin's "Irish heartiness." Although he was seventy years old, Martin radiated a "warmth, fervour and energy" that pulsed through the room, inspiring and rallying the others. The Irishman's every movement projected "indomitable resolution," Hall remembered. When the other men expressed pessimism about Parliament's willingness do anything more to protect animals, Martin burst out, in his strong Irish brogue: "By Jaysus, I'll *make* 'em do it!"

Another prominent man at the meeting was William Wilberforce, the Evangelical Christian MP from Yorkshire who had courageously led the long parliamentary fight to outlaw England's slave trade. Wilberforce was loved and admired by many people for his great charm and his sweet, eloquent voice, raised so frequently and persistently in the service of reformist causes; and he was hated and despised by others who saw him and his fellow "Saints" as joyless, hypocritical apologists for forces of intolerance and repression. Like other Evangelical MPs, Wilberforce had strongly supported animal protection legislation from its introduction in 1800, and lent his considerable moral authority to the continuing battle.

More legislators and Anglican clergymen were at the meeting as well, but those present also included a doctor, a newspaper editor, a poetically inclined barrister, and a Jewish businessman and inventor. Their first priorities, they determined, should be to ensure that Martin's Act was enforced, to educate the public about animal welfare, to investigate the condition of animals in the markets, streets, and slaughterhouses, and to pass stronger laws that would extend greater protection to more kinds of beasts. To do this, they agreed to found an organization: they would call themselves the Society for the Prevention of Cruelty to Animals.

The first several years of the SPCA's existence would prove difficult, as the organization struggled with disagreement and debt; Arthur Broome, the society's first secretary, would end up bankrupting himself supporting the group and be thrown into prison. Despite Martin's incessant efforts, years of heartbreaking failure, contempt, ridicule, and obstruction on many fronts came before the SPCA achieved other parliamentary victories for animal protection. But the group persevered. In 1840, Britain's young queen, Victoria, took the organization under the sponsorship of the Crown, making it the *Royal* Society for the Prevention of Cruelty to Animals—the RSPCA. Twenty-seven years later, on April 10, 1866, the legislature of the state of New York chartered the first American Society for the Prevention of Cruelty to Animals. Other cities, states, and countries followed suit.

THE PASSAGE OF Martin's Act and the founding of the SPCA were early, halting steps, but they blazed a trail that would subsequently be trod and widened by people around the world. These hard-fought early milestones, Richard Martin optimistically proclaimed, represented a new era in legislation, a new era in the treatment of animals. But the official events that inaugurated this new era in the 1820s would not have occurred in the first place if their foundation had not already been laid.

This is the story of the laying of that foundation, of the changes and events that made possible these early milestones in the history of humans' relationship to animals. It is the story of how we came to *care* for animals, both in the sense of assuming responsibility for their well-being and in the sense of feeling a bond with them. This story is complex and multifaceted, for the course of animal protection was never a direct, unimpeded march of progress from some prior historical moment to the years 1822 and 1824 (nor has it been that since). The cause has always proceeded by fits and starts, progressing and regressing. Nor can it be captured in the biography of a single person, although the last part of this book does have a particular champion in Humanity Dick Martin. But he did not act alone. The early history of animal protection actually involved a great many people, most of them unknown to one another, who from different motives, in different ways, and at different times contributed to the cause over a period of many decades.

In order to explain why people would feel moved and outraged enough to take up the fraught, frustrating cause of animal protection, I have had to write, at times explicitly, of the abusive acts commonly perpetrated against animals in their day. The sections that deal directly with the issue of cruelty, specifically chapters two and seven, were sometimes difficult to write and may not be easy to read, either, though I have tried to be as unsensational as I can. These chapters can be skipped, but the anecdotes and information they contain are a fundamental part of this history. Just as the Humane Society of the United States, PETA, and the ASPCA must post painful instances of abuse on their Web sites, so, too, must I give my readers an idea of what animals experienced in eighteenth- and nineteenth-century Britain, and what the vast majority of the human population took for granted. Only by knowing this context can we fully appreciate the courage and tenacity of the early animal protection campaigners, who persevered, in the face of overwhelming hostility and ridicule, in their efforts to change practices so long entrenched.

Many of the men and women who supported animal protection were, like Martin himself, involved in other humanitarian struggles of great significance: to extend legal rights and the vote to Roman Catholics; to improve the terrible conditions in prisons and mental asylums; to restrict the death penalty; to provide relief and legal representation to the poor; to ease England's deadly colonial grip on Ireland; and to end Britain's involvement in the horrors of slavery and the slave trade, to name just a few. Certainly, many reformers had mixed motives, and inevitably they spoke from the prejudices of their class and nation. Some were really more concerned with disciplining the lower classes than with protecting animals. (This concern was evident in many other reform movements as well.) A very few may have been less moved by human suffering than by that of animals. But in most cases, this was an unjust caricature spread by their opponents; rather, many animal protection advocates believed that human and animal causes were interconnected battles against oppression.

The animal protection reformers insisted that just as no society that claimed to be civilized could excuse the enslavement of other humans, neither could any civilized nation continue to countenance the appalling cruelty toward beasts that had too long been associated with the English people. No physical difference, whether that between white skin and black skin or that between bare skin and fur, could justify tyranny. It does not matter, wrote the Reverend Humphrey Primatt,

> whether we walk upon two legs or four; whether we are naked or covered with hair; whether we have tails or no tails, horns or no horns, long ears or round ears; or, whether we bray like an ass, speak like a man, whistle like a bird, or are mute as a fish; Nature never intended these distinctions as foundations for right of tyranny and oppression.

When given voice by the abolitionists, the slave addressed the British people, asking them poignantly: "Am I not a man and a brother?" Horses, cows, dogs, and cats could not speak comparable

words. But there were those who believed that animals, too, were kindred spirits, who were beloved by God and whose suffering was equally
intolerable. And so they spoke for the creatures who could not speak
for themselves, asking: Are not dumb beasts, man's *animal* slaves, worthy of compassion too?

PART ONE

Dumb Brutes

CHAPTER I

OF DUCHESSES AND DUCKS

⁂ ⁂ ⁂

O NE AFTERNOON in late May 1667, an oversized black coach with ducal arms emblazoned on its doors lumbered through the London streets, a multitude of tassels bobbing festively from its horses' harnesses. As it rolled into the mud- and manure-clogged thoroughfare of the Strand, the coach was mobbed by excited crowds straining to catch a glimpse of its passenger. Margaret Cavendish, duchess of Newcastle, always attracted a crowd when, on her rare trips to London, she sallied forth from the family's grand Clerkenwell town house. Though she had arrived at the relatively advanced age of forty-four, the duchess was still a handsome woman. But it was her eccentricity as a controversial writer, her flamboyant dress, and her wholesale flouting of feminine niceties that made her a public sensation—along with her exalted rank, which allowed her to get away with this behavior in the first place.

Earlier that spring, Samuel Pepys, the notable diarist (and equally notable philanderer), had tried very hard to get a look at Cavendish, who fascinated him. "All the town-talk is now-a-days of her extravagancies," he confided to his diary. "The whole story of this lady is a romance, and all she does is romantic." Once he and his friend Sir William Penn heard that she would be taking the air in St. James's Park and rushed there to see her, only to get caught in a horse-and-carriage traffic jam, all "horrid dust, and number of coaches, without pleasure or order." Half of London, it seemed, had come to see the duchess, as a result of which, Pepys reported sourly, "we could not, she being followed and crowded upon by coaches all the way she went, that nobody could come near her." On another day, he caught a glimpse of her coach ahead of him and tried to overtake it, but his way was blocked by "100 boys and girls running looking upon her."

Margaret Cavendish had earned this degree of fame—of notoriety—because, almost astonishingly for a seventeenth-century woman, she was a prolific published writer who over the span of many years issued a torrent of contentious, brilliant, and singular books. Her literary output consisted not only of poems and fiction but also of discourses on a variety of topics in the masculine realms of "natural philosophy"—what we today call science—and philosophy. And she had much to say about the arrogance and downright stupidity of the beliefs most people in her day held about animals.

Cavendish lived in a world where the majority assumed that animals existed only to serve human needs; concern for animal suffering or animal welfare seldom arose, either in the bear gardens and cockpits, in the rural fields and forests, or in the city streets and slaughterhouses. In her writing, the duchess confronted these attitudes directly, arguing in defense of the sensibility and intellect of beasts. Nonhuman creatures might not be able to speak or devise mathematical rules, she wrote, "yet may their perceptions and observations be as wise as men's, and they may have as much intelligence and commerce betwixt each other, after their own manner and way, as men have after theirs." As the historian Keith Thomas observes, "in the seventeenth century, no one had greater faith in animal capacity than Margaret Cavendish."

Cavendish published her unconventional opinions in an age before widespread literacy, when only a minority of women, primarily within the upper classes, were able to read and write at all, and very few were given anything resembling a formal education. (This was also true of men, though a higher percentage of men were literate, and a much higher percentage were actually educated.) Those women who did write produced mostly letters; if they wrote poems and devotions, they usually shared these only with a small circle of family and friends. Very few women dared—or even wished—to see their writing in print, since publication was deemed both indelicate for a woman and vulgar for an aristocrat.

Unsurprisingly, then, for all the public's fascination with her, many of Cavendish's contemporaries considered the duchess arrogant and exhibitionistic. Some even called her mad, including other women who saw her as a disgrace to their sex. (As her biographer Katie Whitaker has shown, however, the disparaging nickname by which she is still sometimes known, Mad Madge, was actually not bestowed upon her until the nineteenth century.) After accompanying her husband to Newcastle House, Mary Evelyn, the wife of Samuel Pepys's friend John Evelyn, another well-known diarist of the period, acknowledged that their hostess had a good figure; however, she sneered, the duchess was vainer about her face than she had any right to be, and her talk was "as airy, empty, whimsical, and rambling as her books, aiming at science, difficulties, high notions, terminating commonly in nonsense, oaths, and obscenity." Mary expressed astonishment that there were supposedly wise and learned men (including, apparently, her own husband) who actually admired this monstrous female; "yet I hope," she remarked acidly, referring to Margaret's childlessness, "as she is an original, she may never have a copy."

Cavendish's writing was as wildly original as everything else about her: her extraordinary narrative *The Blazing World,* in which she imagined another world inhabited by Bear-men, Fox-men, Wild-goose-men, Ant-men, Spider-men, and other types of wise and peaceable beast-people, is among the earliest science fiction. In her books on philosophy and science, she dared to engage and attack the work of some of England's, and Europe's, leading intellectuals, all of them male. Cavendish flouted both old orthodoxies and the new, emerging systems of knowledge that were to transform Europe. She was a fierce critic of many of the practices and principles of the "new science" that was developing in her day, finding much about it to be arrogant, including its introduction of what we now call the scientific method, with its emphasis upon experimentation rather than abstract theorizing, and its reliance upon newfangled instruments such as the microscope.

Bracing herself against the intellectual waves of the future, the duchess of Newcastle was not so much conservative as utterly idiosyncratic; her writings would quickly fade into obscurity. But despite her flamboyance, hers was a loud, often brilliant voice, and in some senses also a humble one, particularly when she addressed the topic of animals. Since other creatures do not display intelligence "the same manner or way as man," she observed, "man denies they can do it at all." But just because beasts cannot speak, "should we conclude they have neither knowledge, sense, reason, or intelligence?" This, she scoffed, is "a very weak argument." Despite Cavendish's resistance to modernity, her views of the natural world, which were considered extreme by her contemporaries, can seem to us today both sympathetic and perceptive.

ON THAT PARTICULAR May afternoon in 1667, Cavendish was crossing London not to take the air in St. James's Park or to pay a social call on another aristocratic lady, but to make history of a sort. She was on her way to a meeting of the Royal Society, the organization that more than any other institution in Britain was the representative of the new science. The Royal Society had been founded in 1660 for the purpose of promoting discussion and experimentation in natural philosophy. Cavendish was the first woman permitted to attend a meeting. (No woman was allowed to deliver her own paper until 1904, and women members were not admitted until 1945.) The gentlemen and peers who made up the Royal Society had granted Cavendish's request to visit after much debate and with considerable trepidation. Some fellows objected that the society, already the target of criticism and satire, would suffer more ridicule for opening its doors to a woman, and especially to this one. They feared that, as Pepys said, "the town will be full of ballads of it," making fun of both the duchess and her hosts. Cavendish had some powerful aristocratic friends within the society, however, and they convinced the majority to grant her wish.

Her coach rumbled to a stop in the courtyard of Arundel House, in the Strand. The society had been meeting at the great estate of the earls of Arundel, on the bank of the Thames, since its previous quarters had burned in the Great Fire, which had consumed nearly all of old London the year before. The place was unusually crowded, for Royal Society fellows were not immune to the lure of notoriety and spectacle. Mary Evelyn's husband, John, was there, as was Samuel Pepys, eager to get his long-awaited view of the duchess. Cavendish did not disappoint her spectators as she descended from her coach. Escorted by a group of noblemen, John Evelyn reported, she made her stately progress into the house with "great pomp."

Pomp, indeed. For her visit, the duchess had chosen a gown with an eight-foot train, carried by six female attendants. Cavendish topped her gown with a "justaucorps," a knee-length coat tightly fitted through the torso with skirts that flared stiffly from the waist. In 1667, the justaucorps, or "pirate jacket," was on the cutting edge of fashion—men's fashion. On this occasion the duchess seems to have matched her man's coat, as she often did, with a cavalier's wide-brimmed hat. Quasi-masculine dress was modish at this time among royalist women, but Cavendish, who designed her own clothes, put her own ostentatious spin on the prevailing style. "I endeavour," she remarked in one of the great understatements of fashion history, "to be as singular as I can." John Evelyn, who considered the duchess to be akin to the warrior queen Zenobia, memorialized her Royal Society visit in a ballad (just as Pepys had predicted). She looked "so like a Cavelier," he wrote, "but that she had no beard."

Beards were otherwise much in evidence that day in the primarily male crowd. But to the great disappointment of Pepys, who seems to have expected some kind of scene, Margaret seemed uncharacteristically muted in these surroundings and said little. This extravagant aristocrat, so bold in writing, was actually shy and awkward in company. She was possibly all the more intimidated by the presence of the society's most celebrated fellows, Robert Boyle and Robert Hooke, both of whom she had attacked in print. Pepys, that incorrigible scrutinizer of the fair sex, found the duchess to be "a good, comely woman; but her dress so antick, and her deportment so ordinary, that I do not like her at all, nor did I hear her say any thing that was worth hearing, but that she was full of admiration, all admiration." The fellows treated their admiring guest to a display of the kind of scientific experiments that were the centerpieces of their meetings, including looking at a louse through a microscope and dissolving a piece of mutton in a liquid that, Pepys reported, turned it "into pure blood, which was very rare." ("Rare" had the scientific meaning of "thin"; let us accept the pun as intentional.)

The society's experiments often involved an air pump, a new, expensive device commissioned and redesigned by Boyle that pumped air out of a globe so that researchers could observe the effects of a vacuum on the object within it. On that day, the society used the pump to show Cavendish how to determine the weight of air and how marble disks could be made to cohere. On other occasions, they put the air pump to different uses, including experiments on "animal respiration," when the object placed in the globe might be a mouse, a frog, or a sparrow whose struggles and gasps for breath were dispassionately noted in the record books and published in the society's journal, *Philosophical Transactions*. Sometimes the animals were brought to the point of suffocation and then revived; usually, they died. Animal experiments involving the bell jar, the injection of poisons, and the dissection of live animals were often on the agenda at Royal Society meetings, but the members refrained from them that day, perhaps in deference to the duchess, whose sympathies were well known.

The fellows of the Royal Society, as well as countless other gentlemen natural philosophers who experimented on live animals in their homes, were not particularly hard-hearted men; some of them acknowledged, and regretted, the suffering of their experimental animals. Occasionally, a fellow might even put compassion ahead of science and terminate an experiment examining what happened to an animal trapped in a bell jar as the air was pumped out of it, if the animal happened to survive the first few evacuations. However, many of these experimenters, along with most others in the Western world at that time, believed that the essential differences between humans and beasts allowed humans to claim superiority to, and dominion over, other creatures. Animals existed to provide humans with food, clothing, implements, labor, and, in the case of science, knowledge. In the opinion of Francis Bacon, the intellectual father of the Royal Society, "Man, if we look to final causes, may be regarded as the centre of the world; insomuch that if man were taken away from the world, the rest would seem to be all astray, without aim or purpose." All things in the world work to man's service so completely, he wrote, that they "seem to be going about man's business and not their own."

Bacon was not unsympathetic to animals; he believed that man's God-given dominion over nature must be tempered by the equally God-given quality of compassion: only "narrow and degenerate spirits," he wrote, ignore the instruction of Proverbs, "A just man is merciful to the life of his beast" (12:10). But his science required the exploitation of nature nonetheless, and the language in which he wrote about it can be quite disturbing to modern ears. The advancement of knowledge, Bacon thought, required men to force nature to reveal "her" secrets: nature was routinely represented as female, and Bacon characteristically used imagery of rape and torture to describe his scientific project. Once man had penetrated nature's secret places, he wrote, he would be able to master her, to break her to human service—to make her his slave.

Echoing Bacon's idea that the progress of science necessitated the mastery of man over nature, Robert Hooke and Robert Boyle celebrated the ability of new technologies such as the microscope and the air pump to give humans greater knowledge of, and therefore power over, the natural world—if only they were not barred by ancient scruples and superstitions. "The veneration wherewith men are imbued for what they call nature has been a discouraging impediment to the empire of man over the inferior creatures of God," Boyle complained.

Margaret Cavendish was probably not so eccentric (or so populist) as to join the wild and often radical ranks of seventeenth-century vegetarians (some of whom, such as the religious radicals Roger Crab, the self-described "English hermit," and Thomas Tryon, a merchant and prolific author, would have been both politically and socially repellent to her). But Cavendish did scoff at the notion that the world exists solely for the benefit of humans. She would have agreed with the twentieth-century scholar Arthur Lovejoy, who called this idea "one of the most curious monuments of human imbecility." She also rejected the power relationships and sense of hierarchy presupposed by the new science. Cavendish was one of a small number of intellectuals who believed that all creatures possess their own kinds of knowledge, which are by definition limited to their spheres—and that this is true of humans, too. Rather than superior knowledge, it is actually "the ignorance of men concerning other creatures," Cavendish wrote, that permits them to despise nonhuman animals, considering themselves "petty Gods in Nature." The duchess expressed her contempt for this self-importance in her speech, in her prose, and, most eloquently, in her poems:

> [Man] is so Proud, *thinks onely he shall live,*
> *That* God *a God-like* Nature *did him give.*
> *And that all* Creatures *for his sake alone,*
> *Was made for him, to* Tyrannize *upon.* *

SIX YEARS AFTER he witnessed Margaret Cavendish's visit to the Royal Society, John Evelyn went to see an exhibition called Paradise, a mechanical reenactment of the creation of the world. Evelyn admired

---

*When discussing human and nonhuman animals in a historical context, the question of language is vexed. During the era covered in this book, and often still today, the word "animal" and other words such as "beast" and "brute" referred to nonhuman animals (unless metaphorically applied to humans). I will follow this traditional practice, except when otherwise noted. I will usually use "animal" to refer to nonhuman vertebrates, although it could be applied to insects and other invertebrates as well. The usual eighteenth-century practice of designating the entire human species as "man," however, is one that I generally try to avoid, though it is difficult to do so when attempting to convey a sense of an earlier historical period. The usage does reveal patriarchal attitudes underlying it, as Margaret Cavendish was well aware.

Margaret Cavendish, noblewoman and intellectual
(William Greatbach, after Abraham Diepenbeek, 1846
© National Portrait Gallery, London)

"the representations of all sorts of animals, handsomely painted on boards or cloth, & so cut out & made to stand & move, fly, crawl, roar & make their several cries, as was not unpretty." Clockwork scenes such as this were extremely popular throughout the eighteenth century (and after), whether exhibited at shops and private showrooms or amazing the crowds at Bartholomew Fair. In the early 1700s, the clock-maker Christopher Pinchbeck became particularly celebrated for his remarkable mechanical extravaganzas. The "Wonderful and Magnificent

MACHINE" he displayed in 1729, for instance, featured, among several other marvels, a scene of Orpheus charming the wild beasts and an "Aviary of Birds," whose song (or so Pinchbeck's advertisement boasted) was "imitated to so great Perfection as not to be distinguished from Nature itself." The machine also contained a dog and a duck playing, fish jumping in the sea, and a river in which swans swam, fished, and fledged, "their Motions as natural as tho' really alive."

Human and animal machines had been a sight on the European cityscape since the advent of the great town clocks adorned with figures that creaked into motion at certain hours. The fourteenth-century clock tower in the cathedral of Strasbourg, for instance, housed a mechanical cock that announced noon by crowing and flapping its wings. In the form of animated waxworks, peepshows, panoramas, and the playhouses' increasingly elaborate mechanized pantomimes, such contraptions became the stuff of popular entertainments, where people marveled at the ingenuity of their construction and their "natural" movements. Considered particularly lifelike were automata—in essence, early robots—created in the shapes of both humans and animals. They achieved remarkable sophistication: automaton humans played instruments, and mechanical birds, dogs, elephants, and monkeys sang, stretched, and jumped, to spectators' delight and showmen's profits.

Most remarkable of all the eighteenth-century automata was Vaucanson's duck. In 1739, the French inventor and engineer Jacques de Vaucanson fashioned a duck-shaped automaton of gilt copper that featured hundreds of movable parts and innards made of rubber tubing. This remarkable mechanical duck moved its head, craned its neck, stirred water with its bill and drank it, quacked, stretched its leg, flapped its wings, shook its tail, swallowed grain, and "digested" food—then excreted it. Open panels in the duck's sides allowed one to view its rubber intestines in action. Having created a sensation in Europe, Vaucanson's duck crossed the Channel to London in 1742, where it flapped, ate, and shat in the Royal Opera House four times a day, to the delight and wonder of the British public.

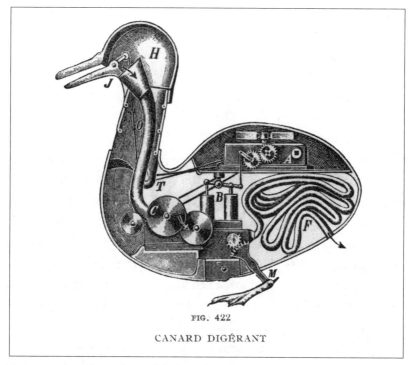

FIG. 422

CANARD DIGÉRANT

A cross section of a mechanical duck, with arrows showing how what goes in at one end comes out of the other. From Alfred Chapuis and Edouard Gélis, *Le monde des automates*. (Courtesy Biomedical Library, University of California, Los Angeles)

Vaucanson's duck, a metal and rubber machine, was so convincingly able to imitate the movements of its feathered counterparts that it, too, seemed to live. Perhaps an automaton could appear so credibly "alive" because the nature of animal life itself was still a matter of intense speculation and heated debate. There were many people in the seventeenth and eighteenth centuries who believed that a *real* duck was a machine as well.

One of the most prominent lines of thinking about animals was the "mechanical philosophy" of the French philosopher René Descartes. The bodies of both human and nonhuman animals, Descartes thought, are essentially organic mechanisms (though very sophisticated ones, since they were designed by God rather than man). However, unlike both animals and true machines, we humans possess rational souls, which are completely independent of our bodies and do not die when our bodies do. Lacking rational souls, animals are, in essence, biological automata—"beast-machines" (*bêtes-machines*). In fact, he argued, when we see an animal automaton, we have no way of knowing whether its nature is any different at all from that of a beast made of flesh and blood.

Descartes and his followers believed that since animal and human bodies were both mechanical, they followed the same laws; man's position was not privileged in this sense. But he also argued that because, as he presumed, animals had no language and could not communicate, they lack rationality. Among humans, he noted in his *Discourse on the Method,* those who are physically incapable of speech can still communicate through signs. That even dull-witted children and madmen can string words together to form meaningful utterances shows that it takes only a small amount of reason to be able to use language. Animals cannot speak, and they lack the ability to reason; therefore their being is very different in nature from ours. If this were not so, Descartes argued, a particularly talented parrot or monkey should be able to speak at least as well as a brain-damaged child. Furthermore, the fact that many animals can do some things better than we can does not prove they have intelligence. A clock keeps time more accurately than we can do, but this is mechanical action, not understanding. Animals are essentially biological clockworks—as we would be, too, were it not for our rational, that is immortal, souls.

Descartes also called into question animals' ability to feel sensations, including pain. Because animals are simply material systems of organic responses, beast-machines that have no consciousness, he wrote, they also lack "real feeling or emotion." If they appear to experience human feelings such as joy, fear, and hope, these are simply the responses of their mechanisms to stimuli, utterly different from what we experience. As for pain, Descartes wrote, it "exists only in the understanding"—and only we humans possess understanding. A dog may jump away if he puts his nose on a hot iron or cry when cut with a knife, but this is a reflex action, not a response to pain.

Descartes had been a visitor to the Cavendish lodgings in Paris where Margaret and her husband, William, having supported the royalists in the English Civil War, lived in exile during Cromwell's rule. Descartes and William Cavendish also engaged in philosophical correspondence. Margaret would certainly have read and disapproved of Descartes's letters, such as the one from 1646 in which he told her husband, "I cannot share the opinion of Montaigne and others who attribute understanding or thought to animals. I am not worried that people say that human beings have absolute dominion over all the other animals." While some animals might be stronger or more cunning than we are, he continued, they are only our equals or superiors in actions that do not involve the ability to think.

Descartes was setting himself in opposition to the opinions of the Renaissance writer Michel de Montaigne (1533–1592), who wrote that when he considered how close a relationship and "mutual obligation" exist between animals and us, he willingly abdicated that "imaginary kingship" we assume we have over other creatures. It was arrogance, vanity, and presumption, Montaigne wrote—the duchess would later use the same kind of language—that allowed us to deny "soul, and life, and reason" to our "fellows and companions." We might consider animals stupid, but since we did not understand them any more than they understood us, was it the animals' fault that we could not communicate, or was it ours? "When I play with my cat," Montaigne famously remarked, "who knows if I am not a pastime to her more than she is to me?" (That we are certainly our cats' pastimes seems obvious to cat lovers today, but this was a radical thing for a sixteenth-century European to say.)

Montaigne had his followers in the seventeenth century, but Descartes scoffed at their notion of a bond between humans and animals and dismissed the idea that animals possess minds and some form of understanding. He argued to William Cavendish that while we might be able to train parrots and dogs to *appear* to act like humans, they were expressing not rationality but only their "passions," which are not conscious states but purely bodily movements. We are sadly mistaken if we think that animals are trying to speak with us and we just don't understand them: "Since dogs and some other animals express their passions to us, they would express their thoughts also if they had any." Just because a dog is made of flesh, as we are, does not mean that the dog is like us in other ways, he said elsewhere: "I observe no mind at all in the dog, and hence believe there is nothing to be found in a dog that resembles the things I recognize in a mind."

For animals themselves, the legacy of Cartesian thinking about nonhuman creatures could be disastrous. Some of Descartes's early supporters logically extended his ideas about pain to appalling degrees: one follower argued that when you pound an organ's keys it makes a sound, but this does not mean that the organ is feeling pain; so, too, when you beat a dog it cries, but this does not mean that the dog is suffering. If beasts could actually feel, Cartesians observed, then no God who is truly good would permit us to be so cruel to them; in order to believe in God's goodness, we must believe that animals are machines.

Descartes's thinking about animal nature was not adopted by everyone in Europe, either in his own day or thereafter. Voltaire, for instance, launched a scathing attack on Cartesian ideas in his *Philosophical Dictionary,* where he observed how readily canaries can be taught tunes, and castigated the "barbarian" experimenters who would cut open a living dog to display its nerves, yet deny that the presence of those nerves meant it could feel. (Voltaire's liberal ideas about animals, however, were unusual, especially in France.) In England, there was nothing like a consensus among writers and philosophers about his ideas. The enormously influential John Locke remarked that it seemed obvious to him that beasts did reason; their reasoning was inferior to humans', since they were incapable of generalizations and abstraction, but they were not mere machines. Writing in Addison and Steele's *Guardian,* Eustace Budgell mockingly imagined a pretentious undergraduate who shows off his abstract university learning by pinching one of his sister's lapdogs and then arguing that the dog cannot feel it. In 1724, the philosopher Bernard Mandeville movingly described the slaughter of an ox and then asked: "When a creature has given such convincing and undeniable proofs of the terrors upon him, and the pains and agonies he feels, is there a follower of Descartes so inured to blood, as not to refute, by his commiseration, the philosophy of that vain reasoner?"

Anatomists dissecting animals found that their nerves and senses functioned very like humans'—and if such creatures had feeling, might not they have minds, and reason, as well? John Bulwar, following Montaigne's lead in asserting that animals could communicate in their own ways, wrote a book about hand gestures, which he understood to be a universal, natural human language analogous to that of animals, who both reason and express themselves through their own gestures. The qualities they express, he said, included honor, generosity, industriousness, intelligence, courage, magnanimity, love, fear, subtlety, and wisdom.

Margaret Cavendish certainly found it absurd to think that other animals cannot communicate just because they cannot speak. First of all, she observed pointedly, speech is overrated as a sign of intelligence, since people often say very stupid things. Other creatures have their own forms of expression and understanding. Confronting the idea that man is superior to animals because he alone can generalize and theorize, she retorted:

> Who knows whether fish do not know more of the nature of water, and ebbing and flowing, and the saltness of the sea? or whether birds do not know more of the nature and degrees of air, or the cause of tempests: or whether worms do not know more of the nature of earth, and how plants are produced? or bees of the several sorts of juices of flowers, than men.

When the English philosopher Henry More, who criticized the anthropocentrism that would deny animals any existence in and for themselves, nonetheless described man as the "flower and chief" of all of nature's products, Cavendish protested that man is hardly a disinterested party when it comes to the question of his status. For her part, she said, she could not see that man has greater abilities than beasts do. He may build a grand house, but cannot build a honeycomb; he can plant a seedling, but he cannot make a tree; he can forge a sword, but he cannot make the metal. And just as man uses other animals, so do they use man—"as far," she qualified, "as he is good for any thing."

Still, as Keith Thomas observes, Descartes "had only pushed the European emphasis on the gulf between man and beast to its logical conclusion." Though modern scholars disagree about the extent to which the Cartesian animal-machine concept was influential in Britain, it was, Thomas points out, "the best possible rationalization for the way man actually treated animals." Among those who even required a rationalization, the notion that animals were organic machines helped to influence at least some thought and behavior, whether by the scientist suffocating a bird or by the gentleman in a hurry commanding his coachman to whip the horses until they dropped. Cartesianism assuaged any guilt humans might feel about their brutal exploitation of animals, and exonerated the God who allowed it. Descartes himself commented that his system was not so much cruel to animals as kind to humans, since it absolves us of culpability for harming them.

IF MARGARET CAVENDISH set herself against the contemporary current of Descartes's "mechanical philosophy" as a theory of animals' natures, she also stood at odds with the long philosophical and theological tradition that underlay prevailing British and European attitudes toward animals. These traditions extended back to ancient Greek and Roman philosophers, particularly Aristotle and the Stoics, and from them into Christianity, where they underpinned the strongly anthropocentric worldview promulgated by theologians. At the center of the mainstream Western tradition of thinking about animals was the belief, most influentially articulated by Aristotle, that animals possess very low forms of intelligence at best, and are incapable of higher reason. Although the question of animal rationality was certainly debated among the Greeks and Romans, and some writers, among them

Plutarch, stressed the importance of treating animals kindly, Aristotle's position came to hold the greatest authority after his work was rediscovered in the West during the late Middle Ages.

Aristotle believed that humans are the only truly rational animals because only we can think. He argued that while animals possess appetite and sensation and are capable of pleasure, pain, and desire, they are not capable of "calculation and thought." The order of nature, he said, is a hierarchy in which animals make use of plants and humans make use of animals. These assumptions, as the historian of philosophy Gary Steiner puts it, "are foundational for the entire subsequent tradition of Western thinking regarding the relationship between human beings and animals."

The Roman Stoic philosophers added that the concepts of justice and injustice apply only to humans. Although the Stoics believed that humans should live in conformity with nature, they also held that since animals are irrational, humans have no fellowship with them and no moral obligations toward them. The Stoics believed, in Steiner's words, that "nothing that we do to animals can . . . be considered an injustice."

When Christianity incorporated and superseded the ancient philosophical traditions, similar attitudes prevailed. St. Paul denounced the Egyptian practice of worshipping gods in the form of beasts; God punished their corruption, he asserted, by instilling in them "vile affections," that is, homosexual lusts (Romans 1:23–27). He also denied the literal interpretation of the passages in Mosaic law that require animals to be treated humanely: allowing work animals a day of rest on the Sabbath, for instance, and forbidding the muzzling of the ox that treads the grain (Deuteronomy 5:14; 25:4). "Doth God take care for oxen?" he asked. "Or saith he it altogether for our sakes?" (I Corinthians 9:9–10). He saith it altogether for our sakes, he answered: the passage must be read allegorically, meaning that it is the *plowman,* not the ox, who may hope for a share of the crop. As one modern commentator remarks, "For Paul, the ox is not even a co-worker."

The influential thinkers of the European Middle Ages adapted the ideas of Aristotle and the Stoics to the Christian context. Although some Christians disagreed, mainstream doctrine taught that God made animals for human use, pointing to the passage in Genesis where God says, "Let us make man in our image, after our likeness: and let them have dominion over the fish of the sea, and over the fowl of the air, and over the cattle, and over all the earth, and over every creeping thing that creepeth upon the earth" (1:26–27). A passage from Psalms expresses the same idea: "Thou madest him [man] to have dominion over the works of thy hands; thou hast put all things under his feet; All sheep and oxen; yea, and the beasts of the field" (8:6–7). In both the Jewish and Christian traditions, there was more than one way of interpreting "man's dominion." As early Christian theologians vied to establish mainstream Christianity's core doctrines, some saw this concept as containing limitations on our use of animals and incorporating obligations to them. But other powerful and influential traditions viewed "dominion" to mean man's complete subjugation of other living things.

One tradition, which persisted into the seventeenth century, held that, with the Fall, humans lost our dominion over animals; the fact that many beasts were now dangerous to us was a fitting punishment for Adam's sin. But although St. Augustine agreed that the existence of wild predators was a punishment, he echoed his Stoic predecessors in arguing that there was no "community of right" between humans and animals and therefore no restriction at all on our use and killing of them.

The late medieval philosopher St. Thomas Aquinas, who was strongly indebted to Aristotle, did the most to establish subsequent mainstream Christian doctrine on these questions. "All animals are naturally subject to man," he wrote; lacking the higher functions of reason and language, animals lack conscience, moral responsibility, and an immortal soul. Man alone is made in the image of God; therefore, it is proper that other animals are governed by him. "By the divine providence [animals] are intended for man's use according to the order of nature," Aquinas wrote. "Hence it is not wrong for man to make use of them, either by killing or in any other way whatever." Unlike Descartes, Aristotle, Aquinas, and the others did believe that beasts can feel sensations, including pain—but they did not think that this entails any particular moral obligations to them. Aquinas acknowledged that Scripture sometimes appears to instruct us to be kind to animals, as when we are counseled against killing a mother bird with its young (Deuteronomy 22:6–7). But such passages really refer to *human* behavior, he asserted, since being cruel to animals might lead to being cruel to people.

By no means were all early and medieval Christian writers comfortable with the notion that God intended humans to exercise unrestricted power over the lives of animals. Some took at face value the many exhortations in the Hebrew Bible to treat animals humanely, rather than deemphasizing these passages or reading them only as allegories applying to humans. Such positions were in some ways more in line with Judaism: as the twelfth-century philosopher Moses Maimonides argued, Genesis depicts the world as good *before* God created man; therefore, it contravenes Jewish belief to hold that all creation exists only for man, when clearly all other creatures, who were here before us, were intended for their own sakes.

Some early Christians also emphasized that we are all God's creatures, and thought of animals as man's brethren. A few, such as Clement of Alexandria and St. John Chrysostom, argued for vegetarianism, saying that all humans were vegetarians before the Flood. This belief was based upon Genesis 1:29: "And God said, Behold, I have given you every herb bearing seed, which is upon the face of all the earth, and every tree, in the which is the fruit of a tree yielding seed; to you it shall be for meat." (After the Flood, this changes; God tells Noah, "Every moving thing that liveth shall be meat for you; even as the green herb, have I given you all things" [Genesis 9:3–4].)

In medieval times, some Christians also felt a connection with animals. The legends that circulated around Francis of Assisi, the patron saint of animals, told of wild beasts approaching him without fear. He tamed the vicious wolf that had been terrorizing the people of Gubbio, convincing "Brother Wolf" to give up his bloodthirsty ways. He also preached to the birds, exhorting them to praise God, who out of great love for them gave them the feathers that clothe them, the earth for their food and shelter, and freedom from toil. Although recent scholarship has called into question St. Francis's credentials as an animal protector (he advocates respect for beasts in his writing, but never actually calls for compassion for them), his status as the Catholic church's best-known friend of animals remains firm in the present day.

The beautifully illustrated medieval Christian bestiaries—books of beasts—were, in essence, early nature writings, based upon biblical injunctions to learn from the examples of animals, such as "Go to the ant, thou sluggard; consider her ways and be wise" (Proverbs 6:6). The bestiaries, along with other medieval churchly writings on animals, posited a world of nature in which beasts possessed both virtues and vices, and were created by God to serve as moral examples to humans. This was certainly a form of anthropocentrism, in which the human world could see itself in the world of animals and learn from them the way to redemption; the habit was analogous to that of reading scriptural references to animals as allegories of human concerns. But it did show that animals could be positive (as well as negative) examples. One early-thirteenth-century British bestiary, for instance, describes how long and faithfully crows tend their offspring, comparing them favorably to irresponsible women who wean their babies as soon as they can; the author advises: "Men should teach themselves to love their children from the crow's example."

Furthermore, for all that medieval theologians had to say about the unbridgeable gap between man and beast, long-established folk traditions often saw the animal world as deeply connected with—and akin to—the human one. Dix Harwood, in his groundbreaking (and recently reprinted) 1928 book *Love for Animals and How It Developed in Great Britain*, points out that strains of popular anthropomorphism at times coexisted with, and contradicted, the official anthropocentric line. The assumption that animals "feel and act like men" was expressed in numerous stories of animal intelligence and emotion: the greyhound who saved a child from a poisonous snake; the horse who let no one but his master ride him; the grateful lion from whose paw St.

Jerome removed a thorn; and the raven who fed St. Benedict. Aesop's fables first appeared in English in 1484 and went through dozens of editions, translations, adaptations, and imitations throughout the eighteenth century. In their Latin form, stories such as "The Tortoise and the Hare" were used to teach schoolboys grammar, while their English versions inculcated into all types of readers moral lessons based upon these animal characters.

BUT DOMINANT CHRISTIAN doctrine stressed a different set of relationships between the human and animal worlds. Melding the authority of Aristotle with that of Scripture, Aquinas and his followers fixed anthropocentrism firmly in the religious, philosophical, and political institutions of the West. Most of Margaret Cavendish's contemporaries, even if they dismissed the Christian rationale for man's superiority and the extremer consequences of the Cartesian beast-machine, believed that only humans possess true rationality, language, and immortal souls. Her countryman Thomas Hobbes, for instance, rejected the idea that God created the world for us—"When a lion eats a man and a man eats an ox, why is the ox more made for the man than the man for the lion?" he asked, provocatively. But he also believed that man rightly dominated beast. Humans in a state of nature must control and kill animals in order to survive, he said, but we are able to do that not because of God's anthropocentric ordering of the world, but because of the superiority conferred upon us by our reason, language, and dexterity.

Some dissenters from extreme anthropocentrism were quite prominent: Isaac Newton, for instance, believed in the duty of mercy to animals and thought that the injunction to love one's neighbor encompassed four-footed as well as two-footed neighbors. Taking an even more outré and (for her day) idiosyncratic position, Cavendish considered man's arrogant attitudes about the natural world downright sacrilegious. She credited animals with religious feeling as well as with rationality. "I should rather think it irreligious to confine sense and reason only to Man, and to say, that no Creature adores and worships God, but Man," she wrote, "which, in my judgment, argues a great pride, self-conceit, and presumption." To Cavendish, man becomes downright blasphemous when he supposes that reason and reverence exist in only a single, human form.

Throughout history there have been individuals who, like Cavendish, dissented from mainstream thinking about animals. However, the great majority of people in her day took for granted the notion that the rest of creation was made by God to serve humans. Richard Bentley, an eighteenth-century Anglican priest who was also a distinguished classicist and a member of the Royal Society, proclaimed that nature is "principally designed for the being and service and contemplation of man." Keith Thomas remarks that it is difficult for us today to fully comprehend how "breathtakingly anthropocentric" was the spirit in which the clergy of Cavendish's time interpreted the Bible. And she was dissenting not only from the philosophical and theological traditions known to the educated elite but also from the beliefs of most ordinary people, who were utterly unaware of the intellectual arguments and even the scriptural authority that underlay, or justified, their attitudes and behavior. Most people simply used, and abused, animals as labor, food, and sport because that was what people had always done. One did not have to be a conscious Cartesian to believe that sympathy for an animal's suffering when we injure it was nearly as preposterous as concern for a tree's pain when we prune its limbs.

CHAPTER 2

RUDE AND NASTY PLEASURES

✳   ✳   ✳

O N A late afternoon in August 1666, Samuel Pepys, his wife, Elizabeth, and Elizabeth's companion, Mary Mercer, joined the crush
of carriages and carts squeezing past the ancient, top-heavy houses
crammed together on London Bridge. In less than three weeks a few
embers left unattended in a bakeshop oven would blaze into the Great
Fire, which would consume most of medieval London, including half
of the buildings on the bridge, leaving nearly two hundred thousand
people homeless and changing the cityscape forever.

The Pepyses' thoughts were fixed on pleasure as they made their
way onto the south bank of the Thames and the raffish borough of
Southwark. Notorious as the home of the Clink, Marshalsea, and the
King's Bench prisons, Southwark also had long hosted a multitude of
morally suspect pleasures such as alehouses, brothels, and, in Shakespeare's day, theaters. By the later seventeenth century, the playhouses
were located elsewhere, but the district could still offer other entertaining spectacles. The Pepyses' destination that afternoon, very near the
sites where Shakespeare's Globe Theatre once stood and its replica
stands today, was the Bankside Bear Garden. The Pepyses were going
to see the bullbaiting.

The bear garden was an arena surrounded by walls, above which
ranged seats and boxes for the spectators. The Pepyses watched from
their box as men led a bull into the center of the pit and tethered him to
a stake by knotting a fifteen-foot rope around the base of his horns.

Then they surrounded the bull and, during the entertainment that ensued, released as many as thirty bulldogs, in waves of two or three, to attack him. The dogs leapt at the bull, tearing at his flesh and trying to fasten their jaws on his throat, ears, lips, tongue, and scrotum, while the bull defended himself as well as he could within the confines of his tether.*

Faced with this onslaught, a "green," or inexperienced, bull that did not know how to protect itself might be horribly mangled. But a bull that had been baited before knew that his best defense was to lower his head to guard his nose and get his horns under the dogs, tossing them high into the air, where their owners would try to break their fall with poles, not always successfully. If the dogs tried to attack him from underneath, the bull would attempt to trample them to death. The bull that day was obviously an old hand, for, wrote Pepys in his diary, he provided "some good sport," flinging the dogs about and even hurling one dog high up into a spectators' box. The Pepyses seem to have taken pleasure in their outing, but, Pepys admitted, it was "a very rude and nasty pleasure."

Pepys made no mention of the condition of the dogs and the bull at the end of this good sport, but all would have been torn and bleeding, at the very least. The dogs usually got the worst of it, sustaining wounds and broken bones; they often died, necks snapped, bodies gored, or backs broken. From the human perspective, baiting was less a contest between dogs and bull than a competition among dogs, with gamblers feverishly placing bets on their favorites. As newspaper advertisements explained, the dog that went "the fairest and farthest"—inflicting the most damage and getting the firmest grip on the baited animal—won the contest. If a dog was killed or ran away, those who bet on it would lose their money. A dog would lock onto the flesh of the bull or bear so

---

*The dogs in question, Old English bulldogs, are extinct today, though a modern version of the breed has been re-created; its closest descendants are the American bulldog, the American pit bull terrier, and forms of the Staffordshire terrier. (The modern English bulldog—a short, stocky dog with bowlegs, sagging jowls, and an underbite—would fare poorly against a bull or bear.)

tightly—"like a leech," marveled a visiting Frenchman, Henri Misson—
that if the bull did not swing it hard enough to break its teeth, its jaws
would have to be pried apart by its owner. Particularly brave and tenacious dogs were much celebrated, while they lived.

Pepys's friend John Evelyn—a well-educated, highly cultivated
gentleman—once reluctantly accompanied some acquaintances to the
bear garden, a venue he had managed to avoid for twenty years. There
he saw a bull kill two dogs and toss one dog "full into a lady's lap as she
sat in one of the boxes, at a considerable height from the arena." In addition to the bullbaiting that day—it being, he said dourly, "a famous
day for butcherly sports"—Evelyn also saw cockfighting, bearbaiting,
and a dogfight between an Irish wolfhound and a mastiff. The entertainment ended with dogs being set on an "ape" (probably a macaque
or a chimpanzee) tied to a horse. The afternoon left him feeling "most
heartily weary of the rude and dirty pastime."

In 1710, a young German tourist named Zacharias Conrad von Uffenbach went to the bear garden in the disreputable neighborhood of
Hockley in the Hole, located on the banks of the Fleet Ditch near
Clerkenwell Green, to see a bull baited. After the bull, a small bear was
tethered in the ring and the dogs were set on it. The bear probably was
muzzled or had its teeth and claws filed down, so it would have tried to
crush the dogs with its powerful arms or roll over on them as they attempted to tear its body through its fur. After this had gone on for a
time, the proprietors retired the bear and led a donkey into the ring
with an ape tied to its back. As the dogs attacked, the donkey raced
around the ring kicking and biting at them, while the ape clung to its
back, screaming in fear. When a dog came close enough, the ape
grabbed it in his mouth, shaking it until it howled. For the finale that
day, another bull was brought into the ring covered with firecrackers.
The firecrackers were lighted and dogs let loose on him, producing "a
monstrous hurly-burly." Thus, Von Uffenbach wrote in his journal,
concluded "this truly English sport, which vastly delights this nation."

Bullrunning, like bullbaiting, was a long established English custom. Bullrunning involved humans chasing a frenzied bull throughout

town, beating and jabbing him and cutting off bits of his flesh. The bullrunning in the Lincolnshire market town of Stamford, the country's most famous, reputedly dated back to the twelfth century, when a nobleman, William, Earl Warren, happened to see two bulls fighting over a cow in a field, and at that moment the butchers' dogs began to chase one of the frenzied bulls throughout the town. So entertaining did the earl find this spectacle that he gave the meadow to the town's butchers in which to graze their cattle in perpetuity—on the condition that every year, six weeks before Christmas, they find a mad bull to repeat the diversion. (Obviously, "finding" a bull that was mad usually required them to madden one.) Ancient statutes in many towns required butchers to bait their bulls before slaughtering them, for baiting was believed to tenderize their flesh, although these laws became steadily less enforced in the later 1600s.

Blood sports involving animals occurred in other European countries as well as England. The Spanish bullfight was one instance. However, the English passion for animal baiting, bullrunning, cockfighting and dogfighting, cockthrowing, and human prizefighting earned them a reputation for cruelty among Europeans. The Spanish visitor Don Manuel Alvarez Espriella, no admirer of his own country's bullfighting, nonetheless thought that at least, with its free-running bull, it involved a skill and courage utterly lacking in the cowardly English bullbaiting. And the French traveler Misson commented that the English loved animal blood sports more than any other people; indeed, "any thing that looks like fighting is delicious to an Englishman."

Richard Steele regretfully acknowledged the justice of this reputation when he wrote in the *Tatler*, "I wish I knew how to answer this reproach which is cast upon us, and excuse the death of so many innocent cocks, bulls, dogs, and bears, as have been set together by the ears, or died untimely deaths only to make us sport." That these were the entertainments of the common people, he acknowledged, "but they are the entertainments of no other common people." Besides, he added, "there is a tincture of the same savage spirit in the diversions of those of higher rank." The poet Alexander Pope commented disgustedly that to take pleasure in watching animals tear each other apart is a "temper that is become almost a distinguishing character of our own nation."

In provincial market towns, blood sports had traditionally been associated with official community festivals, and as these waned in the eighteenth century, bullrings were often maintained for unofficial entertainments. In London, such sports took place in established bear gardens and cockpits. Rowdy and violent, these arenas were notorious as the haunts of all sorts of shady characters and criminal riffraff, but in Pepys's day, they were not at all so disreputable as to place them off limits to respectable citizens. London's cockpits included three located in Westminster in the vicinity of Parliament and Whitehall Palace; two of these enjoyed royal patronage, and in them noble lords made great sums of money on the fighting cocks they owned. And although the adjective "bear garden" connoted lowness and vulgarity, their audiences were by no means limited to the poor, squalid, or criminal. During the Renaissance, bearbaiting had enjoyed royal patronage—Queen Elizabeth I was an avid fan—and aristocratic families had employed their own bear keepers. Though the sport's heyday had passed by the dawn of the eighteenth century, His Majesty's Bear Garden flourished in Hockley in the Hole, with another bear garden in Marylebone, and drew wide audiences.

On a baiting day, the bears and bulls would be paraded through the streets to the garden, accompanied by a beating drum, as bills describing the day's entertainment were handed out. (Passersby would want to give these animals a wide berth, for they posed real danger. One unwary hatmaker's apprentice was walking along Tooley Street in Southwark carrying his basket of hats on his back when another person passed him leading a muzzled bear. The bear grabbed the calf of the boy's leg in its claws and ripped it off.) Bulls would have names such as Emperor, Goldilocks, and Dash; bears might be named Robin Hood and Don John. Bulls sometimes had their horns cut off and replaced with the great horns of oxen, fastened to their heads with pitch and tipped with leather to protect the dogs; either bull or bear might have a large rosette glued between its eyes, to which a daring dog might get close enough to rip off. A successful combatant bull or bear would perform repeatedly.

Not only bulls, bears, apes, donkeys, and (less often) horses, but also other animals provided sport. Bear gardens and cockpits might set boars against each other, or keep a supply of badgers on hand. A badger would be stuffed into an artificial underground den made of a barrel heaped with earth, and it was the dog's task to grab it in its teeth and pull it out, sometimes with the assistance of his handler. Then there was ducking, in which a duck was placed in the middle of a small pond and dogs sent swimming out to attack it as it frantically dived to escape them. In London there were ponds for this sport in Clerkenwell and Mayfair, among other neighborhoods; the Clerkenwell pond had an adjoining tavern called the Ducking Pond House, while Mayfair's was the Dog and Duck.

Occasionally, more exotic and challenging creatures featured in these sports. In 1699, the Royal Cockpit in St. James's Park advertised an event held "at the request of several noblemen and gentlemen": the baiting of an "East India Tyger" by "three large bear dogs, one after another." This was advertised as a "re-encounter," so this was not the first time this tiger had been baited. The ad promised that the pit would provide elegant accommodation for gentlemen and ladies, with particular care taken to ensure the ladies' comfort and respect their delicacy. Whatever the situation in the spectators' boxes, the conditions in the pit were far from delicate. The tiger nearly killed one of the four dogs sent to bait him, but the other three dogs fought so well that they brought the match to a tie; the newspaper reported that had it not been for the collar protecting the tiger's neck, the dogs probably would have ripped its throat—and the tiger's owner would have lost a moneymaker.

This spectacle was so popular that, according to John Evelyn, a parliamentary bill concerning the old East India Company lost by ten votes because so many of its supporters in the House of Commons had gone to see the tigerbaiting instead. At Bartholomew Fair two years later, a tiger had easier work; a newspaper advertisement promised a repeat performance by this tiger, which the day before, had given "such satisfaction to persons of all qualities, by pulling the feathers so nicely from live fowls."

Proponents of baiting and animal fights often argued that these sports were a cultural asset to the country, building English manly character through their displays of courage and honor. John Gay's satiric play *The Beggar's Opera* offers a trenchant commentary on this attitude when the thief-master's wife, Mrs. Peachum, instructs the young pickpocket Filch, "You must go to Hockley in the Hole and Marybone, child, to learn valour." Though the popularity of animal baiting in most parts of the country would begin to wane in the later eighteenth century, most forms of baiting were not outlawed until 1835, after years of parliamentary battles.

IN THE FALL of 1762, nearly a century after the Pepyses' outing to the bear garden, James Boswell, just turned twenty-two, arrived in London from his family home in Scotland. It was his second trip to the metropolis but his first since coming of age, and he was determined to take the town by storm. With his rather endearing mixture of cockiness and insecurity, Boswell was ambitious to make his mark on the world, and secretly afraid that the world was not particularly interested. Everything he did was self-conscious as he went on his rounds of London, so it was utterly in character when, on December 15, this young Scotsman resolved to play the role of "a true-born Old Englishman."

Enemies of the English people represented them as "selfish, beef-eaters, and cruel," he wrote in his journal. (Presumably he had the French in mind, but English-hating Scots would have been plausible candidates, too.) So selfish, beef-eating, and cruel he would try to be. First Boswell went to Dolly's Steakhouse in the City, where he dined alone, thus being selfish as he ate his beef. Then he returned home, dressed himself in old clothes and a laced hat, filled his pockets with gingerbread and apples (for such, he noted, was the custom), took care to leave his watch, purse, and pocketbook behind him, picked up a stout oaken cudgel, and set off to watch cockfighting in order "to fulfill the charge of cruelty." What he saw at the cockpit amused, confused, depressed, and disgusted him.

The cockpit was a circular arena, with rings of benches for the spectators surrounding a round matted table where the cocks fought. The audience was male; this particular blood sport was not attended by women. The cocks, which probably had been bred on Cock Lane, near St. Paul's Cathedral, were armed with silver spurs, most likely made on Cockspur Street near the present-day Trafalgar Square. (Both streets still exist, and silver cockspurs from this period are on display in the Museum of London.) Their wings clipped and their beaks sharpened, the cocks, Boswell said, "are set down and fight with amazing bitterness and resolution," tearing at each other's eyes and trying to drive their metal spurs into their opponent's brain. Sometimes one killed the other quickly; but one match lasted three-quarters of an hour before a combatant succumbed.

Von Uffenbach, who in 1710 ventured into the famous cockpit near Gray's Inn, saw some terrified cocks try to escape by running among the spectators, only to be driven back to probable death by those who had wagered on their opponents. The din was horrific, he said, with the audience shouting and betting and acting like madmen. He noted that the upper and lower classes sat all jumbled together; no distinction of rank was preserved, and none of behavior, either. One mid-eighteenth-century Englishman wrote to a friend in Paris that he should come to England if only to see a cockfight and an election: "There is a celestial spirit of anarchy and confusion in these two scenes that words cannot paint."

During the fights, Von Uffenbach was amazed at how viciously the cocks "peck at each other and especially how they hack with their spurs. Their combs bleed terribly and they often slit each other's crop and abdomen with the spurs." Later, he visited the cocks' coops in the attic and was told how they were fed strong wine and carefully tended by their keepers. (A 1723 manual for cock-keepers detailed instructions on the treatment of injured roosters, which included sucking their wounds and washing them thoroughly with hot urine; the cocks' damaged eyes required the juice of chewed-up ground ivy to be spat into them, while if their wounds became infected they needed to be sucked clean and then filled with fresh butter.) Cocks were very expensive to keep; their owners, Von Uffenbach noted, were great lords who made large profits from them.

Misson, who called cockfighting "one of the great English diversions," observed of its frenzied gambling that a man could be "damnably bubbled [cheated] if he is not very sharp." Boswell was amazed by how much money changed hands during the fights, and how rapidly these wagers were placed. Shocked by the "distraction and anxiety" of the gamblers, Boswell found himself feeling a bit sorry for them, until he considered the poor cocks being "mangled and torn in a

William Hogarth, *The Cockpit* (1759). The figure at the center is the blind earl Lord Albemarle Bertie, who is being cheated by the "lower orders" around him. In the background, a bulldog watches the fight with interest, while at left a Frenchman turns away in disgust. (Courtesy of the Mandeville Special Collections Library, University of California, San Diego)

most cruel manner." Looking around to see if others seemed to take pity on the creatures, too, he saw not the smallest sign of compassion on anyone's face. After five hours at the cockpit, this young Scotsman made his way home "pretty much fatigued and pretty much confounded at the strange turn of this people."

Boswell did not mention it, but cocks were central to another, very particularly English sport: cockthrowing or cocktossing. This amusement, which sometimes made use of disgraced roosters that had been defeated but not killed in the pit, was traditional at Shrove Tuesday (the English equivalent of Mardi Gras). A cock was tethered by a yard-long cord to a stake in the center of a ring, and contestants took turns hurling cudgels at it, battering the animal and breaking its bones until someone finally succeeded in delivering a death blow. Cocks were trained to try to dodge the sticks, so the sport could continue for some time before an animal succumbed. Some accounts say that this sport originated in medieval times as a way of punishing roosters for St. Peter's three denials of Jesus before the cock crowed on the night of the Passion in the Garden: "Mayest thou be punished for St. Peter's crime,/And on Shrove Tuesday perish in thy prime," wrote the Restoration wit Sir Charles Sedley, to a rooster.

Cockthrowing was the first blood sport to be seriously attacked by critics. During the second quarter of the eighteenth century the attacks escalated in certain periodicals (although they subsequently waned, and at this historical point were seldom connected to protests against animal suffering in general). The *Tatler* published one of the earliest attacks in the form of a humble petition concerning this sport from "Job Chanticleer," a cock destined for that "inhumane barbarity of a Shrove Tuesday persecution." Chanticleer begged for protection from "the insolence of the rabble, the batteries of catsticks [sticks used in certain ball games], and a painful lingering death."

In 1749, the *Gentleman's Magazine*—which until the 1760s appears to have adopted criticism of cockthrowing as a particular cause—published the imagined dying speech of a hen who has been broken and bloodied by the cudgels. Addressing her owner, who "has known me for many months," she asked, "What have I done to deserve the treatment I have suffer'd this day, from thee and thy barbarous companions? What have I ever said or done amiss? Whom have I ever injur'd?" The hen ends with a wish that the legislature might consider the chickens' plight—an early suggestion that animals might deserve legal protection.

England's cockpits hosted not only cockfights but also baitings and other animal fights, such as ratting. For this amusement, a squirming heap of rats would be dumped into a round or square pit with boarded sides, and a dog would be set to kill them as fast as possible. Betting raged on all sides as the dog snapped at the rats while they frantically tried to escape the pit. The match ended when all the rats were still. Fights between dogs and boars were also common, and fights could pit a dog against a raccoon or even a monkey. In 1799, the *Sporting Magazine* reported an "unusual" fight in Worcester between a dog and a monkey named Jack. So uneven was this fight expected to be that the wager turned on whether the dog would kill the monkey within six minutes, or take longer. Jack's owner, however, stipulated that the monkey be given a foot-long stick. When the dog rushed him, Jack jumped on his back, grabbed his ear so that he could not move his head, and proceeded to batter his head with the stick until he died.

The long-established tradition of blood sports throughout Britain contributed words to the English language: "cockpit" was used early on to designate a section of a theater, subsequently the aft section of a man-of-war's lowest deck, and now the pilot's cabin of an airplane; whereas dogfighting gave a name to airplane combat and underlies the expressions "top dog" and, of course, "underdog."

Despite the overwhelming popularity of blood sports, there were always individual voices raised against them, although for a long time they were ineffectual. Some people disapproved of such pastimes for reasons that had little to do with the welfare of the animals themselves: concern for public order at the bear gardens and cockpits; disgust at the squandering of time and money; the desire to police the lower classes; resentment against aristocratic privilege. A writer to the *Weekly Register* in 1732 lumped together upper- and lower-class sports as all parts of the same universal human savagery: "Throwing at cocks, bullbaiting, duck-hunting, cockfighting, and horse-racing are barbarities in the highest vogue, and ladies are now as fond of the last, as the most savage amongst us."

WHILE ARISTOCRATS AND gentry ventured at will into the bear gardens and cockpits where they rubbed shoulders—sometimes literally—with the "rabble," other animal sports belonged exclusively to upper-class "savages." Racehorses were owned by aristocrats, and the track was a modish gathering place for aficionados of both sexes, as the *Weekly Register* complained. (The complaints against racing targeted both human immorality and the frequent injuries and deaths suffered by the horses.)

Hunting with hounds had long been the province of royalty and those ecclesiastics and noblemen who were either granted royal privileges or hunted in their own vast forests and parks. Aristocrats and landed gentry employed keepers to protect their property from encroachment by the common folk, who steadily had been deprived of their traditional rights to common land and the game on it by the practice of enclosure. The aristocracy and gentry not only absorbed as their own private property land that traditionally had been communal, but also claimed private ownership of the wild animals that under common law had not been subject to such claims. Game laws ensured that hunting remained an upper-class privilege; an act passed in 1670 required that a man be "lord of a manor, or have a substantial income from landed property, even to kill a hare on his own land."

Starting at the beginning of the eighteenth century, a series of statutes reasserted and strengthened the penalties for unauthorized hunting and fishing that ranged from stiff fines to a year in prison. In 1723, Parliament passed the notorious Black Act, under which the penalty for hunting deer and poaching fish or hares under certain circumstances was death. This act was repealed in 1827, but, as the early-nineteenth-century jurist Sir Samuel Romilly complained, someone who snared a rabbit could still be sentenced to transportation, that is, being shipped to an Australian penal colony, a punishment that itself could turn into a death sentence. The preservers of game were at least as savage as the poachers, Romilly exclaimed, since the practice was becoming common of setting deadly traps, including spring guns and giant man-traps, that often killed or maimed innocent people.

By the later seventeenth century, landed elite hunters of birds had largely replaced hawking with shooting. The noble stag ("the king of the English forests"), the lowly hare, and badgers were hunted with hounds. By the seventeenth century, foxhunting had become an acceptable aristocratic sport, despite the fox's despised status. Indeed, foxes' designation as vermin and predators would later provide rationalizations for hunting them: pest control, and retaliation for their own bloodthirstiness. As early as the sixteenth century, however, observers were pointing out that foxes would have been extinct already if the gentry had not been preserving them to hunt. (One official commented that the hounds did far more damage to farmers' chickens and sheep than the foxes did.)

The preservation of foxes had become commonplace by the eighteenth century, and many individual aristocrats kept their own packs of hounds. Gervaise Markham (who wrote books on gentlemanly country life), thought that the cry of a pack of dogs as they pursued the fox or hare produced a sound more "ravishingly delightful" than music. But hunting also had an ancient rationale quite different from refined pleasure: as military training of the aristocratic warrior classes. Hunting was a type of war game that bred horsemanship, stamina, and courage, with the boar, stag, or fox standing in for a human enemy. It was argued that hunting bred and maintained manliness, the willingness to shed blood. This was an argument that took on new meaning in the later part of the eighteenth century, when, along with the advent of the politer, more decorous Regency came the Napoleonic wars. Some feared that the good old British fighting spirit was endangered by the overrefinement of feeling and manners that made more people want to ban blood sports.

Among royalty, hunting could be rather less strenuous than galloping after a pack of hounds, however. Henry VIII liked to have deer herded into a paddock, where he set his dogs on them. In her prime, Queen Elizabeth I had been a great hunter; when she grew old she would ride into a paddock on her horse and shoot her crossbow at the deer huddled there. (The elderly queen's sport seems to have been an early version of the "canned hunts" so popular among politicians and corporate executives today.) Many royal and aristocratic women after Elizabeth also enjoyed the sport, albeit also in a cosseted form, by following the hunt in their carriages. When the quarry was a deer, the huntsmen would at times do a lady the honor of giving her the knife, so that she could slit the deer's throat herself and plunge her hands into its blood. Ladies believed that this made their skin white.

However, at least one great lady refused to wash her hands in the blood of a slaughtered deer. Margaret Cavendish was so tenderhearted, she said, that it troubled her to kill a fly: "The groans of a dying beast strike my soul." In her aristocratic milieu, hunting was the blood sport that she observed most closely, and she found it despicable.

The duchess wrote two remarkable poems that, quite unusually for her day, imagine the hunt from the perspective of its terrified, doomed victims. "The Hunting of the Stag" narrates with painful vividness the valiant stag's attempts to escape the dogs and the sportsmen who urge them on: "The Stag with feare did run, his life to save, / Whilst Men for love of Mischiefe dig his Grave." Cavendish portrays with great compassion his heaving sides, his hot flanks, and his trembling legs as he is run to exhaustion and killed. And in her extraordinary poem "The Hunting of the Hare," Cavendish puts herself into the place of poor Wat, the hare, who flees from the hounds with pounding heart and trembling body. When he thinks he has escaped the dogs, he sits on his hind legs and licks his paws to wipe the dirt from his face and ears—a poignant moment. Wat's respite is only momentary, however, for the hounds pick up his scent and his desperate flight begins again. Finally he can run no more and they tear him to pieces. There is much jubilation among the poem's aristocratic male hunters, but their triumph is not shared by its aristocratic female poet. Man, Cavendish wrote,

> . . . *for Sport, or Recreations sake,*
> *Destroy those Lifes that God saw good to make:*
> *Making their Stomacks, Graves, which full they fill*
> *With Murther'd Bodies, that in sport they kill.*

For all the worlds of social difference between a great country estate and a bear garden, the passion for blood sports shared by the upper and lower orders would long provide a bulwark against the animal protection movement that began to coalesce more than a century after Margaret Cavendish wrote these lines. While a few localities managed to outlaw certain blood sports as nuisances, parliamentary reformers' attempts to ban bullbaiting nationwide would be squelched by upper-class legislators concerned to protect their own pleasures of hunting and shooting against possible interference. Opponents of reform would ridicule the notion that to set dogs upon a tethered bull or bear was a cruelty in itself; even if it were cruel, they argued, animals deserved no legal status as anything other than human property. As we shall see, animal protection advocates would initially have to turn their attention to forms of cruelty not entailed by the privileges and pleasures of aristocrats.

The impetus for the growth of the animal protection movement would owe a great deal, however, to a different kind of relationship with beasts, a relationship that the upper orders had in common with those below them. Animals had long played other prominent roles in aristocratic lives—most importantly of all, as pets. By Margaret Cavendish's day, pet keeping was spreading among people of all ranks, as animals took the prominent place in the homes of all Britons that they have never relinquished. Pets were instrumental in encouraging some people to feel that the rude and nasty pleasures of blood sports, as well as other kinds of cruelty perpetrated upon beasts, were wrong.

In the history of the changes in attitude that underlay the rise of the animal protection movement, arguably the most powerful force countering Cartesian mechanism, Christian anthropocentrism, and the long traditions of exploiting animals in every way was not the philosophical discourse of unorthodox intellectuals. Rather, it was something much more mundane: the fact that many people were sharing their lives with animal companions.

CHAPTER 3

PETS AND THE CITY

✳   ✳   ✳

I MAGINE A gray, chilly day in November, rain pounding on the roof of the house, water dripping from its eaves. Inside, gathered around a glowing hearth, a mother is writing a letter to her faraway son, her quill rhythmically scratching and pausing as she dips it into her pot of ink, while the other members of her family doze, basking in the warmth. The year is 1707, and the other family members are a dog, a cat, and a monkey.

This cozy scene of contentment took place in a great aristocratic house. The mother was Isabella, Lady Wentworth, and her son was Thomas, Lord Raby, England's ambassador to the Berlin court. Her son would laugh, wrote Lady Wentworth, if he could see her fireside: "Fubs upon a cushion, the cat on another, and Pug on another lapped up all but her face in a blanket." Fubs was the lapdog, and Pug the monkey; the cat's name was Puss. On other, more wakeful occasions, Fubs, Pug, and Puss sent their greetings to Baden and Folly, Lord Raby's dogs.

The widowed Lady Wentworth filled her letters with doting anecdotes of her pets' antics and adventures. Pug was greatly upset when her mistress gave away the last puppy of Fubs's litter, for the monkey loved those puppies as much as Fubs (always an excellent mother) did. Then there was the exciting day when Pug won the lottery. The monkey had picked out the winning ticket herself, and Lady Wentworth had written her full name on it: Jenny Pug. Her prize was a silver needle case and a thimble.

Pug's eyes "sparkle like two diamonds," wrote her fond owner, and she knew many tricks, though she was only willing to perform them "when she has a mind to it, not else." Lady Wentworth's friend Charles Arundel acquired a monkey, too, but that poor creature was "so kept under that it dare not stir except as they bid it." Pug certainly was not kept under, at least not at home. But when she accompanied her mistress on an extended visit to Lady Wentworth's niece, things were different, for the niece was afraid of the prankish monkey. The niece was even wary of Fubs at first, fearing that the lapdog would jump on her, but the little dog was more successful at ingratiating herself than poor Pug: she was "so subtle," Lady Wentworth reported admiringly, "as to fawn upon her [the niece], and kiss her, and come gently to her, that she cannot stir without her." The niece, now thoroughly besotted, insisted upon taking Fubs to church, where she sat very quietly, presumably not even barking at any other lapdogs that might have accompanied their ladies to divine services. Back at home, Fubs now joined the family dinners, where she drank her water from a glass on the table.

Whenever Lady Wentworth heard that a dog had been shot in the neighborhood—as apparently happened with some regularity—she flew into a panic until Fubs was located, safe and sound. Fubs was never shot, but in 1708, she died. Lady Wentworth's letters, usually so chatty and cheerful, became very bleak as she described this "most dismal" event, as emotional as a tragic heroine's demise in the final act or the lingering deathbed scene beloved by sentimental novelists. Fubs left this world as she had lived in it, full of love. She rested her head in her mistress's bosom and, though she was obviously suffering, did not snap at anyone. As the end drew near, she nuzzled Lady Wentworth and Sue, her maid, looking "earnestly" at them. When Fubs died, Sue cried for three days, "as if it had been for a child or husband." Surely, Lady Wentworth mourned, there would never be an equal to Fubs: she had "so many good qualities, so much sense and good nature and cleanly and not one fault; but few human creatures had more sense. . . . I could write a quire of paper in her commendation." Lady Wentworth wept that she would have given a small fortune to save poor Fubs. Instead, she buried her beloved dog in the garden, and laid a gravestone at her head.

At the end of the letter in which she wrote of these painful events, Lady Wentworth mentioned, almost as an afterthought, the news of another death. The prince consort—Queen Anne's much-loved husband, Prince George—had died, at age fifty-five. But she would leave the account of *that* death, Lady Wentworth told her son, to his brother, who had been the prince's equerry. Lady Wentworth herself had once been at court, serving as lady of the bedchamber to Queen Mary of Modena, Queen Anne's stepmother. But now, her mind was more occupied with the loss of the incomparable Fubs than with the queen's sorrow. (It is tempting to imagine that when she put on the requisite mourning to honor the prince, Lady Wentworth was, in the recesses of her heart, really commemorating her dear Fubs.)

Lady Wentworth felt that she would never love another dog so much again. Inevitably, however, other lapdogs won her heart: there was one named Flirt, and then another, of whom she said, "I shall never think it possible for any dog to compare to charming Pearl, I never go anywhere without her except to church." Perhaps, for all her charm, Pearl did not sit as quietly during services as had Fubs.

At the end of 1712, a new sorrow came. Lady Wentworth's daughter-in-law, Lady Strafford, wrote to her husband (now elevated to an earldom) from their family home in Twickenham, that she probably should not have written such a long letter to him that day, "for I am sure you'll have a very long one from Lady Wentworth with very great lamentation; for her monkey is dead." Lady Wentworth was so distraught that she had been unable to leave her room for dinner. Lady Strafford complained that she dared not even laugh in her own house, for fear of upsetting her mother-in-law. Lady Wentworth eased her grief by commissioning two portraits of her dear Pug, one life-sized and the other a miniature.

LADY WENTWORTH WAS far from the only person in her day to become deeply attached to companion animals. In fact, as the eighteenth century approached, increasing numbers of people of all social classes were adopting pets. This is not to say that pet keeping was a new phenomenon. In the fourteenth century, the bishop of Winchester, William of Wykeham, had felt the need to chastise several convents where, anticipating Lady Wentworth's niece, the nuns liked to bring their "birds, rabbits, hounds, and such like frivolous things" to church with them, and, "to the grievous peril of their souls," paid more attention to the animals than to the priest. What had changed in the eighteenth century was the scale on which pets firmly established themselves in the homes of the middle and working classes throughout town and country—and the intensity of the bonds people were forging with these animals in their homes. As Keith Thomas observes, "By 1700 all the symptoms of obsessive pet-keeping were in evidence."

Probably no other development in the history of humans' relationship with beasts had such a profoundly positive impact upon the status of animals as did the spread of pet keeping. As more and more people of all social classes shared their lives with pets—those lucky creatures whose most important role was to provide companionship, rather than labor or food—it became increasingly difficult to think of animals as soulless machines or irrational bundles of appetites. The cat purring as it settled into a lap, closing its eyes in trustfulness, or the dog resting its head on a knee, gazing up with what one had to believe was love— surely these beasts had some kind of soul, perhaps even something equivalent to one's own, and surely cats and dogs possessed understanding, even intelligence and empathy. Then, as now, people reciprocated the love and admiration they were certain they received from their pets, just as Lady Wentworth eulogized Fubs's good nature, cleanliness, faultlessness, and possession of more sense than most humans. The Irish novelist Lady Morgan, who was rather cynical about the status given pets in many homes, nonetheless sniffed that a playful kitten was "infinitely more amusing than half the people one is obliged to live with in the world."

In a 1739 treatise that was immediately translated into English, the French Jesuit priest Guillaume Hyacinthe Bougeant used the example of pets as evidence for his anti-Cartesian argument that animals do possess understanding and language (an argument that got him exiled to the provinces until he recanted). No one can convince us that animals are machines when we love our pets and believe that they return the feeling, he said. Imagine a man who loves his watch and thinks that it tells him the time because it loves him in return. If Descartes were correct, said Bougeant, then all of us who believe our dogs love us would be as ridiculous as that man. But in fact our experience makes us *know* that our dogs and cats have feelings and understanding, no matter how much certain philosophers try to convince us of the contrary.

How did Britons distinguish pets from the other animals that served (or were served to) them? Lapdogs and cats, monkeys and macaws, larks and linnets were not the first or only animals to loom large in people's affections. Horses and hunting hounds, in particular, were much admired, even cherished (at least as long as they were young and healthy; old or weakened animals were often disposed of quite unsentimentally), yet they generally did not achieve the status of pets. Thomas succinctly itemizes the criteria that defined a pet and separated these privileged creatures from other beasts: they lived inside the house, whereas other animals were relegated to separate buildings or to the outdoors; they were given individual names (in England, in particular, these were increasingly *human* names, a tendency that became very pronounced in the eighteenth century); and they were not to be eaten.

The historians' usual definition of pets as "inessential animals" is a designation based upon animals' traditional function of providing humans with labor and food. By the eighteenth century, pets arguably provided another kind of essential service: affection. Many modern commentators point out that the phenomenon of obsessive pet keeping was a product of the modern urbanized society that was rapidly establishing itself at this time, where traditional ties to the natural world and to larger human groups were greatly attenuated and animals became important objects of attachment as well as nostalgic reminders of a vanishing rural past.

UNSURPRISINGLY, THOSE WHO first became accustomed to keeping pets were the upper ranks of society, who could easily afford the luxury of buying and feeding them, and who employed servants to clean up after them. Dogs, for instance, had long occupied privileged places within royal circles. Henry VIII had a spaniel named Cutte, and the doomed Mary, Queen of Scots loved dogs, finding solace during her captivity in the company of her lapdogs. One even accompanied her to the scaffold, hidden under her skirts; the blood-splashed animal was discovered only after her mistress was beheaded. The fashion for smaller pet dogs was entrenched at court by the Stuarts. Charles I's queen, Henrietta Maria, kept a number of the small, floppy-eared dogs that would come to be called the Cavalier King Charles spaniel after her son Charles II.

Beyond the palace, aristocratic women like Lady Wentworth doted on their lapdogs, and their husbands might cherish a favorite terrier. While in the great country estates, hunting hounds and the estate farm's sheepdogs and watchdogs were kenneled outdoors, inside the house greyhounds lounged in the hall, and pugs perched at the dinner table, eating from china dishes. In one late-seventeenth-century comic play, an old country squire waxes nostalgic for the good old days, when "signs of good house keeping" meant that great halls of country houses were filled with long tables, the house smelled of meat and beer, and the halls were decorated with "dogs' turds and marrow bones." (The standard of housekeeping was clearly changing, especially in smaller urban quarters. Thomas suggests that the increasing popularity of cats—who, in desirability as pets, initially lagged behind dogs, but caught up in the nineteenth century—coincided with higher standards of domestic cleanliness.)

The subsequent spread of pet keeping from the upper ranks into the middling stations of society was partially a result of the disposable income that more people were beginning to enjoy, which allowed them to purchase and maintain more expensive animals. At the center of a newly prosperous middle-class family might well sit a greyhound or a monkey or a macaw, upon which affection and money were lavished. But the lower orders also had their animal companions, their birds, cats, and mongrels. By the eighteenth century, there may have been no more convent churches where rabbits worshipped, but the sailor's monkey, the shopkeeper's cat, the tinker's mongrel, and the milliner's linnet were all sights even more common than ladies' lapdogs at Sunday services.

Far removed from the aristocratic and middle-class households of her day, the wildly eccentric cross-dresser Mary Frith, also known as Moll Cutpurse, lived a raucous, brawling life in the streets and bear gardens of seventeenth-century London. But she also kept a more decorous home, which she shared with an array of pets that became part of her larger-than-life legend. Moll, who was immortalized in Middleton and Dekker's play *The Roaring Girl,* kept several bulldogs, one of which she taught to perform tricks and never allowed into the bullring. She also lived with several parrots and nine lovely "shocks" (shaggy lapdogs) "who were trimmed and looked to with the same care as other folks did their children," she wrote. These little dogs had no reason to envy their aristocratic brethren, for they slept on sheets and blankets in individual trundle beds, and Moll boiled meat in broth for their meals. She prided herself on their being completely house-trained, never sullying her quarters. (Keeping her house clean, said this roaring girl notorious for her masculinity, was "the only part of womanhood I did.") Completing her family circle were baboons, apes, squirrels, and a "strange cat" who would follow her through the streets.

The upper-middle-class Samuel Pepys—who, quite unlike Moll, was a thoroughgoing member of the establishment—was another great animal lover (despite his attendance at the bear garden and cockpit) who kept a veritable menagerie in his house near Tower Hill, including an eagle and a lion cub as well as less exotic pets. He filled his diary with animal encounters and mishaps. One day, for instance, the cat got locked in the bedroom and made a racket and jumped on the bed. Another day,

Pepys arrived home after a trip to find "all well, but the monkey loose." This made him so angry that he beat the monkey severely, after which he was tormented by guilt for having reacted so violently. Pepys admired how well his blackbird whistled, but was less admiring when it woke him up between four and five in the morning. The bird knew many tunes, but annoyingly never seemed able to get beyond the first few bars. Pepys was very upset to arrive home one evening and find that the canary had died. His pet eagle had the appeal of exoticism, but it "fouled the house mightily," so he gave it away.

Even in an era with less exacting standards of hygiene, where many streets had open sewers running down the middle and people still threw the contents of chamber pots out of the window instead of taking them down to the outhouse, pets fouling the house must have been a perennial problem. Dog turds might be relatively ignorable in the hall of a great country house, but in closer urban quarters they could be difficult to overlook. Presumably dogs and cats, at least, were encouraged to go outside, where they added to the foul muck that covered the roads and footpaths. Sir Isaac Newton, who first described gravity and the laws of motion, was also a cat lover; he is said to have been responsible for another great advance in civilization, the cat door. (Cat litter, alas, was not invented until 1947.)

Samuel and Elizabeth Pepys staged a domestic drama lasting several months when her brother gave her a cute but incontinent black dog. The dog's habit of pissing in the house enraged Samuel, who got into a huge row with his wife when he threatened to throw the little dog out of the window. He never acted on the threat, but he did banish the dog to the cellar, precipitating another fight with Elizabeth. Both were still angry when they went to bed, where Samuel slept very poorly—"troubled all night with a dream," he wrote revealingly, "that my wife was dead."

But Pepys was more tenderhearted about the beasts of his household than he often cared to show. One afternoon, he, Elizabeth, and his father took a boat to Woolwich. They were en route down the river when they realized that they had left their little dog, who had followed them from the house, at the waterside. Elizabeth was very upset by the prospect that the poor dog would get lost, and so, Pepys confessed in his diary, was he—"more than was becoming to me." They went back, dropping off Elizabeth and her maid to look for the dog while Samuel and his father went on to Woolwich. As they strolled along the river to Greenwich, Pepys was distracted by worry until his wife appeared with their dog, "which made us all merry again." Pepys seemed to have inherited his affection for animals. When Towser, a mastiff that he had given his father, was killed by five other dogs, he wrote, "I am a little and he the most sorry I ever saw man for such a thing."

THE DOG HAD undergone a major redemption in order to arrive at its eighteenth-century status as most favored animal—or at least upper- and middle-class dogs, the pugs and spaniels and greyhounds, had risen thus. The bulldogs and ratters had their circles of admirers, too, but few admired the mongrels and curs who accompanied beggars or roamed half starved through the streets, foraging for offal, or slaved in the kitchens of the larger houses turning the spits and being scorched by the fire. In earlier days, Christian moralists had lumped all dogs together with pigs as the nastiest of creatures, filthy scavengers possessed of vices such as lust and gluttony. Dogs returned to their vomit, it was said. Pet keeping seemed a particularly dangerous threat to the boundary that had always to be maintained between the human and the bestial. Moralists particularly railed against those animals that were allowed to come to the dinner table and ate better than the servants, as was undoubtedly sometimes the case. (Lady Wentworth's servants may have eaten well, but it was Fubs who drank from a glass at the table.)

Quite exacting standards could be applied to the purchase of ladies' lapdogs, the tinier the better. A very insistent notice in the *General Advertiser* of 1746 sought "An Exceeding Very SMALL Little Dog." The dog might be any color, with or without white in its coat, as long as it was "Very, Very SMALL, with a Very SHORT ROUND SNUB NOSE."

Apparently, this advertisement had already elicited some inappropriate animals, to the advertiser's obvious exasperation. Eighteenth-century typography can be very expressive:

And to prevent any Farther Trouble, If it is not exceeding SMALL, and has any thing of a Longish Peaked Nose, it will not at all, do.

And, whereas some Persons have not Rightly Understood this Advertisement. Whoever will bring any Thing as SMALL, and

The infant heir to the throne and his long-suffering spaniel (unknown artist, *King Charles II*, 1630, © National Portrait Gallery, London)

with as *Short a Round* SNUB Nose, as have been lately Bought, they will find the Advertisement, *still* LITERALLY True, in *still* having a Purchaser.

Dogs occupied privileged places in royal and aristocratic portraiture as symbols of fidelity and signs of status. In London's National Portrait Gallery, a painting of Charles II as an unusually large four-month-old baby shows the infant heir to the throne sitting propped up with one of his mother's spaniels in his lap, pulling its ear. The Cavalier King Charles spaniel immortalized in this portrait wears a resigned expression eloquent beyond words.

Later in his career, George Stubbs, justly famed for his beautiful depictions of horses, also developed a sideline in painting the dogs of his aristocratic patrons.

As the eighteenth century progressed, when greater numbers of individuals and families began to be painted and poses became less formal, dogs were often included as treasured members of the family. Or ostensibly so: some successful portraitists, such as William Hogarth, who owned pugs, and Johann Zoffany, who had a striking white German spitz, sometimes used their own dogs in paintings of people who apparently desired the cachet of including a dog in their family picture without actually having to keep one. (If you were to walk today around the National Portrait Gallery, you might notice that the very same dog appears in pictures of different families.) Hogarth, who was widely known as a dog lover, put his own pug in a famous self-portrait.

Newspaper advertisements for missing animals poignantly testified to the affection people had for their dogs. An ad for a little spaniel specified that she had

4 liver coloured spots on her left side, a large liver colour marked cross [on] the middle of her back, with a few white hairs in the middle of it, a liver colour spot on the top of her tail, long ears, one sore within-side, and a white blaze on her fore-head, her feet and nose mottled, and 3 or 4 of her teeth lost

on the lower side, before her upper lip of the left side held up by one of her teeth.

If this obviously beloved (and certainly interesting-looking) dog was brought to Lord Abergevenny's house in Leicester Fields, the finder would receive the handsome reward of three guineas.

Many of the missing dogs described in newspapers must have been stolen. Valuable, cherished dogs were lucrative commodities. So it is not surprising that organized rings of dog thieves would operate, particularly in London. Often their purpose in stealing a dog was to obtain a ransom. (This was a frequent motive for thefts of canes, watches, and wigs, too.) If no ransom was forthcoming, the animal could readily be sold in another location.

Not even royal dogs were safe. Among the many advertisements for missing horses and dogs carried in the *Mercurius Publicus,* one spoke on behalf of King Charles II, asking for the return of a "black dog, between a greyhound and a spaniel, no white about him, only a streak on his breast, and his tail a little bobbed." This was the king's own dog, and, the advertisement noted, it must have been stolen, "for the dog was not born nor bred in England and would never forsake his master." Whoever found him should tell anyone at Whitehall Palace, for the dog was well known at court. The king's pets seemed to disappear on a regular basis, for the ad concludes rather plaintively, "Will they never leave robbing his Majesty? Must he not keep a dog? This dog's place (though better than some imagine) is the only place which nobody offers to beg."

Alas for the poor owner and even poorer pet, ransom was not the only motive behind such abductions. Jane Sellwood, an old woman, and Thomas Pallet, a boy, were arrested for stealing dogs in order to sell their skins. Police raiding Sellwood's house found about thirty decaying carcasses piled in one room, and many more buried throughout the property. One owner was able to identify the remains of his pug "from a particular mark in its mouth." Apparently it was a common practice for such dog stealers to rent a house and, when it was filled

William Hogarth, *Self-Portrait* (1749). The pug seems as much the portrait's subject as Hogarth, and the resemblance between the two is striking. (Courtesy of the Mandeville Special Collections Library, University of California, San Diego)

with as many carcasses as it could hold, to abscond without paying the rent; such had happened in a nearby street, "where the neighbors were almost poisoned by the stench."

Alexander Pope loved dogs and featured them in his poems. Pope, who suffered from a spinal disfigurement, stood four and a half feet tall, and had in succession at least four Great Danes, all named Bounce. The frail, hunchbacked poet and his large, powerful dog must have made a striking pair. One of Pope's friends planning a reunion with him wrote that in his great joy at seeing the poet he might knock him down, "like Bounce when you let her loose after a regimen of Physick, and Confinement." One of Pope's biographers characterizes their affection nicely: "Tiny poet, great dog, and a relationship in which, as many besides Pope have discovered, a damaged body makes no difference."

The aristocratic writer, antiquarian, and man-about-town Horace Walpole doted upon his pets, who figure as personalities in his lively letters. To placate his dog Patapan, who was sulking after he had been wormed, he tied a rainbow-colored ribbon around his neck as a promise never to worm him again. Walpole especially loved his black spaniel Rosette, who had saved his life by barking when the chimney caught on fire. Being Walpole's pet could be something of a high-risk occupation, however. His dog Bettina fell to her death from a balcony and, in a particularly horrible episode, his black King Charles spaniel, "the prettiest, fattest, dearest creature," was seized by a wolf on a trip across the Alps and carried off as his master screamed helplessly. "It was shocking," Walpole said, "to see anything one loved run away with to so horrid a death." Bad ends came not only to Wapole's dogs: his cat Selima was granted literary immortality as the subject of Thomas Gray's poem "Ode on the Death of a Favourite Cat, Drowned in a Tub of Gold-fishes." It comes as a relief to hear of other Walpole pets who closed their lives more peacefully, such as the cat Harold, who lived more than fifteen years, and his elderly black spaniel Tonton (who had been bequeathed to him by his friend Madame du Deffand, along with her snuffbox decorated with the dog's portrait). Tonton, like his former mistress, died at a ripe old age.

Cats' popularity as pets increased from the seventeenth century on; then as now, however, cats were particularly associated with woman and female sexuality, and—a phenomenon that at least in some instances was related—could inspire dislike or fear. The 1759 periodical the *Busy Body* called them "the most hated and beloved of all animals." Cats had to overcome the bad reputation they had gained in the Middle Ages as creatures of the night, devils' companions, and witches' familiars, or just as slothful animals that spend most of their time sleeping. Pet cats retained their function as mousers, so they were less completely detached from their traditional duties than were lapdogs from the work of farm and household. But in the eighteenth century, kittens became doted upon as cuddly pets for children, and many adults loved their cats as well.

The antiquary William Stukeley spoke of his cat in much the same language Lady Wentworth used about Fubs, remarking that she had superior sense and "inimitable ways of testifying her love to her master and mistress." This cat was his loving companion as he smoked his pipe in the evenings. When she died, he was heartbroken and thereafter avoided the area of his garden where he had buried her. John Lawrence, a well-respected authority on horses who confessed himself as fond of playing with his cat as Montaigne had ever been, affectionately described his pet's "eyes beaming fondness, and its feet kneading in unison with the grateful thrum." He rejected the slurs against cats made by the Comte de Buffon, whose popular *Natural History* accused them of being the most self-interested of all animals.

Cats'-meat men peddled their wares from door to door: these itinerate vendors sold skewers of horsemeat used for cat (and dog) food, customarily trundling their goods in a wheelbarrow and often depicted as trailed by a horde of extremely interested felines. In the nineteenth century, a cats'-meat man reported that there were twice as many cats in London as dogs.

John Rich, the eighteenth-century manager of the Theatre Royal, Covent Garden and London's leading pantomime Harlequin, notoriously did not care much for actors. But he did care very much for cats. An early biography of the famous actress Peg Woffington described her visit to Rich at his home, where she found him lounging on the couch, a playbook in one hand, a cup of tea in the other, and twenty-seven cats, of all ages, sizes, and colors, "round him, *upon* him, and *about* him." The cats were thoroughly at home: "Some were staring him in the face, some eating the toast and butter out of his mouth, some licking the cream out of a cup, some frisking about, some lying down, some perched upon his knee, some upon his head." In his drawling manner, Rich introduced Peg to Sally, Jenny, and Sharlotte, and recounted in some detail the "amours" of his he-cat Tom Devil among all

A nineteenth-century depiction of a cat's-meat man, greeted by some very interested cats and dogs (Courtesy Guildhall Library, London)

the females. (It is clear how this eighteenth-century male version of a cat lady acquired so many cats.) To the author of the memoir, the fact that Rich was so fond of these "odious animals" was yet another proof of the manager's legendary eccentricity.

The great Dr. Samuel Johnson had at least three cats, but the cat that became part of his legend was Hodge, whose modern statue sits today in front of London's Johnson House museum. Johnson used to buy oysters for Hodge himself, fearing that his servants would resent this extra task and thus bear a grudge against the cat. Boswell, who reported all this, confessed (to his readers, if not to Dr. Johnson) that he himself was a cat hater—and he often had to suffer Hodge's company when he visited Johnson. Fortunately, he was able to control his antipathy (or his allergy) enough to record two endearing anecdotes:

Peg Woffington visited the famous pantomime actor and theater manager John Rich and found him taking tea with his twenty-seven cats. (G. C. Finden, engraver, after F. Smallfield, painter, collection of the author)

I recollect him one day scrambling up Dr. Johnson's breast, apparently with much satisfaction, while my friend smiling and half-whistling, rubbed down his back, and pulled him by the tail; and when I observed he was a fine cat, saying "why yes, Sir, but I have had cats whom I liked better than this;" and then as if perceiving Hodge to be out of countenance, adding, "but he is a very fine cat, a very fine cat indeed."

Boswell also wrote of the time Johnson was talking about a young gentleman who had fallen into such a "despicable state" that he was running around town shooting cats. "And then in a sort of kindly reverie, he bethought himself of his own favourite cat, and said, 'But Hodge shan't be shot: no, no, Hodge shall not be shot.' "

Cats generally were not represented in portraiture until the eighteenth century, when they began to be shown in family groups, particularly

The two "Fisher kitties" (Nathaniel Hone, *Catherine Maria ("Kitty") Fisher*, 1765
© National Portrait Gallery, London)

middle-class urban families, as playful, beloved pets. A cat also occupies a
playful position in the portrait of a famous mid-eighteenth-century cour-
tesan, Kitty Fisher. To paint the human Kitty with her animal kitty was
an obvious pun, but more subtle and amusing is what the kitten is depicted doing: she is dipping her paw into a fishbowl, trying to snag a
goldfish—a "kitty fisher," like her mistress, for gold. (This detail also
gives us a graphic illustration of how Horace Walpole's Selima met her
fate. "What female heart can gold despise? / What cat's averse to fish?"
asked Thomas Gray, amusingly if misogynistically.)

Misogynistic representations of women could make effective use of the femininity customarily ascribed to cats. When news of an adulterous affair conducted by the young, flirtatious countess of Strathmore hit the newspapers, among the damning stories told about her was that she preferred her cats to her young son—a variation on stories of society women preferring their lapdogs to their husbands. When, after years of unhappy marriage to an abusive husband, the countess finally left him, he hired the satiric cartoonist James Gillray to produce a series of prints accusing her of promiscuity, bad mothering, and cat loving. In one of these prints, the countess sits at a table, suckling two cats who cling by their claws to her enormous bare breasts; her pathetic little boy stands beside her wailing, "I wish I was a cat—my mama would love me then."

Dogs and cats were not the only favored animals of the day. Songbirds, too, had became extremely popular by the end of the seventeenth century. Finches, larks, and linnets caught in the English countryside and captive-bred canaries were sold by vendors with the cry "Buy a fine singing bird." Cages for pet birds, then as now, could be quite elaborate. Caged singing birds invoked the nostalgia of the transition from country to city, for while their size made them practical in cramped city dwellings and their inexpensiveness made them affordable to many, their individual melodies carried reminders of the birdsong that filled the countryside. Birds deemed "clever," such as magpies and imported parrots and macaws that could imitate the human voice, also were popular, if more expensive, pets.

Monkeys, for obvious reasons, were associated with sailors and ships. One could buy monkeys from sailors at the docks, and just as all sailing ships had their resident dogs and cats, so too many had monkeys, at least after they had called in southern hemisphere ports. In the earlier part of the century, monkeys, like lapdogs, were associated with fine ladies, though they were probably considerably less common: they were much more difficult actually to manage, and some women were afraid of them for their trickery or their "indecency."

Wild animals also might find their way into people's homes and hearts. The poet William Cowper was a shy, gentle man and devout

Christian who suffered from some unknown mental illness. He had just emerged from one of his bouts of insanity when someone gave him a baby hare that had been saved from the dogs. Soon he added other hares to his family, and before long his circle of pets had expanded to include "five rabbits, two guinea pigs, a magpie, a jay, a starling, a linnet, two goldfinches, two canary birds, two dogs, and sixteen pigeons." Cowper became one of the finest British poets to write about the human bond with animals. Thinking about his hare rescued from the hunt, he wrote in his major long poem, *The Task,* "Well—one at least is safe." Now the "innocent partner of my peaceful home," she plays on the floor and has a bed of straw where she can sleep without fear. He has gained her confidence, Cowper writes; and he pledges to keep her safe. When she dies, he will be able to say, poignantly, that there has been "at least one hare that had a friend."

WIDE-SCALE PET KEEPING was a development whose social, psychological, and commercial importance cannot be overstated, especially in connection with the rise of animal protection sentiments. Keith Thomas nicely sums up its profoundly transforming effects on British society: "It encouraged the middle classes to form optimistic conclusions about animal intelligence; it gave rise to innumerable anecdotes about animal sagacity; it stimulated the notion that animals could have character and individual personality; and it created the psychological foundation for the view that some animals at least were entitled to moral consideration."

Their loving bonds with their pets gave increasing numbers of people a foundation for questioning the idea that animals lack understanding, feelings, and the ability to communicate. At least as far as their own dogs, cats, and monkeys were concerned, firsthand experience revealed something quite different to Lady Wentworth, Alexander Pope, Horace Walpole, William Hogarth, and many, many others—famous names and ordinary folk alike. It was no coincidence that so many of the early animal protection advocates had their own beloved pets.

Pets became the animals with whom most people, especially in the cities, had the most direct and frequent contact. However, in city and country alike, people had other encounters with animals besides using them for food and labor, encounters that in their own ways worked to undermine received wisdom about animal capacity and the human-animal connection. Not only in the pets basking at one's fireside, but also in animals encountered in the streets and fairs, one could experience a sense of the commonality between humans and beasts that would help shape the attitudes that gave rise to animal protection. Just as a loving lapdog broke through the barrier supposedly separating human qualities from those of beasts, animal performers seemed to offer more evidence that intelligence, communication, and perhaps even the soul were attributes not exclusively human.

CHAPTER 4
DANCING DOGS AND HORSES
OF KNOWLEDGE

✳ ✳ ✳

JOHN EVELYN disliked the disreputable South Bank, but in September 1660, he braved the crowds of Southwark Fair to indulge his scientist's interest in curious sights. Rope dancers, jugglers, and contortionists were everywhere, but one troupe of acrobats particularly captured his attention. They were monkeys and "apes" (probably chimpanzees), and they put on quite a show. The apes danced on the rope while carrying lighted candles in their hands without extinguishing them, they balanced tubs of water on their heads without spilling a drop, and they even turned somersaults with buckets of eggs on their heads without cracking a single one.

Dressed in the latest fashion, they also imitated human high society, and did it uncannily well. "They were gallantly clad *alamode*, went upright, saluted [kissed] the company, bowing, and pulling off their hats," reported Evelyn, adding, "They saluted one another with as good grace as if instructed by a dancing master." These monkeys and apes, like other animal performers to be found at fairs, inns, and street corners, displayed such a remarkable ability to dance, bow, calculate sums, and read that they seemed to call into question on a popular level the position challenged by Margaret Cavendish on a philosophical level: the assertion that animals are incapable of "knowledge, sense, reason, or intelligence."

The spread of compassion for nonhuman creatures in the eighteenth century was fueled in part by various, mutually reinforcing ways in which people were coming to perceive similarities between themselves and animals. At the same time that, for example, anatomists' dissections were revealing marked correspondences between the organs and nervous systems of animals and those of humans, popular encounters with animals were revealing other correspondences—or apparent correspondences—to those inclined to see them. Animal performers reinforced this perception by demonstrating their remarkable ability to learn relatively complex tasks. When these tasks involved mimicking human behavior, as they often did, the family resemblance, as it were, was striking.

London's summer fairs sprawled throughout the streets, fields, and inn yards of neighborhoods in different sections of the city: May Fair to the west, Tottenham Fair to the north, Bartholomew Fair in the ancient parish of St. Bartholomew (abutting the stinking Smithfield livestock market), and Southwark Fair. There, engulfed by crowds of all classes, besieged by a cacophony of trumpets, pipes, drums, and human voices, people ate roasted meat and apples, drank more than their fill of ale, scrutinized elaborate clockwork scenes featuring hundreds of moving parts, watched dancers cavort on the high wires and rubber-limbed contortionists twist their bodies into knots, and marveled at feats of magic and sleight of hand. (If they were wise, they also kept their own hands firmly clenched around their purses, for pickpockets lurked everywhere.) Fairgoers also attended performances ranging from puppetry and pantomime to concerts and the traditional drolls enacting imaginatively pared-down and hammed-up renditions of Shakespeare's plays.

Animals, unsurprisingly, were among the fairs' star attractions, beginning with the butchered pigs hanging in Bartholomew Fair's cook-shops, which filled the air with the aroma of roasting pork. Beasts provided more than food, however: animal dancers, acrobats, and comedians were an integral part of the fairs' spectacle, as were displays of animals whose appeal lay in their curiosity value. One attraction was the Giant Hog, whose awe-inspiring bulk seemed as subject to inflation as the economy: in the early eighteenth century, a pig was considered massive at ten feet long; by 1748, standards had increased to twelve, and by 1779, a hog had to stretch fourteen feet to merit the title "giant."

Spectators were drawn to animals in distorted, grotesque shapes. Some of these creatures possessed more or fewer than the usual number of legs (such as the "goose with four feet—and a cock with three" viewed by Samuel Pepys in 1663) or seemed to have parts of other species growing on their bodies. Other beasts attracted crowds because of their sheer exoticism. As England's ships sailed into new areas of the world to trade and conquer, establishing its empire and encountering new peoples, plants, and animals, specimens of all of these exotica regularly arrived at the ports of London. "Apes" (chimps and macaques) and tigers, in fact, had been arriving in such quantities for so long that by Pepys's and Evelyn's day they had become almost commonplace. (As early as the 1630s, the story went, one English merchant had written to request that his overseas agent send him "2 OR 3 apes," but since he hastily omitted the "r," his agent understood him to request 203 apes—which duly arrived at the London docks.) A 1713 poem about Bartholomew Fair referred to both a rhinoceros and elephants as typical sights.

Strange and marvelous creatures could be seen everywhere in London, displayed not only at the fairs but also around town, in showrooms and inns, at other times of the year. In 1730, for instance, the newspapers reported that "a very curious animal, alive, called a hog in armour"—a tortoise—had been presented to the Prince of Wales by a sailor who brought it back from the West Indies. Henri Misson was intrigued by the live opossum and rattlesnake he saw at the Royal Society. John Evelyn wrote in great, fascinated detail about his visit to the Belle Savage Inn on Ludgate Hill to see a rhinoceros, which he, following the precedent of the King James Bible, understood to be a kind of unicorn. He described with awe her scaly, sagging skin, her set of "most dreadful teeth," and her enormous bulk. When she lay down, he said, she appeared like an overturned coach: "if she grow proportionable to her present age, she will be a mountain." The famous rhinoceros, named Clara, caused a sensation when she capped her seventeen-year tour through Europe with a visit to London in early 1758. Displayed in a tent in Lambeth's Horse and Groom Inn from eight in the morning to six in the evening, Clara was visited by the cream of London society, including the royal family, before she died suddenly that April.

Evelyn also viewed another novelty, a West Indies crocodile, whose "sharp & long teeth" were terrible, but whose belly was a "lovely green." This creature, too, he worried, could grow to be dangerous—though there had long been some tame lions around town; apparently less worried about their teeth, Evelyn once stuck his hand into the mouth of one, which fortunately for him proved as docile as reported.

During the eighteenth century, several collections of animals were on display, forerunners of the Zoological Society, which would open in 1828 in the new public space called Regent's Park, where the London Zoo still is today. Some of the zoo's creatures were transferred from an older collection, the royal menagerie in the Tower. For centuries the passion for collecting rare, exotic animals—apes, leopards, giraffes, elephants, and camels, among others—had raged among the royal courts of both the Christian and Muslim worlds. In Britain, menagerie-collecting came in with the Norman Conquest. In the thirteenth century, Henry III received gifts from fellow monarchs of three leopards, an elephant, and a polar bear (who fished for his dinner in the Thames), and the menagerie expanded with subsequent rulers to include camels, lions, tigers, eagles, and many other beasts. People flocked, fascinated, to get a look at the wonderful creatures. For centuries every visitor to London was expected "to go see the lions at the Tower."

In his typically dyspeptic manner, Ned Ward reported in the *London Spy* of 1699, no doubt accurately, that the menagerie stank like a dog kennel. There, Ward saw four lions, or "Beelzebub's blood-hounds, or lap-dogs for a she-devil," as he engagingly called them. One of the lions swiped at him with claws "like pruning hooks." Ward told the story of the keeper's young female assistant who had grown too confident and careless around the lions and ended up being ripped apart by one. The keeper himself had once come face to face with a lion, but, fortunately for him, this one decided to put its paws on his shoulders and lick his face. Ward also saw a tiger, a wildcat, three eagles, two owls, a hyena, two stuffed lions, and a domestic cat and dog who were included in that exotic company because each had only two legs. He also visited the bad-tempered leopard that had "grown as cunning as a cross Bedlamite that loves not to be looked at." His allusion was to Bedlam, London's mad-house, which was a major tourist attraction despite the fact that the in-mates had been known to throw the contents of their chamber pots at gawkers. This leopard (who indeed must have been driven mad by his own confinement) would "stare in your face, and piss upon you, his urine being as hot as aqua fortis, and stinks worse than a pole-cat's."

A decade later, when Von Uffenbach made his own obligatory trip to the Tower, the menagerie appears to have diminished. He saw two fierce "Indian cats," some wolves, two eagles—one of which, he was told, was forty years old—and a tiger. He also saw four lions caged together amica-bly with a dog, although, he remarked, if the lions were not adequately fed, their attitude toward the dog might change. He did not mention whether this dog had more or fewer than the usual number of legs, but he was disappointed to hear that the two-legged cat was dead.

Beasts were not only passive (or not so passive, considering the ill-mannered leopard) displays in London's fairs, menageries, inns, and streets. They were also—as John Evelyn witnessed—active entertain-ers. In 1718, a booth at Southwark Fair advertised a French troupe of dancing dogs freshly come from entertaining royalty at Hampton Court and Richmond, "their dresses, as well as their dances, being en-tirely after the French mode, particularly Miss Depingle in her Hoop petticoat and leading strings." The hoop petticoats of this period were enormous, radiating rings stiffened by whalebone, much enjoyed by satirists, who pictured women colliding with each other on the streets, trying in vain to stuff themselves through coach doors, and tipping over without being able to get back up. Miss Depingle presumably sported a miniature version. Leading strings were strips of fabric at-tached to the dress of a child that were used to help the infant—or, as in this case, the dog—learn to walk.

Dancing dogs inspired one of Samuel Johnson's most memorable witticisms. When Boswell mentioned one Sunday that he had been to a Quaker meetinghouse where he had heard a female preacher (a great novelty), Johnson uttered a famous line: "Sir, a woman's preaching is like a dog's walking on his hind legs. It is not done well; but you are surprised to find it done at all."

On the last day of performances of an "animal pantomime" at the Haymarket Theatre, the newspaper ran a related account of a concert given in Paris by a band of animal musicians. "A number of cats, clothed uniformly, were placed on stools, with music books before them, and a monkey in the middle who beat time. On a signal given by the monkey, the cats set up a mewing, and were accompanied by some violins; which form'd a very diverting dissonance." This act was a great hit with the Parisians. Similar feline musicians who "sang" to musical accompaniment were later to be seen in London, too. There may have been local versions of the seventeenth-century "cat piano," in which cats were lined up in compartments attached to a keyboard, and with every note, a hammer drove a sharp spike into a cat's tail, causing it to "sing." The cruelty of this was overt, but the behind-the-scenes methods used to train other animal performers were often at least as cruel.

MUCH OF WHAT was fascinating and unsettling about these animal entertainments was precisely the way in which nonhuman creatures so astutely "held the looking-glass" up to humans. A variety of animals could be pressed into human-imitating service. In 1679, for instance, Robert Hooke saw at Bartholomew Fair an elephant that waved flags, fired a gun, bowed with bended knee, and carried a man on its back in a castle. A Bengalese marmoset danced and a hare beat a tambourine before audiences at Sadler's Wells. Dancing bears had long been a mainstay of popular entertainment, seen frequently in the streets: a bear might be forced to stand on its head, or dance with a monkey on its back. A juggler named Breslaw exhibited in Cockspur Street a regiment of little birds, wearing cone-shaped grenadiers' hats made of paper and carrying tiny muskets under their wings. The birds conducted military drills, and then they marched a "deserter" into place facing a small brass cannon that had been packed with gunpowder. The designated executioner, clutching a lighted match in its claw, hopped up to light the fuse. When the cannon fired, the condemned culprit immediately fell over and lay still—only to rise from the dead at its master's command.

That many animals were more powerful, or more skilled at certain tasks, than most humans was obvious. Even Descartes acknowledged this with no sense of alarm, for to him their superior facility, like that of the clock that kept better time, was simply mechanical. When it came to types of performances, such as acrobatics, that both people and animals engaged in, superiority might be credited to certain animals— simian performers, for instance, equaled or outstripped humans in acrobatic balance and dexterity. (Humans performing feats of climbing or tumbling might more aptly to be said to imitate monkeys than the other way around.) In 1766, for instance, "Signor Placido's Company," performing at the Little Haymarket Theatre, featured a monkey on a tightrope who, his advertisement promised,

> walks, dances, and turns about on the tight rope with the pole . . . he walks blindfolded in a sack, balances various equilibres, and rolls a wheelbarrow with a dog in it on the wire, with and without a pole; he vaults and turns the Katharine wheel on the slack rope to admiration.

But some of these entertainers also staged human scenarios, like the monkeys Evelyn saw, thus exercising a more unsettling fascination. Von Uffenbach, roaming along Fleet Street one October afternoon, came upon a street performance featuring an ape who juggled and smoked tobacco. About the same time, a type of simian advertised as never having been seen in England before, a supposedly West Indian "Man Teger" (probably, conjectures the literary scholar Richard Altick,

Who rewards the Posture Masters.

Monkey imitating man imitating monkey: Marcellus Laroon's
Joseph Clark the Posture Master, from *Cryes of the City of London,*
1687 (**Courtesy Guildhall Library**)

a West African baboon), was said "from the head downward [to]
resembl[e] a man." This creature, "taking a glass of ale in his hand like
a Christian, drinks it, also plays at quarter staff." When Samuel Pepys
took Elizabeth to Bartholomew Fair in 1663, where they saw a monkey
tightrope dancer, he was not impressed, finding the creatures' antics
"strange, but such dirty sport that I was not pleased with it." Perhaps
their resemblance to humans made him uneasy.

If monkeys looked uncannily like people, especially when they wore clothing and imitated human behavior, other performing animals seemed to encroach upon a different aspect of humanness: rationality. Particularly fascinating to many people were the animals that seemed to exercise reason and its corollary, language—the supposedly exclusive human capabilities that fundamentally separated mankind from brute beasts, according to dominant religious, philosophical, and scientific traditions. Talking parrots and mynah birds were popular pets that, like monkeys, were brought to England by sailors. Pepys encountered a mynah bird that "talks many things, and neighs like the horse and other things, the best almost that ever I heard bird in my life."

In his late-seventeenth-century *Essay Concerning Human Understanding,* John Locke told a story reported to him, he said, by a credible observer, of the "rational parrot." An elderly Brazilian parrot, brought into a room with a group of Dutchmen, allegedly exclaimed, "What a company of white men are here!" When asked who he was, the parrot responded, "A Portuguese," and when asked what he did, the parrot said, "I guard the chickens," elaborating that he knew very well how to do his job and making the "chucking" sounds people use to call chickens. Locke's philosophical point was that identity is based upon the body: no matter how much sense this bird's discourse might make, no one in their right minds would think that the speaker was a human who happened to look like a parrot. In order to make this point, he appeared to accept the *possibility* of a "rational parrot"—the possibility that a bird can possess reason and language.

Some of the most popular acts staged at the fairs and at the inns and theaters around London and the provincial towns were "learned animals," and they seemed to proliferate as the eighteenth century progressed. Like the talking birds and the wig-wearing apes who bowed and curtseyed, these creatures, too—a "horse of knowledge," for instance, or a "sagacious pig"—seemed to blur the lines between human and animal. During the Elizabethan period, William Banks's remarkable horse Morocco astonished people with his ability to dance, count, fetch, identify people, play dead, and defecate on command (apparently a particular crowd-pleaser). John Evelyn attended a performance at a private house of "a dog that seemed to do many rational actions," and that shared the bill that day with a man who ate live coals (by contrast with whom the dog might well have appeared rational).

At Bartholomew Fair, Samuel Pepys enjoyed an encounter with a learned mare, who, he said, could dance and count money. One of her many gifts, apparently, was her ability to spot an incorrigible womanizer. Asked by her owner (to whom Pepys had given twelve pence beforehand) to identify "him of the company that most loved a pretty wench in a corner," the mare headed straight for Samuel. This, Pepys reported happily in the polyglot words he used to recount his sexual adventures in his diary, gave him "occasions to besar [kiss] a mighty belle fille that was in the house, that was exceeding plain but forte belle." Unhappily but probably all too typically for the mare, when Pepys (perhaps hoping for a repeat performance with the belle fille) returned to the fair a few days later with some friends, he found the horse "to act much worse than the other day, she forgetting many things, which her master did beat her for and was mightily vexed."

In the mid-eighteenth century, a retired cavalryman and impresario named Philip Astley established a riding school in Lambeth, near Westminster Bridge, that became the predecessor of the modern circus. He began staging shows that featured bareback riding stunts; eventually he built a great amphitheater in which he expanded his repertory from horseback stunts to include other entertainments such as acrobatics, animal dancing, and pantomimes. In 1768, Astley bought a small horse named Billy at Smithfield Market. Within a decade, Billy, billed as the "Little Military Learned Horse, three feet high from the deserts of Arabia," was giving demonstrations in which he counted and figured sums, shot a pistol, played dead, danced, read minds, and spelled out Astley's name in the dirt with his hoof.

Perhaps no learned animal in the eighteenth century excited the public more than the Wonderful Pig, which first appeared at Charing

Cross in 1785 and went on to perform to great acclaim at Sadler's Wells. His original trainer, one S. Bisset, previously had acts featuring dogs, horses, monkeys, canaries, a rabbit, turkeys, and cats. His "Cat's Opera" starred three felines who played the dulcimer and sang. But the pig outdid them all. Using cards with letters printed on them to read, spell, do sums, and tell time, the Wonderful Pig created a sensation.*

The Amazing Learned Pig, or Scientific Pig, as he was also called, had his detractors. Sylas Neville, a mid-century diarist, thought that pigs were "the least docile [animal] in nature," and, referring to this beast's popularity, contemptuously sniffed, "any thing will do in London." The historian Joseph Strutt, writing in 1800, called the Learned Pig a "large unwieldy hog" and thought his performance was "a very ridiculous show." When he transferred to Sadler's Wells, the pig outraged the resident troupe of rope dancers and tumblers, who took offense at being expected to take second billing to a swine. They gave the proprietor, Richard Wroughton, an ultimatum: either the pig went or they would. Needless to say, the pig stayed. (The human performers had to find new jobs at Astley's Circus.)

These lowered expectations about swine in general would have made the Wonderful Pig's performances all that much more astonishing and appealing to large numbers of people, including those in the social and cultural elite. High society flocked to see this hog use its alphabet cards to read people's minds. Fashionable women reportedly waited four hours in line to gain admittance. The Wonderful Pig, the poet Robert Southey remarked with a certain acerbity, was "in his day a far greater object of admiration to the English nation than ever was Sir Isaac Newton." Among the several other pigs of knowledge who followed his trail, one successor, the very popular "Sapient Pig" named Toby, published his autobiography in 1817, entitled *The Life and Adventures of Toby, the Sapient*

*Today we recognize pigs as among the most intelligent nonhuman animals, but the eighteenth century held them in low esteem, apparently because of their bulk and their supposedly slovenly habits. Their status in the Hebrew Bible and medieval Christian bestiaries as unclean animals (not to mention their documented taste for human flesh) may have contributed to antiporcine prejudice.

Pig: with his opinions on Men and Manners. Written by Himself. He said that he had been taught to write by his mother, who had educated herself by devouring an entire library.

When Samuel Johnson's old acquaintance the poet Anna Seward (known as the Swan of Lichfield), told him about seeing the marvelous pig in its earlier appearance at Nottingham, Johnson was interested, joking that the pig's learning proved that swine have been "unjustly calumniated." Now it was clear, he said, that pigs were not stupid after all, but that humans prevented them from realizing their potential by butchering most of them when they were a year old. When another person present at this conversation remarked that the pig's trainer must have inflicted "great torture" upon the animal in order to instill learning into such a creature, Johnson agreed that this was undoubtedly true. But, he observed, the Wonderful Pig, now three years old, had no reason to complain, for he would have been killed in his first year had he not been undergoing his schooling, however torturous. Surely, said Johnson (who was in the last months of his own long, often tormented life), "protracted existence is a good recompense for very considerable degrees of torture."

By making people think about the similarities between beasts and humans, animal performers contributed, at least potentially, to the changing attitudes that would create the animal welfare movement. But they also figured in the rise of the animal protection cause more directly, for they were yet another category of abused animals. The cruelty involved in these entertainments was often (though not always) less visible than that of bullbaiting, for it took place behind the scenes. Yet it did not go unnoticed by contemporary observers that many animal dancers, acrobats, musicians, and intellectuals paid a high price in suffering for the monetary rewards they brought their owners. Not everyone took that as lightly as Dr. Johnson.

Performing beasts were often subjected to serious abuse, such as that inflicted upon the learned mare Pepys saw. (He did not seem particularly distressed by her owner's violence.) Writing over a century later, when sensitivities toward animal mistreatment were much more developed, however, Strutt attacked the cruelty of animal trainers, calling Bisset, the Wonderful Pig's showman, his "tormenter" and reporting that this man had "lost" three earlier pigs during the course of training them. Bisset also owned a troupe of turkeys that he made to "dance" by lighting a fire under the floor they stood on. Another showman had taught his bears to "dance" by applying hot irons to their feet while a fiddle was played. And of the drum-playing hare that performed for a crowd of spectators without running away, Strutt commented, "It is astonishing what may be effected by constant exertion and continually tormenting even the most timid and intractable animals."

Punishment to instill fear was considered more effective than rewards to encourage affection. A nineteenth-century animal welfare publication detailed the abuse that went into training animal entertainers by using the example of a monkey famous for performing twelve different acts. Its owner admitted that it had taken two years of incessant beatings to break the monkey of its natural behavior. Even once it was trained, she severely caned it before each performance—in order, she said, "to quicken its faculties"—and continued to "tap" it as it went through its complicated routines. This, then, concluded the outraged writer, is "the inspired learning of this wretched monkey, as well as of other *learned* animals."

As popular spectacles in which cruelty played an integral if often covert part, animal performances, whether acrobatic or intellectual, had much in common with overtly violent pleasures such as bullbaiting and cockfighting. But unlike the animals in traditional blood sports, many of these performers, through their apparent intelligence and anthropomorphic behavior, seemed to participate in the human world in humanlike ways. Animal performances are as old as human history. But in the eighteenth century, a time when other encounters between humans and beasts were undermining species boundaries, these animal performances contributed to an emerging sense of kinship and identification with beasts. That sense of kinship was altering perceptions of the animal world and fostering the growing sense of responsibility to it that would inspire animal protection. In their blurring of the boundaries between human and animals, and in the abuse that often underlay them, the performances also shared elements with another kind of entertaining animal spectacle. But instead of the playhouse and the fairground, these animals performed in the courtroom and the gallows.

CHAPTER 5

ANIMAL CRIMES

❋   ❋   ❋

D URING THE summer of 1677, London's criminal court, the Old Bailey, was packed with spectators who had gathered there to see one of the most talked-about trials of the year. The defendant was Mary Hicks, a married woman who lived in the working-class neighborhood of Cripplegate, outside the City walls, whom the court records characterized as "that monster rather than woman." Hicks stood accused of having committed "the crime of buggery with a certain mongrel dog, and wickedly, devilishly, and against nature had venereal and carnal copulation with him, &c." Her neighbors testified that Mary was a woman of "lewd conversation," and that through holes in the walls of her room, they had often spied on her while she engaged in unclean behavior with men. Three witnesses testified that they also had seen Mary engaged in acts with her dog that were "unfit to be described" in the court records, and that they had several times seen her "practicing this beastliness." Mary denied the allegation, claiming that the witnesses were motivated by malice.

The most dramatic moment in this sensational trial came when the accused dog was led before the court. The mongrel sealed Mary Hicks's fate, and his own, by wagging his tail when he saw her and "making motions as it were to kiss her," just as he had done, the witnesses said, when they coupled. Within this highly charged courtroom scene, the dog's natural greeting behavior was taken as the final proof of culpability: the verdict was guilty, the sentence death. A few days later, Mary Hicks and her canine lover were paraded together in the condemned cart from Newgate Prison to Tyburn Tree, the gallows located near the spot in Hyde Park where the Marble Arch stands today. Before she was executed, Mary was forced to watch while her dog was hanged.*

Prosecution and execution, as well as the religious penalty of anathematization (declaring someone or something accursed), of animals had been practiced in Europe, especially in France, since the later Middle Ages and were most common during the Renaissance. But they continued throughout the seventeenth century and persisted, though greatly lessening in frequency, during the eighteenth and nineteenth centuries. Records exist for nearly two hundred of these trials, and there were probably more whose documents do not survive. While they took place more frequently on the Continent, they did occur in England, too: the ability (and the desire) to criminalize animals in certain contexts was shared throughout the Western world. Edward Payson Evans's fascinating book *The Criminal Prosecution and Capital Punishment of Animals,* published in 1906, remains the definitive account of this phenomenon.

Ecclesiastical courts in Europe conducted proceedings against pests such as rats, mice, locusts, and caterpillars for destroying crops. (The church based its authority over brutes upon biblical precedents such as God's curse on the serpent; as beings created prior to man, however, animals were also supposed to be treated with clemency, insofar as this was consistent with justice.) Secular courts heard sodomy and murder charges against domestic animals—dogs, cows, pigs, and bulls. These prosecutions took place in the context of other human-animal connections, such as the practice of rural people living under the same roof as

---

*In 1704, one Mary Price was indicted at the Old Bailey for the "horrible and abominable Sin of Sodomy," committed with a dog. The accuser again was a neighbor, but this time, witnesses in the accused's defense testified that the accuser and her mother had often quarreled with Mary and shown malice toward her. When asked what color the dog was, the accuser said she could not tell, nor did she know whether the dog belonged to Mary or not. *This* Mary was acquitted.

their working beasts and the widespread belief that animal behavior reflected or predicted something of consequence for human society. Forbidden interactions such as those of which Mary Hicks and her dog stood accused were in some ways more extreme consequences of the deep, daily intertwining of animal and human lives.

The prosecution, conviction (or exoneration), and execution of beasts implicitly endowed animals with humanlike characteristics, assigning them legal and moral responsibility for their actions. This view of animal culpability would become outmoded in the eighteenth century, displaced by some of the same changes in thinking about beasts that underlay the rise of animal protection. But insofar as this new thinking about animals involved a developing sense of kinship to them, it was in certain respects anticipated by the phenomenon of animal prosecution. Just as a sagacious pig or performing ape might seem in its own way to bridge the supposed gap between people and beasts, so, too, did these early spectacles of the courtroom and gallows suggest some kind of shared identity.

The accounts of these early criminal trials of animals indicate that, as a general practice, the treatment of a beast accused of a serious crime did not differ from the treatment of its human counterpart. People and animals were held in the same prisons, fed at the same levels of expense, and assigned defense lawyers.* The animal's legal right to a proper trial was usually taken very seriously: when a sow accused of wounding a child in Franconia, Germany, in 1576 was summarily executed by the hangman before she could be tried, the hangman had to flee town, so great was the court and public outrage at his usurpation of the judicial process. Courtroom verdicts could be nuanced, too. In

---

*The sixteenth-century French lawyer Bartholomew Chassenée made his name defending rats accused of eating grain. When the rats were summoned to appear in court but never showed up, he invoked the right exercised by humans to refuse to obey a summons to a place where they would be in danger. The rats could justifiably fear for their lives were they to make the trip to court, since all along the way lurked cats waiting to pounce. (The 1993 British film *The Advocate*—released in the U.K. as *The Hour of the Pig*—features Colin Firth as a Chassenée-like lawyer, assigned to defend a pig charged with homicide.)

1457, a sow in Sevigny was convicted of "murder flagrantly committed" on a five-year-old boy and sentenced to be hanged; her six piglets, which had been found with blood on them, were indicted as accomplices, but since no proof could be brought that they had actually assisted their mother in the crime, they were acquitted.

When the accusation was sodomy, the accused man or woman and the implicated animal stood trial together and, if both parties were found guilty, were executed together. (In Britain, bestiality became a capital crime in 1534 and, except for a brief lapse during that century, remained one until 1861.) The standard sentence was for the pair to be burned alive, but sometimes they were hanged first, or the animal was compassionately strangled or knocked on the head before being thrown into the flames.

Evans points out the grim irony that medieval Christian sodomy laws, which were based on Mosaic law, considered sex between a Christian and a Jew as a capital offense equivalent to human copulation with a dog. Also, seventeenth-century English moralists and legal writers aligned male homosexuality with bestiality committed by both men and women as forms of "buggery." Sir Edward Coke, the lord chief justice of England in the early years of the century, adjudged this sin a felony: "Buggery is a detestable, and abominable sin, amongst Christians not to be named, committed by carnal knowledge against the ordinance of the Creator, and order of nature, by mankind with mankind, or with brute beast, or by woman-kind with brute beast." The stated penalty for all these offenses was burial alive.

The most commonly cited biblical prohibition against bestiality occurs in Leviticus 20:15–16: "And if a man lie with a beast, he shall surely be put to death: and ye shall slay the beast. And if a woman approach unto any beast, and lie down thereto, thou shalt kill the woman, and the beast: they shall surely be put to death; their blood shall be upon them." Some people argued that animals, being irrational, were incapable of culpability for such crimes, although putting them to death was necessary for other reasons. The twelfth-century churchman Gerald of Wales reported the story of a woman in France who submitted herself to a lion's "beastly love"; both human and animal were "worthy of a shameful death," he explained. "The beast is ordered to be killed, not for the guilt, from which he is excused as being a beast, but to make the remembrance of the act a deterrent, calling to mind the terrible deed."

Bestiality was considered the gravest sexual crime because it violated the separation between human and animal. Raging against a story of intercourse between an Irishwoman and a goat, Gerald specified that the unnaturalness of the act lay in a woman's lowering herself to the level of a beast: human reason succumbing to animal sensuality. (Sexual intercourse itself was considered by many to be brutish, and bestiaries itemized a large number of animals associated with lust or adultery.) The clergyman Richard Capel, writing in 1633, exclaimed that sex with an animal "turns man into a very beast, makes a man a member of a brute creature." Yet bestiality was also understood as a particularly human offense, for beasts themselves, as the seventeenth-century moralist William Gouge remarked (not entirely accurately), never attempted to mate with those outside their own species: "Brute beasts content themselves with their own Kind." Still, the later consensus followed the biblical condemnation of the animal victim as well as the human initiator: even if not guilty in a moral sense, the animal was still in some sense a transgressor, tainted by the sin—a reminder of it. In a treatise on the Ten Commandments, a seventeenth-century moralist wrote: "Buggery with beasts is . . . a sin so hated of God, that the innocent and harmless beast should die as well as the party that committed the fact."

In the realm of comedy and satire, women's fondness for their lapdogs, monkeys, and squirrels was an apparently inexhaustible source of humor, and was often described in ways that suggested the sexual. A joke that never seemed to get old was that women were much more attached to their lapdogs than they were to their husbands. In an era when many upper-class marriages were arranged and husbands notoriously unfaithful, there may have been some truth to this witticism. In the middle of the eighteenth century, the clergyman John Hildrop related a conversation with a "very pretty lady" who was bestowing endearments and kisses on her lapdog. Hildrop asked her how she could waste on a dog the affection that many men would be grateful to receive. "Sir," she replied, "I love my little dog, because he loves me; and when I can meet with any one of your sex, that has half so much gratitude and sincerity as my poor Totty, he shall never find me insensible or ungrateful."

The satirist Tom Brown told a story about a despairing woman who suffered the "double Widowhood" of losing "upon the same day the best husband, and the prettiest little lap-dog in London." She cries harder, tearing her hair and beating her breasts, when her dog Dony is mentioned than she does when thinking of her husband. The human does finally seem to outweigh the animal, however: it takes a new lap-dog just eight days to make her forget entirely about poor Dony, whereas it takes a full three months before she marries a new husband. In Jane Austen's *Mansfield Park*, the indolent Lady Bertram cares more for her pug than her children, with inevitably disastrous consequences.

Alexander Pope repeated this idea in his mock-heroic poem *The Rape of the Lock,* writing of the two great crises in women's lives: "when Husbands or when Lap-dogs breathe their last." The same poem contains a more explicitly off-color joke: Belinda's lapdog Shock "wakes his mistress with his tongue"—another way in which women apparently preferred their dogs to their husbands or human lovers. In Nahum Tate's 1685 comedy *Cuckolds' Haven*, a servant offers his sexual services to his master's wife thus: "Dear delicate Madam, I am your little parakeet, your sparrow, your shock, your pug, your squirrel."

OF THE CRIMES allegedly committed by domestic animals acting without human accomplices, by far the most common was homicide. Small children were often the victims, especially of hogs who killed and devoured them. Pigs were, in fact, the most frequent animal offenders in murder trials. Evans assumes that this was because there were so many of them, roaming freely through towns and villages; hogs were seen everywhere in British cities, too, including London, and were reported as killing children into the nineteenth century. (Their fates in the courtroom may also have been influenced by medieval Christian symbolism, in which sows represented sinners and heretics, an echo of the pig's status in Hebrew law as an unclean animal.) Animals found guilty of homicide were often burned alive, though sometimes they were hanged before, or instead of, being sent to the pyre. In 1386, a sow convicted of murdering a child in Normandy was forced into men's clothes before being hanged in the public square.

THE EXECUTION OF convicted animals was often held to be necessary, to expiate bloodshed within a community or to banish the demons that had possessed the creatures. Exodus 21:28 established the principle: "If an ox gore a man or a woman, that they die: then the ox shall be surely stoned, and his flesh shall not be eaten." While putting a dangerous beast to death freed the community from the threat that it might kill again—and punished the owner by depriving him or her of a valuable animal—the ritual of trial and formal execution indicates that a more complicated social function was being served. Dix Harwood conjectures that such executions arose "among primitive peoples as *lex talionis*" (the law of compensation: "an eye for an eye") intended "to appease the injured party." Other modern scholars have seen these trials as rituals that served the purpose of maintaining community standards of morality and the rule of law, or as ascribing meaning and intention to the animals' otherwise arbitrary, inexplicable acts of violence.

Whatever their rationale in either Europe or Britain, the trial and punishment of animals for buggery or murder implied that, however harmless and innocent they might be considered and however much their status as property subjected them to human control, they nonetheless had committed crimes and should answer for them. Even when the rationale for the condemnation seemed to reject anthropomorphic thinking by exonerating the animal of moral responsibility, the process of the scrupulous formal trial, conviction, and official execution nonetheless implied that beasts had some kind of equivalence with humans, some kind of accountability before the law (and therefore also a possibility of being exonerated by it). To force a sow into men's clothes for the occasion of her execution suggests that the crime she had committed was a human one, or that condemnation and punishment, at least, transformed the animal into a symbolic person.

Mary Hicks's dog was not only a damning courtroom witness against his mistress but also a malefactor himself. During the trial, he did not have the same status as a defendant that she did, and his hanging in front of her eyes was clearly part of *her* punishment (and part of the spectacle that served as warning to other people who might be harboring lustful thoughts about their own dogs). But the mongrel's execution also implied that he was killed for his *active* participation in the crime, as that incriminating attempt at a courtroom kiss illustrated.

In 1750, however, when Jacques Ferron of Vanvres, France, was accused of sodomy with a she-ass, Ferron was convicted and executed but the donkey was not punished. Unlike the wretched Jacques, the she-ass had character witnesses eager to testify on her behalf. The parish priest and leading members of the community submitted a document declaring that they had known the donkey for four years, and, as Evans summarizes their report, "she had always shown herself to be virtuous and well-behaved both at home and abroad and had never given occasion of scandal to any one, and that therefore 'they were willing to bear witness that she is in word and deed and in all her habits a most honest creature.'" Deciding that she had not acted of her own free will, the court acquitted her. The man was deemed bestial, while the beast was considered virtuous—a human attribute. (The word "virtue" derives from the Latin *vir,* man; when used to describe a woman, "virtue" implied chastity.)

In the cases of both Mary Hicks's dog and Jacques Ferron's she-ass, both the species and the sex of the animals seem to have been significant in their fates. The trials invoked vestiges of attitudes stemming from associations with the various types of animals in medieval Christian tradition. Dogs had traditionally been associated with filthiness and lust, and although by the late seventeenth century some types of dogs had been elevated to the top of the animal hierarchy as helpmeets of humans, the negative stereotype persisted—particularly for dogs such as this mongrel, who, like his mistress, was lower-class. Medieval Christian tradition associated the ass either with lechery or with meekness: apparently the latter association was paramount during the Vanvres she-ass's day in court.

Human gender associations clearly played a part as well, for these animals were assigned stereotypical traits attached at that time to men and women: criminal male lust and honest female virtue. The male dog was presumably a willing, active partner, the she-ass presumably an unwilling, passive victim. The terms of the donkey's acquittal imply that it would have been possible for such a beast to possess a *disreputable* character, in which case she would have been found guilty and executed along with Jacques. Whatever her defenders actually had in mind when they referred to the ass's freedom from scandal and her honesty in word, deed, and habits, their description suggested a human feminine ideal.

Sparing the life of a female donkey because of her good moral character and dressing a pig in men's clothes as part of the execution ritual may have been unusual, but the anthropomorphic assumptions behind these acts stressed the way in which the criminal trials and punishment of animals contradicted the absolute distinctions between humans and beasts so often asserted in official Christian doctrine. On the one hand, executing a murderous sow seemed to reassert the hierarchical differences of species and power between humans and beasts—after all, humans "murdered" sows every day. But, on the other hand, imprisoning, trying, hanging and/or burning, and explicitly *not* eating the animal, rather than simply butchering her and serving her for dinner, implied that the commission of murder moved the sow out of one category of being and into another that more closely approximated the human.

ALTHOUGH IN BRITAIN and its colonies official trials and executions of animals were much less common than on the Continent, a long, unofficial tradition of holding animals responsible for bad behavior certainly flourished. People felt, Thomas comments, "that men and beasts inhabited the same moral universe and that terms of praise or reproach could be applied interchangeably to either." Humans injured in some way by miscreant animals routinely retaliated against them, and often used them as cautionary examples to other animals: a farmer might shoot a crow plundering his fields and nail its body to a fencepost, for instance. William Byrd, an early-eighteenth-century writer, statesman, and planter in the colony of Virginia, punished a dog that had killed a lamb by putting her into a stall with a ram "that beat her violently to break her of that bad custom." In *The Merchant of Venice*, Gratiano compares Shylock to a wolf "hanged for human slaughter." The practice of hanging an offending canine was common enough to give rise to the expression "a hangdog look." James Woodforde, a country parson, wrote in his diary that his young greyhound named Fly had stolen a shoulder of mutton from a nearby farm and eaten it. The neighbors complained so vehemently about Fly's theft that, he said, "I had the greyhound hanged in the evening." Probably, as the owner of the miscreant (itself an expensive animal), he also accepted a degree of the blame and paid them compensation.

In 1711, Tom Gerrard, age twenty-four, was hanged at Tyburn Tree for housebreaking. Poor Tom had been a rather hapless housebreaker: he had already been burned in the hand for an earlier burglary attempt that, so the story went, had been foiled by a parrot. According to the *Newgate Calendar*, Poll's owner was a "profane gentleman" who had taught the bird to curse. When Gerrard sneaked into the parlor where Poll lived and tried to make off with a few pieces of plate, the parrot "set up her throat and fell a-screaming out: 'Thieves, God damn you! Thieves, thieves, by God, make haste!'" The servants ran in and caught the burglar red-handed. (While accounts in the *Newgate Calendar* obviously must be taken with a large grain of salt, this anecdote at least seems to show that in the popular mind a parrot was perfectly capable of understanding which words in her limited but expressive vocabulary were suited to the occasion.)

When Gerrard was executed for a subsequent break-in, his attractive little dog was adopted by a Presbyterian parson, who was quite fond of the animal. But one day when he was shopping near Newgate Market, the dog ran off and brought back a purse containing a considerable amount of money. When the dog did it again, the shocked parson realized that Gerrard had taught his pet to pick pockets. An apparently incorrigible miscreant, the canine suffered his first master's fate: when they got home, the parson "called this criminal to justice, and very fairly hanged the poor cur, for fear he should at last pick pockets in his meeting-house." When, at the end of the eighteenth century, the member of Parliament John Dent introduced a bill to levy a tax on dogs, he told the story of a dog that had been seen killing sheep, but had bathed in a pond afterward, washing off the incriminating blood. This was reported to his master, who put the dog to the question by hanging him by his hind legs, whereupon he vomited a quantity of blood, thus proving his guilt. In this case, as with Woodforde's Fly, the master probably was deemed financially accountable for his dog's damage, and certainly the dog would have been killed.

Sometimes baiting was a means of punishing animals deemed criminal. Unlike the customary bear garden baiting in which the baited bull or bear usually survived (however wounded), punitive baitings were intended to continue until the animal was dead. In the early seventeenth century, King James I ordered the baiting to death of a bear that had killed a child. Later that century, John Evelyn recorded the news that a horse accused of having killed a man was to be baited to death by dogs. The event was advertised as a special entertainment. That this equine capital punishment was made into an amusement was not so remarkable in a society in which the hanging of human criminals at Tyburn Tree was a spectator event complete with gin and gingerbread vendors.

The description of the horse as a murderer raised the stakes of the sport, adding the novelty appeal so desired by bear garden proprietors. But it probably also provided an additional pretext for baiting a species of animal that was usually admired as the most noble of beasts, and one of the two species that most faithfully served humankind—the other being dogs, which in this spectacle, as the attacking animals, were the executioners. Horses were baited less frequently than other animals (although as working animals they often suffered appalling abuse and cruel deaths despite their idealization). Evelyn believed that the accusation against this horse was false, simply a pretext for brutality, and refused to attend. But he reported hearing that on the day of the baiting, the "gallant horse" fought off one after another of the fiercest dogs, until the dogs' owners finally stabbed him to death with their swords.

WHILE BOTH THE official and unofficial trials and executions of animals symbolically elevated the accused beast to a human level, human criminal or ill-mannered behavior was (and still is) "often characterized as sinking to the level of a beast. Human failings ranging from crude table manners to drunkenness to violence were described as bestial; similarly deemed animal-like were behaviors that included eating, excreting, lust, adultery, swimming, working at night, and keeping pets. Speaking more sympathetically—and more perceptively—than most such moralists on the topic of drunkenness, Samuel Johnson remarked that "he who makes a beast of himself gets rid of the pain of being a man."

The irony of these comparisons was that many had nothing to do with brutes: behaviors such as lechery, drunkenness, immodesty, and gluttony were termed "bestial," though they were human failings. (Usually, that is. Woodforde recorded that his pigs once located a barrel containing some leftover grounds from beer brewing and "got so amazingly drunk by it, that they were not able to stand and appeared like dead things almost, and so remained all night from dinner time today." The next morning, the porcine tipplers were still unable to walk: "They tumble about the yard and can by no means stand at all steady yet." But by the afternoon, he was pleased to report, "my 2 pigs were tolerably sober.")

To compare a human to an animal was a common insult. When César de Saussure visited London in the 1720s, he found to his dismay that a well-dressed Frenchman in the streets "will, without doubt, be called 'French dog' twenty times perhaps before he reaches his destination. This name is the most common, and evidently, according to popular idea, the greatest and most forcible insult that can be given to any man, and it is applied indifferently to all foreigners, French or otherwise." Such a person ran a real risk of being not only spattered with mud but also pelted with dead dogs and cats. The Spanish traveler Don Manuel Alvarez Espriella observed that "a flatterer is called a spaniel, a ruffian is called a bull-dog, and an ill-looking fellow an ugly hound; whelp, cur, and mongrel, are terms of contemptuous reproach to a young man; and if a young woman's nose turns upward, she is certainly called pug." While "you dog, you" could be used in a playfully admiring way, it still usually insinuated either sexual profligacy or caddishness. Whether playful or insulting, "dog" used in this way referred exclusively to men, as, of course, in the related epithet "son of a bitch." (The use of "dog" to mean an unattractive woman is a twentieth-century U.S. slur, vaguely similar to, though more denigrating than, the U.K.'s "cow.") "Bitch," of course, has long been a term of choice to abuse women: the earliest such uses cited in the *Oxford English Dictionary* come from the fifteenth and sixteenth centuries. In his late seventeenth-century poem "A Ramble in St. James's Park," the earl of Rochester lashed out at a former mistress who, having had sex with him, was sullying herself with lower-class men. Displaying both his wounded ego and the double standard typical of his time, this profligate libertine referred to his ex-mistress as a "proud Bitch" leading a pack of curs (her uncouth lovers) that followed her "savoury scent."

The use of animal analogies to insult displayed, by negative example, the desire to maintain absolute distinctions between humans and animals: it was degrading, indeed dehumanizing, for a person to be compared to an animal. Many of the legal practices surrounding violent and sexual encounters between animals and humans, however, seemed paradoxically to reveal and reinforce the idea of sameness rather than difference. Although animals, like people, were punished for crossing the line between human and beast, the very act of punishing them, as well as the ways in which they were judged and condemned, often had the effect of anthropomorphically blurring that line.

After their heyday in the Renaissance, the criminal prosecutions and executions of animals steadily declined. Although the last trial of an animal reported by Evans took place in the early twentieth century, by the nineteenth century the notion of beasts' moral responsibility had largely been replaced by the modern idea that animals cannot be held legally accountable for their behavior. Although animals that killed humans were usually put to death as dangers to society, legal retribution was reserved for their owners—as remains the case today.* And for other crimes against people, the beast did not necessarily pay with its life. Harriet Ritvo mentions the nineteenth-century case of a farmer sued by a plaintiff injured by his ram: the farmer had to pay damages, but the ram's aggressive behavior was assumed to be natural to its species, so it was not punished.

Evans, writing at the turn of the twentieth century, celebrated the cessation of these trials and punishments as the unequivocal (and in his day, relatively recent) triumph of enlightened humanitarianism against medieval barbarism. Qualifying his view, Ritvo points out that this humanitarian attitude cut two ways, for in some respects it diminished animals' status: "Their independence and power that had been implicit in the ability to intentionally transgress was withdrawn." As animals' legal accountability for transgressing against humans disappeared,

---

*The 2001 killing of Diane Whipple by her neighbors' Presa Canario mastiff in San Francisco is a striking example of our modern treatment of animal-related crimes. The dog that killed Whipple was put to death immediately and the other dog that had participated in the attack was euthanized a year later, both upon the order of the police department, which deemed them incorrigibly dangerous. The humans involved were tried, and one of them, Marjorie Knoller, was found guilty of second-degree murder (an unusually severe verdict), while her husband was found guilty of involuntary manslaughter. The presiding judge reduced Knoller's conviction to involuntary manslaughter as well, but an appeals court reinstated the jury's original judgment of murder. At this writing, the California Supreme Court has ordered the original trial judge to reconsider Knoller's sentence, stating that the judge had been too lenient while the appeals court had been too harsh. (*The New York Times*, June 1, 2007.)

however, humans' accountability for intentionally transgressing against animals increased.

The cruelty often suffered by animals in these judicial proceedings was, in a sense, the price they paid for the symbolic humanness with which the trials endowed them. The waning of official animal executions (and probably of unofficial, impromptu ones as well) was, as Rod Preece observes in his history of attitudes toward animals, a result of the greater understanding of beasts' own natures that grew during the eighteenth century. It was also a consequence of the related changes in sensibility that produced the rise of the animal protection movement—a movement that would be dedicated to, among other goals, bringing humans into the courtroom to answer charges of crimes against creatures that were deemed essentially "innocent," rather than the other way around.

The criminal prosecution of beasts was a real-world practice that implied a kinship between humans and beasts, despite established church doctrine and philosophical theories that stressed differences. As a new appreciation of animal nature developed, and people rejected the kind of anthropomorphism implied in the trials, their frequency greatly diminished. But at the same time, a more nuanced conception of kinship with animals arose—one that challenged old views of beasts' lack of rationality, language, feelings, and even immortal souls. At the same time that widespread pet keeping made it a common experience to have a loving animal companion one might even treasure more than one's spouse, and to observe performing animals that appeared to display knowledge and intelligence, some naturalists were exploring and attempting to chart the kind and the degree of affinity between various animal and human groups.

In the eighteenth century, old doctrines that asserted animals' "otherness" would be undermined on a variety of fronts, both deliberately and inadvertently. The consequences would be widely significant in contexts ranging from philosophy, science, and religion, to the practices and self-justifications of British imperial expansion, to the rise of reform movements such as animal protection. Not all manifestations of potential kinship were as comfortable for people as their relationships with their pets. Perhaps no creature more disturbingly exemplified the newly emerging challenges to species boundaries and human uniqueness in the eighteenth century than the age-old figure of the monster.

CHAPTER 6

PARLIAMENTS OF MONSTERS

✳   ✳   ✳

O NE SEPTEMBER day in 1727, in the town of Guildford, Surrey, an impoverished cloth worker named Joshua Toft pounded on the door
belonging to a respected surgeon and midwife, John Howard. When he
was admitted to Howard's presence, Toft opened the bundle he was
carrying to reveal the monster that had just been stillborn to his wife,
Mary. There lay a misshapen lump of flesh that could have been a cat's
torso, except that it appeared to have the backbone of an eel. Howard
initially scoffed at Joshua's story that his wife had just given birth to this
aberration, but he was curious enough to visit the Tofts at their home
in the neighboring village of Goldaming the next day.

The Tofts showed Howard some more cat-shaped flesh that Mary had
borne in the interim. Then, while he was there, she went into labor
again, producing two cat legs. Howard remained skeptical, but his skepti-
cism wavered when soon thereafter he himself delivered her of another
cat's foot and the head of a rabbit. The rabbit head was just the beginning: over the next few weeks, Howard assisted Mary Toft in giving birth
to a series of stillborn whole rabbits, sometimes in rapid succession.
Reaching under her skirts to feel the rabbits in her vagina and seeing
with his own eyes the violent contractions and obvious pain Mary suffered as she delivered them, he became convinced that he was witnessing
a marvel of nature. Her story of the events leading up to these monstrous births had the ring of truth, too, for it echoed other stories current
in his day explaining why women might bear animal-like creatures.

The several versions of Mary's story differed in the details, but the substance was this: Mary and some other women had been weeding a field when one or more rabbits ran into it. The women tried to catch a rabbit, but failed. That night, Mary dreamed of rabbits and woke up feeling ill. Soon after that she developed a powerful craving to eat rabbit. In August, she miscarried a lump of flesh that, Howard later surmised from her description, must have been a mole. In September she was overcome with violent cramps and gave birth to the monster that her husband took to Howard.

Howard wrote news of the births to certain important persons in London, including members of the Royal Society, to whom he offered to present specimens of the rabbits. He also rushed an account of them into print. These wondrous events, taken up by the newspapers, soon became the talk of the town, and other hastily written pamphlets on the subject added more details to Mary's story, such as the color of the rabbits she saw in the field, and the fact that she allowed her pet cat to sleep on her bed at night. Eminent medical men, including Nathanael St. André, the surgeon and anatomist to the Royal Household of King George I, came to examine her—and believed. The king himself grew interested. After Mary had given birth to a total of seventeen rabbits, St. André and others, acting at his majesty's command, brought her to London, installed her in Mr. Lacy's bagnio in Leicester Fields, and watched and waited. Physicians and noblemen came to visit her, expecting any moment the arrival of another rabbit. The ordinary public also waited, ravenous for news. But no more rabbits appeared.

Mary Toft had become a sensation, but she also became the subject of growing controversy as Britain's leading physicians and scientists— some of whom had been skeptical from the beginning—debated heatedly whether these monstrous births were real. The skeptics began to gather evidence of rabbit purchases made by Joshua Toft, and suspicion grew that he and his sister had dreamed up the hoax in order to attract sightseers who would pay to view such wonders—"sensation tourism," as it were, could be quite profitable. They secretly stuffed Mary's vagina with the parts of a butchered cat and then the rabbits that first she and subsequently Howard delivered. Her contractions were initially counterfeited, but soon her pain and the violent convulsions that seemed so convincing to the doctors became very real, for, unsurprisingly, she had developed a bad infection. Confronted with the evidence, Mary admitted the hoax, and was incarcerated in Bridewell prison to await trial on fraud charges. The press hurled recriminations, satirists wrote squibs and drew cartoons, and the embarrassed medical men who had either genuinely believed that a woman was giving birth to rabbits, or who had jumped into the story for their own aggrandizement, tried to salvage their reputations.

In the eighteenth century, many people—by no means only the uneducated—were prepared to believe that a poor cloth worker's wife in Surrey might give birth to rabbits. It was no accident that the

Long after the hoax had been exposed, William Hogarth depicted Mary Toft and her rabbit offspring in his satiric painting *Credulity, Superstition and Fanaticism,* 1762. (Detail, courtesy of the Mandeville Special Collections Library, University of California, San Diego)

Tofts had hit upon this particular ruse to make money. The phenomenon of the monstrous birth was well established in Mary Toft's day, on levels ranging from illiterate popular culture to the highest reaches of education and sophistication. (Despite the preponderance of evidence, the charges against Mary were eventually dropped, apparently on the grounds that her incarceration had been punishment enough.)

Monsters were discussed in Royal Society meetings and exhibited around town, in houses, in inns, and at the fairs. John Evelyn went to see a sheep that had six legs and used five of them to walk, and a goose possessing four legs, two crops, and two "vents, voiding excrement by both." This, he commented understandably enough, "was strange." At Bartholomew Fair, people's ears would routinely be blasted with calls to come see monsters; Tom Brown complained about the "damn'd *Trumpeter* calling in the Rabble to see a Calf with Six Legs and a Top-knot." An advertisement for the Flying Horse Inn in Bartholomew Close announced "to be seen a most strange and monstrous Living Milk Cow, having Five Horns, Five Legs, Six Feet, and a Cod like a Bull." A house in Hosier-Lane, Smithfield, advertised "A Surprising and wonderful Young MERMAID, caught on the Acapulco Shore, after six Hours dangerous Pursuit, whereby three Men belonging to the Adventurous Privateer were dangerously wounded in endeavouring to take her." When the poet William Wordsworth left his country retreat to visit Bartholomew Fair in 1802, he encountered an overwhelming scene where, he wrote, "All out-o'-the-way, farfetched, perverted things, / All freaks of nature" were "jumbled up together." He called Bartholomew Fair "a Parliament of Monsters."

The word "monster" in the eighteenth century already carried the meaning it has today of something hideous and frightening, but it also retained associations with its Latin root *monere,* to warn. In the Middle Ages, monsters had been seen as portents from God, prodigies, or marvels, and sometimes as the visible sign that God was punishing the mother for some sinful actions or thoughts. These ideas did continue to echo throughout the eighteenth century, along with the later notion that a monster was a *lusus naturae*—joke of nature—whose deviation from nature's laws served to delineate the form of those laws. But for the most part, in the eighteenth century, older understandings of monsters as God-sent wonders were more generally replaced by natural explanations, whether the cause was understood to be interspecies sex, the workings of the maternal imagination, or some other agent found within the blood or nervous system of the human or animal organism.

Eighteenth-century theories of reproduction generally held that the complete human form—the homunculus—was already contained within either the egg or the sperm (depending upon which warring school of thought one belonged to). But once she was pregnant, a woman's imagination could exert powerful effects upon the development of the fetus. Women were usually believed to be more irrational and more prone to imaginative flights than men anyway. By happening to fix her attention upon a thought or a sight, especially (though not necessarily) an unusual or shocking one, or even by dreaming of something, a pregnant woman might imprint its shape upon her child and thus produce a living or stillborn monster. These powerful influences upon the female imagination were typically other humans (particularly when they were in some way unusual) and animals, such as the rabbits Mary Toft allegedly saw in the field.

The *Philosophical Transactions of the Royal Society* carried numerous accounts of monstrous births to both human and animal mothers, and on occasion published articles addressing cases in which the human and nonhuman intersected by way of maternal imagination. In 1733, William Gregory of Rochester wrote a report of a monstrous birth involving a forty-four-year-old woman he attended. While this woman was pregnant, some traveling showmen had brought a bear and a monkey to her door. She could not keep her eyes from the monkey, which wore a hood and played with a stick. Not long afterward, the woman encountered a "dismal looking" man whose face, she thought, greatly resembled a monkey's. As her pregnancy advanced and her fetus began to move, she could feel it turn over and over in her womb just as the monkey had gamboled with its stick. Later, however, the movement ceased. After ten months, she was delivered of a stillborn monster whose umbilical cord was twisted, showing, according to Mr. Gregory, that the fetus had turned over in the womb just as the woman had described. Gregory took possession of the deformed fetus in order to present it to the Royal Society, adding: "I need not here mention the exact resemblance of the fetus to a hooded monkey: the fetus will show it itself more particularly than I can relate it."

Scientific accounts of the power of the maternal imagination to create monsters were common throughout Europe in the eighteenth century. If a child was born with a harelip, for instance, the mother must have seen or eaten a hare; an infant with a facial deformity might be traced back to her startling encounter with a bear or a pig or a monkey. Though imaginatively shaping the development of a fetus in utero might seem to be an exclusively human phenomenon, at least one instance was reported in an eighteenth-century English journal of a female dog that was similarly susceptible. The mother in question was a lapdog in Berlin. It seems that this dog, while pregnant, was in the habit of venturing into the yard where her owner also kept fowl, and there she was subjected to the attacks of a turkey cock. The turkey would dart at the little dog, pecking at her and making a racket, terrifying her and driving her away. Some time after these events, the dog gave birth to a monstrous puppy whose head very much resembled a turkey cock's. The rest of the puppy's body was normally shaped. The monster had no mouth or nose, but instead a "red bob" that looked just like the red gills of a turkey. It died soon after its birth and was dissected by an eminent surgeon who verified that its head resembled a turkey's head internally as well.

Some monstrous births were popularly suspected to be the result of intercourse between a human and a beast. If a woman gave birth to an infant that looked somewhat canine, it might be identified as the product of her copulation with a dog. So, too, a monstrous lamb that looked rather human, it might be suspected, was sired by a man. When Samuel Pepys was invited to see a "great baboon"—probably a gorilla—he found the creature to be "so much like a man in most things, that (though they say there is a species of them) yet I cannot believe but that it is a monster got of a man and she-baboon. I do believe it already understands much English; and I am of the mind it might be taught to speak or make signs."

There were certainly those who were skeptical about the easy overlap of human and animal. When, in 1699, the physician and Royal Society fellow Edward Tyson dissected a creature he knew as an "Orang Outang" (in fact, it was a chimpanzee), he chose to call it a "pygmie" and acknowledged that it more resembled humans than any other animal he knew. Yet he stated categorically that, however closely it approached the human, this creature was definitely a type of ape and not the "product of a mixed generation." Tyson argued that many accounts in classical authors of supposedly human or half-human pygmies and "wild-men" were in fact these "Orang Outangs."

In the *Philosophical Transactions,* John Floyer reported from Staffordshire that he had been shown a monstrous piglet recently stillborn to a sow. The local people, he said, believed that it had "a human face, produced by the copulations of two species"—that is, a man and the sow. Floyer, however, rejected this explanation, especially since an eyewitness had seen the sow mate with a boar. Upon examining the monster, he also ruled out maternal imagination, since the sow's imagination was unlikely, he thought, to be "so violent as to distort the bones without injuring the rest of the pigs [in the litter], which appeared all sound." Floyer determined that the piglet's head had somehow been distorted by an external force while in the womb, even though no one had seen the sow receive a blow. Recounting many older reports of monstrous births that were popularly supposed to result from interspecies copulation, he concluded, "I believe either fiction, or want of observation has made more monsters than nature ever produced."

While a pig born with the face of a man was deemed interesting enough to occupy the pages of the Royal Society's journal, women born with the faces of pigs became celebrated phenomena of popular culture. Tannakin Skinker, the daughter of wealthy parents in Germany, was born with a head and face that resembled a pig's, and lived a sequestered life, understandably shunning the curiosity seekers who came from all over Europe to see her. An account of her case was published in London in 1640; the cause of her deformity, it was believed, was not mixed generation but witchcraft, for a beggar woman had cursed Tannakin's mother while she was pregnant.

In the mid-eighteenth century and again fifty years later, rumors about pig-faced ladies swept London. In the early nineteenth century, one such woman, who was said to be Irish, supposedly lived in Manchester Square in Marylebone. She was reputed to be very wealthy, have an elegant figure below the chin, dress well, eat from a silver trough, and communicate only in grunts. This story inspired a number of broadsides and satiric prints, and with repetition its details grew more specific: that she was proficient at the piano, for instance, playing the most difficult pieces of Handel with great skill; that she occasionally attended masquerade balls; that she was called Grisly because of her appearance; and that she could be identified as Miss Griselda Steevens, whose brother had founded Dr. Steevens Hospital for the poor and destitute in Dublin on the condition that it take care of her.*

According to the London *Times,* "there is hardly a company in which this swinish female is not talked of; and thousands believe in her existence." The apparent believers included a young woman who placed an advertisement in the newspaper offering her services as an attendant to the pig-woman, and the man ("with a calf's head, we suppose," quipped *The Times*) who wrote offering this heiress his hand in marriage. The newspaper observed that very similar rumors about a pig-faced lady had fascinated the town on two occasions within the previous fifty years, commenting, "Our rural friends hardly know what idiots London contains." But the pig-faced-woman craze, in fact, could

*In the later nineteenth century, the writer and publisher Robert Chambers, in his popular miscellany, *The Book of Days,* pointed out that a portrait of Griselda Steevens, who along with her brother was a patron of the hospital, hung in its library, and that, far from resembling a pig, she was "a very pleasant-looking lady, with a peculiarly benevolent cast of countenance."

not be contained in London: after this rash of reporting, exhibits of pig-faced women became extremely popular throughout the country. One such monster exhibited at Bartholomew Fair was revealed to be a poor brown bear that was tied to a large armchair, its face and arms shaved, its mouth muzzled and its body squeezed into a wig, gown, and gloves. Its head was covered with scars from beatings and its face scabbed from its painful weekly shaving.

EVEN MORE THAN dancing dogs and tobacco-smoking apes, these pig-faced ladies, human-headed pigs, and rabbits and monkeys born to women fascinated people on both the popular and intellectual levels because they seemed to combine the human and nonhuman animal. Even when understood as the effects of imagination rather than the results of interspecies copulation, half-human and half-animal monsters challenged the very idea of human uniqueness. Those deeply invested in the belief that humans were distinct from animals must have found monsters, seemingly biological hybrids, to be even more disturbing than the metaphorical ways in which human beings made "beasts" of themselves. Keith Thomas observes, "Wherever we look in early modern England, we find anxiety, latent or explicit, about any form of behaviour which threatened to transgress the fragile boundaries between man and the animal creation." If drunkenness or sexual desire threatened to sink a human into temporary bestiality, as moralists warned, how much more anxiety-provoking was the physical combination of human and beast. How could humans maintain their belief in their essential difference from animals if half-human hybrids could be produced by interspecies sex, or by the workings of the mind on the body—or if, as was widely believed, being fed the milk of a sheep or a goat could make a child stupid or "goatish"?

So when audiences flocked to the fairs to see the "Man Teger," which resembled a man from the head downward, or the corpse of the "Northumberland monster," which had the head, mane, and feet of a horse and the body of a man—it had been deliberately scalded to death immediately after its birth—or the country lad whose body was covered with hedgehog bristles, or the boy covered in fish scales, or the boy with a live bear growing on his back, or the dried-out body of the "Feejee Mermaid" exhibited at the Turf coffeehouse in 1822, they must have responded with a pleasure that was strongly tinged with horror and anxiety.

As the eighteenth century progressed, the scientific establishment gradually debunked the notion that either imagination or interspecies generation could produce monstrous births and dismissed the belief that such monsters were genuine hybrids illustrating the permeability of the border between the human and the animal. But new, more powerful challenges to the claim of human uniqueness were arising that would have profound ramifications, both for the attitudes of people toward animals and for the lives of animals themselves. Nowhere were both the challenges and the anxiety they produced more brilliantly expressed than in Jonathan Swift's *Gulliver's Travels*.

First published in 1726, *Gulliver's Travels* tells the story of British travel and colonization through Lemuel Gulliver's imaginary voyages to different lands. Swift wrote his satiric fantasy in the context of England's overseas adventurism as the nation pursued the trade and colonization that would establish its vast empire. He was intensely critical of the violence and arrogance of England's imperial mission. Gulliver's experiences in other lands undermine in various ways the character's sense of entitlement and importance as an Englishman. Even more unsettlingly, they also erode his status as a man, for they reveal how faulty and tenuous human claims of significance actually are.

The Lilliputians, whom Gulliver encounters in his first voyage, seem recognizably like the English in their corruption and self-importance, and are rendered preposterous by their utter unawareness of their miniature scale. To them, Gulliver is a monster, but a recognizably human one, a "man-mountain" not unlike (though considerably larger than) the human giants sometimes exhibited in London. However, in his second voyage Gulliver travels to the land of Brobdingnag, where the proportions are reversed, and his own diminutiveness, seen through the eyes of the enormous Brobdingnagians, turns him into a monster in explicitly dehumanizing ways.

When first discovered in a farmer's field, Gulliver is likened by the Brobdingnagians to animal vermin, a weasel or toad or spider—the farmer's wife screams and runs away when she first sees him—but soon he becomes a bona fide, entertaining monster, as the farmer takes him around to perform at inns. Swift drew upon London's monster shows and animal entertainments in describing Gulliver's career as an exhibit and performer. Gulliver finally ends up at court, where he is first mistaken for an automaton, then labeled a joke of nature. Here his Lilliputian-like sense of England's importance and his own significance as an Englishman suffers. His naïve descriptions of English society and politics, intended to display his country's greatness, instead expose its corrupt pettiness, to which the enlightened king of Brobdingnag responds with a mixture of amusement, horror, and contempt. Gulliver stages mock battles for the queen's entertainment, fights for his life against giant wasps, is retrieved by a spaniel and nearly drowned by a frog, and, most damaging to his sense of himself, is abducted and force-fed by a monkey who sees him as one of its own kind.

Gulliver's fourth and final voyage forces him to confront the gravest challenge to the meaning and value of his humanity, when he arrives in the land of the Houyhnhnms, the rational horses. Although in this land he is definitively considered human, the Houyhnhnms' definition of humanness consists of those very elements that the English would call bestial. The intelligent horses, whom Gulliver grows to admire, have an orderly society, whose greatest disruptions are the odious Yahoos, so filthy and disgusting that Gulliver upon his first encounter calls them the most vile creatures he has ever seen. So he is horrified when he discerns human features in the Yahoos—and even more when he realizes that the horses consider him a Yahoo, too, though marginally more rational.

Against the mounting evidence to the contrary, he persists in denying his own resemblance to these despicable creatures, until one day, when he is bathing and therefore naked (moralists usually associated nakedness with animals), a young female Yahoo, smitten with desire, pursues him—forcing him to admit that he, too, is a Yahoo. His anthropocentrism utterly collapses.* For the Yahoos' "bestial" traits—their eating of flesh (the horses, of course, are vegetarians), their violent aggressiveness, their lust, selfishness, and greed—are human traits. Even Gulliver's clothing, at home a marker of civilization that supposedly distinguishes rational humanity from beasts, does not signify such to the Houyhnhnms, for the civilized, intensely rational horses have no conception of immodest nakedness that needs to be covered up.

"In attempting to shore up the distinctions between human and animal," writes Thomas, "men attributed to animals the natural impulses they most feared in themselves—ferocity, gluttony, sexuality—even though it was men, not beasts, who made war on their own species, ate more than was good for them and were sexually active all the year round." It is just this contradiction that Swift exposed in Gulliver's last voyage, where the humans are the most despicable beasts of all.

IN 1726, CÉSAR de Saussure wrote to his family that in St. James's Park he had caught sight of the teenage "wild boy" who had been captured in Germany the year before and brought to England by the king. "His hair was matted and bristling, his nails very long, his skin hardened and tanned by the air—in a word he was a perfect savage, probably born, fed, and brought up with the wild beasts of the forests, and speaking no human language." His eyes were "haggard," he was uncomfortable in his clothes, and he kept taking off his hat and throwing it on the ground. De Saussure was told that the first time he was taken to the park he had climbed high into a tree and could scarcely be gotten down

---

* However, some sense of racial difference and superiority is left to him, since Swift's description of the Yahoos resemble the travelers' accounts of "savages," particularly African peoples, current in his day; even the Houyhnhnms acknowledge that Gulliver seems to have a greater degree of reason than the odious Yahoos. Swift's major point about the Yahoos, however, is their universal humanity: their greed, lust, violence, unteachability, etc.

again. "He frightened me," the Frenchman wrote. Several pamphlets, including one written by Daniel Defoe, the author of *Robinson Crusoe* (the story of a man who, flung alone onto a semideserted wild island, spends twenty-seven years taming it), pondered whether this language-less, apparently irrational, and possibly soulless human-shaped being was actually human or animal.

Samuel Pepys's response to the baboon he saw was that it was half human, that it already understood English, and that it could be taught to speak or use sign language. Edward Tyson, who stated categorically that the "Orang Outang," or chimpanzee, he dissected was an ape, also spent much of his treatise itemizing its essential similarities to humans: "The Orang-Outang imitates a man more than apes and monkeys do." At the end of the eighteenth century, a creature from "Mount Tibet" was exhibited that was said "to approach the human species nearer than any hitherto exhibited." This monster was said to possess "affabil-ity, friendship, and good-nature." The advertisement claimed that it was "the long lost link between the human and brute creation."

The notion of variously defined "missing links" between humans and animals was based upon the concept of the great chain of being. This idea that all the "plenitude" of existence was ordered along a fixed, hierarchical scale had its foundation in Greek antiquity, filtered through medieval Christianity into the eighteenth century. The "Vast chain of being, which from God began," as Alexander Pope described it, was in this period a commonly accepted model of the world. At the top of the vertical chain were the infinite numbers of heavenly beings descending from God, and below them, in order of significance, ranged the mem-bers of the earthly creation, beginning with men. Overall, humans fell somewhere in the middle of the entire chain, above all other earthly creatures but below the heavenly beings above. Some people found in this model justification for the idea of man's dominion over nature, since all other earthly beings ranked below humans on the chain. Oth-ers, however, were acutely conscious of the vast number of beings rank-ing higher, and found the human middle position humbling.

In 1667, Thomas Sprat, the first historian of the Royal Society, wrote that the mission of the society was to discover new natural phenomena and place them into their proper positions on the chain of being. Using language that echoed Francis Bacon, Sprat declared that the task of science was to "follow all the links of this chain, till all their secrets are open to our minds." This, he said, "is truly to command the world; to rank all the varieties or degrees of things so orderly upon one another; that standing on the top of them, we may perfectly behold all that are below, and make them all serviceable to the quiet and peace and plenty of Man's life." Adding discoveries to the chain below had the additional benefit of raising the ground upon which man stood, he said, enabling him "to look the nearer into heaven." And there were many such discoveries: global expansion brought new territories and their creatures—both human and nonhuman—into the British view, while new technologies such as the microscope showed that, in Joseph Addison's words, "Every part of matter is peopled. Every green leaf swarms with inhabitants." From Sprat's point of view, each new subordinate link further elevated man. Addison, however, took a different perspective, noting that the degree of separation between humans and the lowest animal was much less great than the separation between humans and God.

Alexander Pope's well-known poem "An Essay on Man," which he wrote "to vindicate the ways of God to Man," also expressed some of the more humbling implications of the great chain of being. Asserting that there is a unchanging God-given moral order to the universe—most infamously, in the line "One truth is clear, 'Whatever IS, is RIGHT' "—Pope characterized as pure, unwarranted arrogance human claims of uniqueness and centrality, and especially the thesis that nature exists solely for the sake of humans. On the contrary, Pope argued, the animal and human worlds are mutually dependent. God "Made Beast in aid of Man, and Man of Beast; / All serv'd, all serving! nothing stands alone," he wrote.

> Know, Nature's children all divide her care;
> The fur that warms a monarch, warm'd a bear.
> While Man exclaims, "See all things for my use!"

"See man for mine!" replies a pamper'd goose;
And just as short of Reason he must fall,
Who thinks all made for one, not one for all.

Although arrogance might turn a man into a silly goose, Pope thought, the possession of the capacity for reason nevertheless constituted an absolute dividing line—a "nice barrier; / For ever sep'rate, yet for ever near!"—between human and animals. The goose can never understand that man pampers it in order eventually to slaughter it. So, too, the innocent lamb "licks the hand just rais'd to shed its blood." Only rational humans possess awareness of death, and only humans have the hope of eternal life to make that awareness bearable. Furthermore, in Pope's satirical poems, most particularly his masterpiece, *The Dunciad*, comparison of a human to an animal renders the human monstrous.

Pope's insistence upon an absolute division between humans and animals that, when bridged, creates monsters takes on a particular poignancy in light of the fact that, to many people, he was a monster himself. Pope's stunted, frail figure—he was four feet, six inches tall—his pronounced humpback, and his twisted spine made him vulnerable to vicious ad hominem attacks from his enemies. Those who felt the sting of his fierce satiric pen frequently characterized him as a spider or toad spitting venom, as both creatures were thought to do. Perhaps awareness of his physically ambiguous status particularly reinforced Pope's desire to cling to the uniqueness of humans; at the same time, it certainly underlay his strong sympathy for animals.

As the eighteenth century progressed, the search to uncover the existence and meaning of heretofore unknown links on the chain continued, and fascination with those missing links between species, especially between animals and humans, grew. But the very idea of missing links called attention to an ambiguity inherent in Thomas Sprat's orderly hierarchy: when closely considered, the chain metaphor called into question humans' separateness from the brute creation, and therefore undermined the traditional rationale for our supposed dominion over it.

As a structure in which every element of creation occupied a fixed and necessary position along a vertical scale, the great chain of being was a model of hierarchy—but it also implied a potentially troubling interconnection and ambiguity. So far from establishing sharp, absolute distinctions among the various orders of creation, the chain metaphor blurred them, for, if a chain is to remain intact, its links must intersect and overlap. So while each link of the great chain of being had a discrete center, the points of connection at its top and bottom raised questions about what the overlapping of links signified. At what point along the chain were humans actually separated from the creatures below?

This model raised problems for those invested in the belief that there are sharp distinctions between human and nonhuman animals. Furthermore, consideration of humans' position in the *middle* of a vast chain of being whose upper links stretched into infinity could also undermine anthropocentrism. The idea of the great chain of being had always contained these problems for prevailing orthodoxies about human uniqueness, but in the eighteenth century its implications about the interconnection of all existence were particularly emphasized.

John Locke enumerated examples of earthly creatures that seemed positioned at the interstices of the chain's links: flying fish, "fishy" birds, amphibious animals, mermaids, and seamen. "There are some brutes that seem to have as much knowledge and reason as some that are called men," he wrote, "and the animal and vegetable kingdoms are so nearly joined that, if you will take the lowest of one and the highest of the other, there will scarce be perceived any great difference between them." Locke acknowledged that divisions among species were of humans' making, not nature's. In his 1735 taxonomy, *Systema Naturae,* Linnaeus classed humans together with other mammals, specifically primates. Other naturalists of the time debunked the idea of species altogether, arguing that nature progresses upward along the great chain of being so seamlessly and continuously that it is impossible to establish real distinctions among its various stages.

One effect of this blurring of demarcations along the chain has been much noted by recent historians of eighteenth-century thinking about racial difference. The chain metaphor positioned in hierarchical order not just species but categories within species. Within the hierarchy of humans, "inferior" and "less rational" humans occupied the lower positions along the chain, which placed them close to the higher orders of animals. These lower orders of humans were identified racially as nonwhites, particularly Africans, who at this time were understood by many to have such a resemblance to the higher levels of animals, the primates, as to be virtually indistinguishable from them.

While some insisted that there was nonetheless an unbridgeable divide between human and animals, however imperceptible the actual point of difference was, others argued that in some cases there was no divide at all. The naturalist Lord Monboddo, for instance, argued that "Orang Outangs" were, in fact, primitive humans who lacked language. Such racially conceived conflations of certain human groups with animals provided a justification for colonial conquest. It also had the effect of elevating the status of animals, and at a time when British colonization of distant parts of the globe was greatly increasing, elevation of the status of animals could undercut the notion of universal humanness.

In a complementary way, some taxonomies of animals ranked them in order not of their resemblance to humans, but of their usefulness, placing the dog and the horse at the top. These noble, helpful animals, it was observed, valuably assisted the white man in subduing and civilizing savage humans and animals, thus enabling his domination of the globe. (After the first veterinary college was established in London in 1791, it restricted its practice to horses, at least partly because of the need for a veterinary cadre in the cavalry during the wars against France; it would not treat other animals until the 1820s.) And just as the elevation of animals lowered the status of nonwhite peoples in some eyes, so did the lowering of nonwhite peoples raise the status of animals. As the historian James Turner notes, "the very process of pushing blacks down toward the beasts tended to bring animals closer to humanity."

Comparisons between nonwhite humans and animals were not always intended to support a hierarchical ranking of humans, however. In a sermon against cruelty to animals preached in 1810, the Reverend

Thomas Moore drew an analogy between animals and slaves in order to elevate the status of both. Although African slaves were once held to "be a different race of beings" whose humanity was denied, he said, we now know that "the faculties, the moral qualities and the feelings of Africans, are of the same kind, and capable of equal improvement with those of Europeans." Such enlightened thinking, he argued, should also be applied to our duty to exercise compassion toward animals.

IN HIS DEFINITIVE history of the great chain of being, Arthur O. Lovejoy observes that "the sense of the separation of man from the rest of the animal creation was beginning to break down in the eighteenth century." As a corollary, more arguments were being made for the humane treatment of animals that were based upon a sense of kinship with them, even if there was not a consensus about the degree of that affinity or about the extent and nature of animal capacity. In a decisive rejection of Cartesian ideas, what mattered to larger numbers of people was one capacity definitely shared by animals and humans: the ability to experience pain. Believing that animals are kindred spirits, and that the pain they suffer at our hands entitles them to our compassion, some people sought actually to do something about how they were regarded and treated. First calling for changes in Britons' attitudes, they eventually also began to call for changes in the law. In these calls, the animal protection movement was born. Jeremy Bentham, although speaking from the particular perspective of his utilitarian philosophy, nonetheless spoke more broadly for the feelings of many of his contemporaries in the later eighteenth century when he uttered words still quoted by animal defenders today: "The question is not, Can they *reason?* nor, Can they *talk?* but, Can they *suffer?*"

PART TWO

Nature's Cry

CHAPTER 7

STAGES OF CRUELTY

*   *   *

STROLLING PAST one of London's print shops in Fleet Street early in 1751, a passerby might have been drawn into the crowd milling in front of its windows, prepared to snicker at the latest political cartoons and caricatures posted there. Confronted with the four shocking plates of Wlliam Hogarth's new series of engravings, however, the spectator might have been less inclined to smile. The series was entitled *The Four Stages of Cruelty*, and while some in the crowd would inevitably have been hardened or indifferent enough to smirk at Hogarth's impassioned images, others would have responded, as the artist intended, with pity, outrage, and recognition.

At a glance, the first scene appears to be another lively depiction of mid-eighteenth-century London street life, a bustling crowd of people and animals. On closer examination, however, the human population consists entirely of boys, and their relationship to the animals in the scene is far from innocent. In a foreground corner, a grinning urchin ties a bone to the tail of an emaciated dog, which pathetically licks his hand; next to him, three boys prepare to hurl clubs at a tethered rooster. Nearby, another group of boys hang two cats by their tails, laughing as the creatures frantically claw at each other. A third cat struggles to escape as a bulldog, egged on by his master, rips out her guts. A boy frowning in concentration pokes a hot wire into the eyes of a captive bird, while another boy looks on leeringly. High up in an attic window, boys have hurled a cat into the air, wings glued to its back, to see if it can fly. A dog yelps in agony as a swaggering bully rams an arrow up his rectum, while a well-dressed young gentleman tries desperately to stop him, futilely offering up his tart in exchange for the dog. None of these vignettes was unfamiliar in the streets of London; the only thing unusual about this scene is that so many cruelties are happening simultaneously in close proximity. Such was Hogarth's satiric genius—his ability to condense into one eloquent scene so many of the horrific truths of everyday life.

In February 1751, when the newspapers carried notices advertising the new four-plate set of engravings entitled *The Four Stages of Cruelty*, Hogarth was already famous as the creator of the age's most trenchant pictorial satire, particularly the narrative series *The Rake's Progress*, which chronicles the decline of a young provincial man after he inherits a fortune and moves to London to live the high life; *The Harlot's Progress*, which chronicles the decline of a country girl after she goes to London and becomes a whore; and *Marriage à la Mode*, which chronicles the decline of a London husband and wife after their mercenary arranged marriage. In *The Stages of Cruelty*, Hogarth's subject was not the decline of individuals but the brutality of English civilization itself: the inevitable consequences of lifelong depravity and the omnipresence of cruelty in many walks of British life.

The series' unifying figure is Tom Nero—named after the sadistic Roman emperor—who comes from the notorious slum parish of St. Giles and, as the saying went, was "born to be hanged." (Tom does not decline but rather lives out his destiny, ominously predicted in the first plate as a boy chalks his hanged figure on a wall.) As the series progresses, the violence escalates: Nero moves from boyhood to adulthood, from one type of viciousness to another, and from animals to people. The mood of the engravings is grim from the beginning, for Hogarth was illustrating a pervasive evil that he felt particularly deeply.

Hogarth was well known for his love of animals, particularly his pugs, whom he painted into his self-portraits. A cartoon published during one of the outbreaks of disease when city officials ordered all dogs clubbed to death shows him ineffectually trying to stop the slaughter, rather like the young gentleman trying to stop the dog's torture in his own engraving. Hogarth conceived *The Four Stages of Cruelty*, he explained, "in hopes of preventing in some degree that cruel treatment of poor animals which makes the streets of London more disagreeable to the human mind, than any thing what ever. The very describing of which gives pain." Viewing his images, in which one cruelty is piled on another, is indeed painful, for his intention was to stir "the most stony hearts," and to accomplish that goal he spared no detail. To a modern

William Hogarth's *The First Stage of Cruelty* depicts the vicious ingenuity of boys in their torment of animals. (Courtesy of the Mandeville Special Collections Library, University of California, San Diego)

viewer, this is strong stuff. Surely many in his day would have thought so, too—but people in his day could not avoid seeing the many kinds of real-life abuse of humans and animals alike that went on constantly, everywhere around them. *The Four Stages of Cruelty* is both one of the earliest anticruelty polemics created, and one of the most powerful.

The first plate, which introduces Tom Nero—he is the boy torturing the dog with the arrow—depicts the various abuses of animals described above. "Tortur'd Victims bleeding shew / The Tyrant in the Boy," Hogarth's caption explains. The child is already a cruel oppressor who torments animals, and he will become a vicious, criminal man. Addressing the spectator, the plate's caption concludes:

> *Learn from this fair Example—You*
> *Whom savage Sports delight,*
> *How Cruelty disgusts the view*
> *While Pity charms the sight.*

The savage sports here are specifically cockthrowing and catbaiting, the bloody impromptu entertainments of the street urchins. Only one figure of decency appears, the pitying young man who tries to save the dog.

Hogarth's portrayal of the cruelties perpetrated by children, particularly boys, was reiterated in books, sermons, and periodicals commenting on the plight of animals in eighteenth-century British society. Granted that moral writers often exaggerate the practices they condemn, but there were so many accounts of the same type of cruelties that they must have reflected a social reality. In 1789, for instance, an article in the *Gentleman's Magazine* signed "Mr. Humanus" detailed a litany of abuses that parents allowed their sons to commit: tearing the wings from flies, impaling beetles on pins, laming and killing their pets, stealing eggs from birds' nests, tying lanterns to dogs' tails and driving them away "to be hunted to madness and death by all who meet them," setting stray dogs to rip apart cats, and hanging dogs and cats in imitation of human executions at Tyburn Tree. Also, Humanus continued, they will tie two cats together by the tails and then throw them over a line, for the luxury of seeing them tear each other's eyes out. They will tie a string to a rat's tail, pour spirit of wine over it, set fire to it, and betray the most rapturous joy at seeing the unhappy animal run about covered with flame till it expires under this refinement in barbarity.

"It is hard," concluded Humanus, that "there should be no law for brute animals, when they carry so large a proportion of representatives to every legislative assembly." Cruelty to animals was so dire and so widespread that Parliament should act to protect the very creatures, such as their coach horses, on which the members themselves rely.

In *The Second Stage of Cruelty*, Hogarth turns to adult refinements of the boys' viciousness. Tom Nero has grown up and become a hackney driver, whose overburdened coach has crashed because his horse, driven beyond endurance, has collapsed in the street fronting one of the Inns of Chancery. Nero is beating the broken-down horse on its head with the heavy handle of his whip. Complicit in his cruelty to the horse are his social superiors, the fat, greedy barristers who had overloaded the coach by cramming themselves in to save a few pennies of the fare. Although those who physically perpetrate the acts depicted in the first and second stages are all members of the laboring classes, the upper classes share culpability for the violence done on their behalf. The one good man in this scene is taking down the name of the hackney coach's owner in order to report the driver. According to existing law, the driver might be prosecuted, not for cruelty but for damaging the owner's property. However, Hogarth implies, the owner shares responsibility for allowing, even expecting, his driver to maximize profits by overcrowding his coach and then beating the horse to make it go.

Close by the overturned coach, a drover pushes his flock of sheep through the streets en route to Smithfield market. The sheep, which have traveled many miles from the country, are worn and exhausted.

The cruel boy becomes a cruel man in a cruel world. William Hogarth, *The Second Stage of Cruelty.* (Courtesy of the Mandeville Special Collections Library, University of California, San Diego)

One has collapsed and the enraged drover is beating it to death with a cudgel. In the background, a small donkey staggers under the weight of an enormous trunk, heavy barrels, and two large men, while its driver jabs it in the rump with a pitchfork. As in the first stage, blood sports are present in this scene. An escaped bull pitches a dog into the air, as people run toward it with upraised sticks, and bills posted on walls advertise cockfights and their human equivalent, fistfights, at the pugilism amphitheater. In the middle ground, a heavily laden beer wagon whose driver has drunkenly passed out runs over a boy: this, like the hanged figure in *The First Stage,* is a statement of the connection between cruelty—careless or malicious—to beasts and to people. That the victim is a boy also suggests Hogarth's point that cruelty rebounds on the cruel.

Testimony from Hogarth's day indicates that his portrayal is, if anything, understated. His was a world in which human existence was often marginal, and the demands of making a working-class living were often exigent at best. Few people, regardless of their social standing, stopped to consider the suffering of the animals they used. In combination with the pervasive idea that an animal's life was only as valuable as the work one could exact from it, this indifference created a cruel and often deadly mixture.

Carters (or their bosses) routinely overloaded a cart or coach, then savagely beat the horse or the donkey (or sometimes the dog) as it strained to pull the weight, until they crushed its skull or knocked out its eyes. Heavy and cumbersome, stagecoaches were notorious cripplers, and killers, of the horses that drivers—often urged by their passengers—whipped to pull them at breakneck speeds. Costermongers cut incisions in the rumps of their donkeys along the spine and drove wedges into them, using the pain of these perpetually open wounds to control the creatures. One man who had torn a horse's tongue from its mouth—it is striking how often this particular cruelty was reported in the newspapers during the century—was arrested but, since there was no evidence he had done it to injure the horse's *owner,* he was set free.

Because draft animals were often old, ill, injured, or malnourished—sometimes all of these, since the idea was to work a horse or donkey at as little expense to the owner as possible until it dropped—their strength was obviously limited, and often they were seen to be pulling their loads with broken bones protruding and open sores on their backs. For a carter to beat his horse to death with a cudgel seems, in strict pragmatism, to be counterproductive. But when we consider that the animal might well be on the verge of death anyway, there would be little to counteract the driver's rage, perhaps fueled by gin or perhaps simply by his need to make a delivery. In any event, a last few pounds could always be extracted from an animal by selling its carcass to a knacker's shop, where horses and donkeys were rendered into hides and pet food.

Conditions in the slaughterhouses and knackers' yards were desperate. Wounded animals might be left to linger for days before they were killed. It was routine to starve horses as they waited to be slaughtered. Calves' mouths were taped to stifle their cries as their throats were slit and they were hung up to slowly drip out their blood, for it was believed that bleeding an animal to death over a period of days tenderized its flesh and made it white, highly prized at wealthy dinner tables. Live geese were plucked five times a year to provide quills for pens and feathers for beds; in a cold winter, many died of exposure. In wealthy kitchens, peacocks were bled to death by cutting out their tongues, eels were skinned alive, fowls were crammed with food and their orifices sewed up, and fish were "crimped," that is, cut into pieces while still alive. The fur and hide trade was particularly horrific, for many of the skinners of cows, sheep, dogs, and, especially, cats believed that skinning the animal while it was alive produced a better pelt.

The congested streets of London and other large cities obviously provided a more concentrated setting for cruelty, but animal suffering was by no means restricted to the cities: traditional rural communities also inflicted great injury on the beasts they worked and farmed. Poorer farmers saved the expense of harnesses by tying their horses to the plows by their tails, beating them when the pain caused them to stop moving. Sheep had their wool pulled off instead of sheared. Food animals were often abused with indifference. Not only calves but also lambs and pigs were bled slowly to whiten their meat; pigs, roosters, cows, and lambs were confined to tiny crates (predecessors of today's battery farming of chickens and crating of veal calves and sows); pigs were whipped to death, geese had their feet nailed to the floor to fatten them, and chickens' legs were cut off. Thomas quotes one contemporary who observed that rural animals "feed in pain, lie in pain, and sleep in pain."

All the blood sports encountered in London were practiced in provincial towns and villages as well, but there were other blood sports particular to the country: the gentry hunted foxes and deer with horses and dogs, shot partridges and ducks, and chased down hares with greyhounds. Horse races were held in local grounds as well as the fashionable tracks such as Newmarket: the racing could take a brutal toll on the horses, many of which were broken by overrunning and negligence. Timed races—in which men competed to drive their gigs a hundred miles in the shortest possible time—were particularly deadly for the animals. Those horses that managed to survive racing careers would likely spend their latter years pulling wagons and hackney coaches until they were consigned to the knacker's.

The ancient Lincolnshire town of Stamford staged a yearly bullrunning that became a byword for brutality. In this November event, a terrified bull stumbled through town hotly pursued by the roaring populace, who beat him, stabbed him, broke his tail, and exploded gunpowder on his back. Techniques used to madden a bull for running and baiting included sawing off the tips of his horns, cutting off his tail and ears, smearing him with soap, and blowing pepper into his nose. In the Staffordshire town of Tutbury, there was a yearly event in which all these things were done to a bull provided by the lord prior's bailiff, at which point he was driven through town as people tried to cut off a piece of his flesh before he ran into neighboring Derbyshire. If someone succeeded, then the bull would be taken to the ring and baited.

Percival Stockdale, who wrote a tract against such cruelty, reported that an Irish friend had explained to him how bulls were flayed from neck to shoulders. He no longer remembered why this was done, Stockdale said, but he would remember the fact of it with pain for the rest of his life. John Lawrence, a sportsman and well-known expert on horses who later would help Richard Martin draft his animal protection bill, itemized a series of cruelties he had personally seen or been told about: dogs thrown into hot ovens, cats nailed to gates and tortured, birds' eyes put out, hedgehogs burned to death, living animals cut open. The historian Robert Darnton's classic essay "The Great Cat

Massacre" discusses a workmen's revolt in eighteenth-century Paris that took the form of slaughtering the pet cats of their masters; Darnton notes that the torture and killing of animals, particularly cats, was a popular amusement in England and Europe, often propelled by folklore and the sexual symbolism that associated cats with women. Cruelty to animals may or may not have been more inventive in the past than it is today, but the percentage of the public practicing it, and the degree of public tolerance, were much greater.

Cruelty to animals in provincial life figures only tangentially in *The Four Stages of Cruelty*—the principal example being the rural drover who has beaten the sheep to death. Like other, later anticruelty advocates, Hogarth focused primarily on the city. But the third engraving of the series, which he entitled *Cruelty in Perfection*, is the one scene set outside of London. Here Hogarth makes the connection between rural and urban violence as he moves from violence against animals to violence against people. This plate depicts a country churchyard in the middle of the night. A young servant woman, visibly pregnant, lies dead, her throat and arms slit, a bundle of silver plate and an empty jewel casket lying near her body. She robbed her mistress at the behest of her seducer, Tom Nero, who has then murdered her and tried to escape with the goods. Nero has been apprehended, still carrying his bloodstained knife and a pistol. Hogarth's point here was that cruelty against animals and cruelty against people are connected: while Hogarth did not put animal life on an exact par with human life, he showed how the impulse to abuse animals is essentially the same as the impulse to abuse humans. The knife that slaughtered the girl is reminiscent of the knives that slit the throats of calves and cut off the legs of sheep. One type of assault leads to the other. The society that countenances cruelty to animals breeds sociopaths who will eventually turn their violence against people.

This profile has become widely accepted today in discussions of criminals; serial killers often begin with torturing animals, and abusive partners or parents often injure or kill their human victims' companion animals. In the eighteenth century, this connection was given credibility by growing awareness of other ways in which the line between

William Hogarth, *Cruelty in Perfection*. The murdered housemaid, her throat and wrist cut, has been viciously "slaughtered" by the criminal who began to practice his cruelty on animals. (Courtesy of the Mandeville Special Collections Library, University of California, San Diego)

humans and animals seemed less absolute than had often been assumed. But recognition of this trajectory of violence goes back to ancient times. The Roman poet Ovid, for instance, depicted the vegetarian philosopher Pythagoras making an equation between the hard-heartedness it takes to kill a kid or a calf, and the callousness needed to murder a person. St. Thomas Aquinas suggested a similar correlation when he said that when God apparently forbids cruelty to animals, he is really concerned about cruelty to humans, lest the former lead to the latter. Aquinas dismissed animals' pain except as it predicts human pain, which he considered the only kind worthy of divine concern. Hogarth, on the contrary, maintained that animals genuinely suffer and that inflicting this abuse on them is wrong in itself. The people of his day may not have wanted to recognize a common bond with

William Hogarth, *The Reward of Cruelty* in the realms of law and science (Courtesy of the Mandeville Special Collections Library, University of California, San Diego)

beasts, but they should, he insisted, even if it takes the story of a so-
ciopath to convince them.

In the series' final plate, *The Reward of Cruelty,* Tom Nero's life has
come full circle. He has been executed, and his grotesque body, appearing almost alive, is stretched out on a dissecting table in the College of
Surgeons, the hangman's noose still looped around his neck. The surgeons watch, smiling, as his skull is drilled, his eyes cut out, his tongue
torn from his mouth, and his bowels removed. His skeleton will be
boiled to remove the flesh—a cauldron of skulls and bones steams in
the foreground—and hanged on display along with those of other
criminals positioned along the walls of the dissection theater.

The final stage of cruelty echoes and amplifies the earlier stages.
Nero's intestines spilling onto the ground are reminiscent of those
ripped from the baited cat; a knife is stuck into his eye, as the wire
blinded the bird; his skull is opened, as those of the sheep and horse
were crushed; an emaciated dog gnaws his heart, a reminder of the dog
he heartlessly tortured; the surgeons smile as they watch the acts performed upon his body, just as the boys did as they tormented the animals; his supine, cut-open body parallels the gashed figure of the woman
he murdered. A kind of justice has been done; the perpetrator of cruelty has met his harsh reward. But the state-sanctioned violence of the
executioner and the surgeons is cruel as well. While dissections of executed felons were public events—intended to serve as a graphic warning of the consequences of crime—they were also greatly opposed in
Hogarth's day, for both religious and political reasons, by large numbers of people belonging to the social orders whose members were
most likely to be executed and turned over to the surgeons. Furthermore, surgeons were often equated with butchers as professionals
whose work hardened their hearts to cruelty and bloodshed.* Nero's

---

*It was widely, though inaccurately, believed that members of both professions were
barred from serving on juries because their work rendered them pitiless. In fact, surgeons were exempt, not excluded, from jury duty because of the vital services they
performed. Butchers were neither exempt nor excluded, although the presumption
of their callousness often resulted in their challenge and dismissal.

violence in the earlier stages is not unique, we see, but part of a larger context of cruelty going on all around him. So, too, the circumstances of his demise collapse distinctions between high and low, authorities and criminals, humans and animals.

The Four Stages of Cruelty shocks by making connections among various commonplace forms of violence perpetrated against both animals and humans—by boys and by men, by criminals, laborers, barristers, surgeons, and the hangman. Hogarth represents cruelty as both externally shaped and internally driven. Poverty and innate viciousness combine within a culture that is violent on all levels to cause suffering to animals and humans alike. This impassioned work is an operatic spectacle of the cruelty that was performed every day, everywhere.

HOGARTH CONCLUDED HIS depictions of cruelty in the realm of powerful elites—institutionalized medicine and the judiciary—in order to make the connection between the cruelty of the streets and the cruelty of the state. Knowledgeable eighteenth-century viewers would have been able to discern another implicit connection: that between the dissection of Nero's dead body and the medical experimentation that was going on at the time. This was another point at which the human and animal worlds intersected and produced suffering. Live animals were experimented upon and dissected with some regularity during this period, not only under the aegis of the Royal Society (whose vivisections had decreased in frequency since Margaret Cavendish's day), but also as intellectual exercises conducted by scientifically inclined gentlemen in the privacy of their homes, or as staged performances by celebrity doctors in front of curious audiences.

The Royal Society's Register Books for the seventeenth century record numerous experiments on living animals, dogs, cats, sheep, and calves being the most common. Animal respiration experiments suffocated kittens, birds, mice, and frogs and were duly recorded in the record books and sometimes published in the *Philosophical Transactions*. In other experiments, animals were placed in containers of "inflammable air" (hydrogen) to see if they could live—which they could not. Many experiments involved poisons, which would be administered to animals to note their effects: sometimes the poison was injected, other times transferred directly from the bite of a poisonous snake.

Among the animal experiments recorded for the year 1666–67 (the year of Cavendish's visit) were blood transfusion experiments that siphoned blood from one animal into another: from a sheep into a dog, for instance, or from one sheep into another sheep. The donor animal was usually drained of blood and died, but the recipient responded in various ways. Richard Lower performed a transfusion in which, he reported to Robert Boyle, he slowly put one dog's blood into another, letting out the recipient's blood into bowls at the same time. He observed that the donor dog "begins to cry and faint, and fall into convulsions, and at last die by his side," while the recipient "will leap from the table and shake himself, and run away as if nothing ailed him." Boyle queried whether the first dog's characteristics transferred to the second, and, if the donor was fed, whether the recipient could go without eating.

Edmund King conducted an experiment at his house in which he replaced a dog's blood with sugary milk. (The oxygen-carrying function of blood was not known at this time; King apparently wanted to test if the nutrients and energy contained in milk and sugar could sustain life in the place of blood.) The dog struggled so much, he reported, that he almost stopped, but then the animal ceased to struggle, so the experiment continued. The dog lived for several hours, vomiting, and lost the use of his limbs "but seemed to know when he was kindly spoken to," King observed. He eventually died, his body smelling so foul that it made the servants sick.

The experiments that most often troubled the experimenters themselves—and that would greatly trouble antivivisectionists in the nineteenth century—were the true vivisections: the actual dissection of living, often conscious, animals. "Vivisection," whose first usage is dated 1707 by the *Oxford English Dictionary*, refers most precisely to an experiment that involves cutting into or dissecting a living creature; but the term was also used more generally to refer to any painful experiment on a living organism, so the air pump, poison experiments, and transfusions could also be termed vivisections. (I use the term specifically to characterize the live dissections that occurred both before 1707 and after, and refer to the others as "live animal experiments.") In a true vivisection, an animal, usually a dog or cat, would be tied or nailed by its paws to a table and its body cut open. These experiments depended upon the animal's being alive and, since this was an age before anesthetics (for humans or animals), this meant that the animals were usually conscious, at least initially. No attempt was made to do anything that might alleviate an experimental animal's pain, for it was not clear that anything could be done. Whether the animal's suffering was even considered worth alleviating, or to what degree, depended upon the experimenter.

Some vivisections examined the relation between respiration and the circulation of the blood, testing the hypothesis that the lungs worked like bellows activating the heart and pushing blood through the veins: in these experiments, the scientist would open up the living animal to expose the action of heart, veins, and lungs. John Evelyn attended one such vivisection, performed before the membership of the Royal Society by Robert Hooke and Richard Lower: this was a repeat of an experiment Hooke had performed previously, in which a dog's neck and throat were cut away. Evelyn described how they kept the "poor cur" alive after his thorax was cut open by blowing air into his lungs with bellows, "& that long after his heart was out, & the lungs both gashed & pierced, his eyes quick [alive] all the while." Evelyn, who in his diary described matter-of-factly his participation in blood transfusions and trials of various poisons on cats, dogs, and birds, said of this one, "This was an experiment of more cruelty than pleased me."

The early vivisectionists of the Royal Society were well aware that their experiments caused animals pain: the degree of suffering was in fact often an important detail to be recorded, part of the observation of an experiment's effects. The scientist thus paid close attention to a dog or a sheep's physical sensations. In these records, the experimenter sometimes does express satisfaction when he is able to report that an animal seems none the worse for what it has undergone. (This, of course, is not to say that the animal *was* genuinely none the worse, or that it had not suffered.) There were times, too, when the experimenter made decisions in order to avoid extending an animal's pain. Boyle, who described the agonies of some creatures in the air pump quite dispassionately, seems to have felt compassion for three newborn kittens he was using: he killed one in the air pump, but having nearly suffocated and then revived the second, he used the third in the next experiment in order to spare the second one a repetition of the agony.

Lower, who assisted in the vivisection that disturbed Evelyn, was a frequent, apparently enthusiastic performer of animal experiments. But that particular experiment's originator, Hooke, had qualms about its cruelty, and in fact had had to be pressured into undertaking the repeat performance that Evelyn witnessed. After the first experiment in which he cut open a dog, Hooke wrote to Boyle: "I shall hardly be induced to make any further trials of this kind, because of the torture of the creature: but certainly the enquiry would be very noble, if we could find any way so to stupefy the creature, as that it might not be sensible, which I fear there is hardly any opiate will perform." Elsewhere he expressed concern that the suffering inflicted upon animals might so alter their natures as to call into question the accuracy of the scientific observations gleaned from the experiments.

Hooke, Boyle, Lower, and subsequent fellows of the Royal Society performed live animal experiments throughout and beyond the eighteenth century, although the rate of such experimentation slowed. Generally, vivisectionists justified their work by means of the anthropocentric argument that animals existed to serve the greater good of humans. Yet unease at such experiments was growing, especially since many of them were unnecessary repetitions. Alexander Pope expressed severe criticism of the animal experiments performed by his neighbor and friend the Reverend Stephen Hales, a fellow of the Royal Society. Hales, an accomplished scientist, inventor, and enthusiastic vivisectionist, was an admirable man, Pope told another friend. But "he has his hands imbrued with blood," because in his home laboratory he cut up not only rats but also *dogs*. "Indeed," the poet said, "he commits most of these barbarities with the thought of its being of use to man. But how do we know that we have a right to kill creatures that we are so little above as dogs, for our curiosity, or even for some use to us?"

The philosopher Immanuel Kant, who held an anthropocentric position on animal life, nonetheless asserted that "the painful physical experiments for the mere sake of speculation are to be abhorred, if the end may be achieved without them." John Lawrence, who wrote early veterinary treatises on diseases and care of horses, passionately condemned vivisection. And just a few years after Hogarth depicted human dissection as a cruelty, Samuel Johnson wrote in his periodical *The Idler,* "It is time that a universal resentment should arise against those horrid operations, which tend to harden the heart and make the physicians more dreadful than the gout or the stone. Men who have practiced tortures on animals without pity, relating them without shame, how can they still hold their heads among human beings?"

The fact that the Royal Society reported fewer vivisections after the seventeenth century clearly did not mean that others had done so as well. Vivisections flourished in other contexts, both private and public. In 1825, a French anatomist named François Magendie gave a series of lectures in London. In order to demonstrate the functioning of the facial nerves, Magendie cut open half of the face of a living greyhound. He had first nailed the animal to the table by its paws and its ears, using large blunt spikes that would make it harder for the dog to tear itself away. After performing his vivisection, Magendie had told his audience that he would keep the dog alive overnight in order to cut open the other side of his face in his lecture the next day. (He had paid ten guineas for the dog—a large sum, for a greyhound was an upper-class pet—and presumably wanted to get his money's worth.) If the greyhound showed less animation by that time, the French doctor said, he would then cut into his torso to show the working of his heart and viscera.

When Richard Martin described this demonstration in a speech to the House of Commons, he elicited cries of *"Hear"* and *"Shame"* from his colleagues. Martin professed himself no enemy to all animal experiments, just those that, like this one, were egregiously cruel and not justified by scientific necessity. Magendie, he said, had performed this operation thousands of times in Paris, and only exhibited it in London "to produce a dramatic effect." This was showmanship, not science. Martin's account outraged some of his colleagues, not least because the experiment had been performed on a greyhound. Yet other MPs defended Magendie, praising him for his kindness and humanity to people and implying that Martin had slandered him. Although antivivisection sentiment was growing in Martin's day, an organized movement against the practice arose in Britain only some years later.

WILLIAM HOGARTH DECLARED that he was prouder of *The Four Stages of Cruelty* than any of his other works. If his pictures did anything to prevent cruelty, he said, he would rather be the creator of them than of Raphael's cartoons. He professed himself "happy because I believe the publication of them has checked the diabolical spirit of barbarity, which, I am sorry to say was once so prevalent in this country." (This was a noble but, to say the least, overoptimistic view: many of the cruelties cited in this chapter took place well after 1751.)

Hogarth's explicitly intended audience for his series were those who delighted in cruelty or at least perpetrated it—that is, people like Tom Nero—and he addressed them in his captions. But these were obviously not the people most likely to absorb his moral lesson; they certainly were not the purchasers of his engravings, and quite possibly could not even read the captions in a print shop window. The illiterate laboring classes were not positioned to respond to didactic works of art. The audience Hogarth could and did reach comprised middle- and upper-class people who, though they might not have acknowledged it, shared culpability for tolerating such cruelty and in fact often benefited from the overloaded wagon or whip-driven stagecoach. These were also the people who were positioned by class, education, and income to create and support a reform movement dedicated to seeking recourse in the law.

As one of the earliest polemics against cruelty to animals, appearing almost exactly in the middle of the eighteenth century, *The Four Stages of Cruelty* can be said to represent the point of transition in our story: the moment at which earlier, scattered, individual expressions of concern for the abuse of animals began to coalesce into a larger collectivity—into a cause and a movement. Of course, this change did not actually happen in a single moment: it was a long, gradual process of many individual threads beginning to weave together into a fabric. At the point when action could be taken and results possibly obtained, the animal protection movement emerged. In Hogarth's day, that critical point was still more than half a century away, but from now on the story will be one of increasing awareness of animal abuse and the escalation of demands that something on a national scale be done to address it. Some of the earliest voices attempting to influence the British public came from the pulpit.

CHAPTER 8

THE MEANEST WORM
IS OUR SISTER

✳︎　　✳︎　　✳︎

IN THE late 1750s, the poet Christopher Smart was declared insane and committed to Mr. Potter's private madhouse in Bethnal Green (a former country retreat in east London just beginning its decline into poverty). Smart, who had already earned a reputation as a gifted poet, was also a feckless alcoholic, a hack writer, and a cross-dressing theater entertainer who performed under the stage name Mrs. Midnight. The primary symptom of Smart's madness, according to his friend Dr. Johnson and others, was not actual insanity at all, but religious ecstasy of an inconveniently public sort that would cause him to fall on his knees to pray in the street and insist that others pray with him. (Another apparent symptom, said Johnson, was Smart's refusal to wear clean clothes—a position for which the great doctor, none too tidy himself, felt considerable sympathy.)

In Potter's asylum, Smart had access to a garden, a small library, and, most important of all, a cat named Jeoffry—dubbed by one of Smart's biographers the "most famous cat in the whole history of English literature."* While incarcerated, Smart wrote his extraordinary long devotional poem "Jubilate Agno" (Rejoice in the Lamb). The poem is filled with animals, but its best-known passage is the sequence

---

*Puss in Boots, Dick Whittington's cat, Horace Walpole's Selima, and Dr. Johnson's own Hodge could all have taken issue with this assessment. (Although Puss's claim on the title might be weakest, since he was an Italian immigrant who arrived in England via France.)

147

of seventy-four lines that begins "For I shall consider my cat Jeoffry." Here, Smart celebrates both Jeoffry's animality and his godliness, seeing them as complementary—indeed, as inseparably interrelated. In this, Smart joined two concepts that would have seemed directly contradictory a century before. And still in his own day such a conjunction of the animal and the divine would have been considered bizarre, if not downright sacrilegious, by most people.

Smart gives us a cat who, as "the servant of the Living God duly and daily serving him," rises in the morning to perform his feline devotions, "wreathing his body seven times round with elegant quickness." Then, "having done duty and received blessing," Jeoffry turns to "consider himself." He checks his forepaws to see that they are clean, washes himself, sharpens his claws, stretches, picks out his fleas ("that he may not be interrupted upon the beat"), and then goes out to hunt—giving the mice he catches a chance to escape, as one occasionally does. Jeoffry's master lovingly describes how his cat leaps into his bosom, plays with a cork, jumps over a stick, and even fetches and carries.

Jeoffry also "purrs in thankfulness, when God tells him he's a good Cat"—something the Lord seems to do often. Jeoffry is all cat, and therefore he is God's creature; God has given him grace and dexterity as signs of his love. "For every house is incompleat without him," wrote his devoted owner and companion, for where there is no Jeoffry, "a blessing is lacking in the spirit." In his very feline being, Jeoffry both worships and manifests God.

For he knows that God is his Saviour.
For there is nothing sweeter than his peace when at rest.
For there is nothing brisker than his life when in motion.
For he is of the Lord's poor and so indeed is he called by benevolence perpetually—
   Poor Jeoffry! poor Jeoffry! the rat has bit thy throat.
For I bless the name of the Lord Jesus that Jeoffry is better.
For the divine spirit comes about his body to sustain it in compleat cat.

Undoubtedly there were many in Smart's day who would have seen these lines—if they had seen them, for the poem was not published until 1939—as nothing more than the ravings of a madman. But in fact, when Smart claimed that Jeoffry was a creature beloved by God, and when he displayed his own obvious love and admiration for his cat, he was expressing some of the attitudes toward animals that would be articulated with increasing frequency in other, less marginal religious and secular voices in the decades that followed.

Smart wrote his poem in the middle of the eighteenth century, a time when a cultural shift regarding the status of beasts was starting to manifest itself in both secular and religious contexts. Seventeenth-century philosophical debates about the existence and nature of animal intellect and souls that had been conveniently settled (for some) by Descartes's mechanism were revived. Against the complacent anthropocentrism enshrined by dominant church teachings, some devout Christians were now reexamining doctrine and scripture. Questions about the nature of animals had always to some degree been present in theological and philosophical circles, as we have seen. In the eighteenth century, however, these questions started to be answered in a context that, for the first time, would come to have implications for the legal status of beasts. Christian writers departed from traditional interpretations of the doctrine of man's dominion to reconsider that idea and the scriptural authority behind it. Not that cruelty to animals had never been attacked before from a Christian perspective—it certainly had—but now the attacks were increasing in number and beginning to influence orthodox beliefs. Members of the established Church of England, some of whom belonged to its rapidly growing evangelical wing, as well as dissenting sects such as the Quakers and Methodists, were having some impact, albeit still a slight one, upon the status of animals within Christianity.

The Anglican clergymen who took up the cause of animals in the second half of the eighteenth century wished to stop the cruelty routinely practiced on beasts. With one voice, they proclaimed that animals are God's creatures, too—"the brute Creation"—and are beloved by him. Humans have a duty to extend compassion to animals and it is a sin to abuse them. The Romantic poet Samuel Taylor Coleridge expressed this sentiment in his well-known lines from *The Rime of the Ancient Mariner*:

> *He prayest best, who loveth best*
> *All things both great and small;*
> *For the dear God who loveth us,*
> *He made and loveth all.*

People were beginning to argue with more and more conviction that animals obviously feel pain, are capable of affection, and possess some kind or degree of understanding. Their similarities to humans outweigh their differences. One of the earliest clergymen to publish an essay against cruelty to animals, John Hildrop of Yorkshire, asserted in 1743 that the difference between the lowest level of human understanding and the highest level of animal understanding is "hardly perceptible," evident only in humans' greater "fluency of language." But even that is a dubious advantage, he continued, since people's linguistic fluency all too often reveals their empty heads, perverse wills, and iniquitous hearts.

Many of those who came to argue from this position appealed to people's experience of their own animals, usually their pets. Descartes's notion that animals are machines is ridiculous, even criminal, they protested, for animals obviously think on some level, and certainly they feel. How, asked the Reverend Richard Dean in 1768, could anybody possessing even "a grain of common sense" possibly believe that an animal feels no more when whipped or beaten than a log of wood feels when struck by an ax? As Proverbs taught—Dean was citing a passage invoked again and again by these writers—"A righteous man regardeth the life of his beast, but the tender mercies of the wicked are cruel" (12:10). Animals may be lesser beings, and many of them may indeed exist to serve humans, Dean exclaimed, but that does not give us the right to transform our dominion over them into tyranny.

The clergyman Thomas Young, a fellow of Trinity College,

Cambridge, posed a question that neatly reversed the usual implications of the Cartesian model. Even if we weren't conscious of its monetary value, he asked, would we deliberately smash a mechanism as intricately made as a watch? Of course we would not. So how could we so wantonly destroy even the lowest beings—"a mite, a worm or a fly"—when these, divinely created, are so much more complicated than a watch?

These opinions were part of a larger shift in the eighteenth century away from the idea of human domination of nature and toward the concept of stewardship. Keith Thomas points out that while in earlier periods people had viewed the earth as a fallen entity (like man), damaged and decaying, they were now emphasizing its lushness and plenitude: an earth whose abundance exists to reward our responsible cultivation of it. This notion still placed humans at the apex of earthly creation, but it also imposed upon us a new set of responsibilities. The earth would yield rewards, but only if we assumed a proper relationship to it. As the historian Roy Porter explains, the paradigm that came to dominate eighteenth-century thinking about the environment was "not conflictual but cooperative."

In this model of cooperation, God has given humans the earth to cultivate responsibly and animals to help us do this. Man is not earth's tyrant, its dominator, but rather its steward. The prototype of this paternalistic, indeed managerial, model was the farm. "Such images of stewardship—paternal rather than plundering—sanctioned action and ordained environmental ethics and aesthetics," Porter writes. The concept of the domestication of nature certainly served the purposes of management and exploitation, but it also rejected older, cruder metaphors of forcible domination and rape. Although the gentler, paternalistic model did mask (rather than change) the power relationships at the heart of the use of nature for profit, when it came to humans' actual treatment of animals—specifically, the violence inflicted upon them—the rise of the notion of stewardship marked the beginning of a change, however long and slow, for the better.

As it influenced the positions taken by Christian clergymen and theologians, the replacement of dominion by stewardship often entailed a turn to the Judaic roots of Christianity. While they did not question the subordination of animals, and usually accepted the great chain of being, eighteenth-century Christian writers such as Hildrop, Dean, and Young cited as authority for their arguments scriptural passages that were overwhelmingly found in the Hebrew Bible. New Testament writers, by contrast, were much more prone to use animals as metaphors for humans; when they represented people as Christ's flock or chicks, for instance, they were not expressing concern for actual sheep or chickens.

We should bear in mind that concern about cruelty to animals was not shared by all clergymen of any denomination, any more than it was by all laymen: many did not particularly care about animals at all, and neither the Church of England nor most of the Dissenting sects (notably excepting Methodism) took an official stance on animal welfare. They disapproved of cruelty more often because it manifested human depravity than because it resulted in animal suffering. Furthermore, those who did care about animals may have shared a common ground of compassion, but beyond that they disagreed about key theological issues. One of the largest-looming questions was whether animals possess immortal souls and therefore enjoy life after death. Those who supposed that beasts do enjoy an afterlife had to consider the question of what heaven for animals might be like: most (though not all) agreed that beasts' experience of eternal bliss would be less than humans'. Correspondingly, the question of animals' capacity for sin had to be raised: If animals can sin or somehow have defects, what is the nature both of these failings and of the animal moral life that they imply? And if beasts cannot sin, what can account for their fall from grace? For animals are subject to all the ills and sorrows that plague fallen humans, in addition to their brutal treatment by people. If God is just to all his creatures, what have animals done to deserve this fate?

Though these Christian writers agreed that humans have a duty to be kind, different clergymen had different explanations of why we should perform that duty. Those who believed that animals possess an immortal soul based their case for kindness upon the similarity between humans and animals, and the fact that these animal souls are clear evidence of God's love for his creation. Cruelty to animals is displeasing to God, who cares for all creatures and promises them immortality. John Hildrop argued that while animals are indeed placed by God under the absolute dominion of humans, in the Garden of Eden all creatures had lived together happily, worshipping God in peace and harmony. When Adam and Eve fell, they took the other living beings with them, and this was the reason for the "present lamentable condition" of animals, now subject to such abuse by humans through no sin of their own. Hildrop cited numerous passages from the Hebrew Bible where God enjoins humans to be merciful to animals, particularly the familiar Proverbs 12:10. "Brutes have souls," he pronounced; and, like human souls, those of animals are immortal—just as they were before the Fall. "What authority we have to strike out of the system of immortality so great a part of the creation, without an absolute and evident necessity, exceeds my comprehension," he said.

Richard Dean agreed with Hildrop that animals possess souls, but came to a different conclusion regarding their innocence. The curate of parishes near Manchester and master of the Middleton Grammar School, Dean published his *Essay on the Future Life of Brutes* in 1768. Granted that animals, like humans, suffer pain and disease—all the "injuries of the Fall"—Dean was troubled by the question of their culpability: if these injuries are the consequence of sin, how can we understand sin as regards animals, who do not have our "moral rules"? Since God does not punish unjustly, he reasoned, animals must have some sort of faults or defects, too, even if we do not know what those are. But, just like the souls of humans, the souls of beasts will be saved. (It is clear that animals have souls, Dean said, quoting early Hebrew and Christian writers who supported this notion.) A brute is no less entitled to a future life because it is inferior to a human, than we are denied immortality because we are inferior to the cherubim. Since we have greater rational capacities than beasts, we will enjoy our eternal bliss to a greater degree—but animals will have their share of joy in a future life, too.

John Wesley, the evangelical preacher and founder of Methodism, shared the belief in an animal afterlife. He exhorted his congregations to show mercy to animals, observing, "What a dreadful difference is there, between what they suffer from their fellow-brutes, and what they suffer from the tyrant man!" Carnivorous animals, who must kill in order to live, do so quickly, he said, "but the human shark, without any such necessity, torments them of his free choice; and perhaps continues their lingering pain till, after months or years, death signs their release." Surely, he commented elsewhere, "Something better remains after death for these poor creatures also."

In contrast, one of the most important eighteenth-century polemicists against cruelty to animals, Humphrey Primatt, believed that animals deserve special consideration because they do *not* have an afterlife. In 1776, he published his only known work, *A Dissertation on the Duty of Mercy and the Sin of Cruelty to Brute Animals*. Not much more is known about him: the son of a clergyman, he held parishes in Suffolk and Norfolk until, later in life, an inheritance allowed him to resign his position, live comfortably in Kingston-upon-Thames, and commit to paper his thoughts about animals. He died the year after the *Dissertation* was published. It would become one of the central texts of the animal protection movement (and is still quoted in animal welfare and animal rights circles today). Later writers would cite passages from it and repeat its arguments. Arthur Broome, the clergyman who became the driving force behind the creation of the SPCA, published his own editions of Primatt's *Dissertation* just prior to the society's founding.

"An hereafter for a beast has a strange sound in the ears of a man," Primatt wrote. "We cannot bear the thought." We do not know the truth, of course, but because we can see no indication of a beastly heaven and have no scriptural authority upon which to assume it, we must suppose that there is none. However, Primatt continued, "from this very supposition, we rationally infer that cruelty to a brute is an injury irreparable." The injuries suffered by an innocent human will "be overbalanced in a future and happy state," and the affliction will have been but a moment in comparison to eternity. But nothing can undo what we inflict upon animals. Far from justifying their abuse, their final mortality gives us an extra degree of responsibility for them—more, in fact, than we have for other humans. The "cruelty of men to brutes," Primatt argued, is "more heinous (in point of injustice) than the cruelty of men unto men"—because animals are dependent upon humans, because they cannot speak for themselves, and because they have no reward in heaven.

Alexander Pope also believed that animals do not have an afterlife. His influential early essay on cruelty to animals was often cited by later eighteenth-century writers including several of these clergymen. In it, he argued that since animals do not possess a soul, and therefore cannot look forward to a heavenly salvation that might compensate for ill-treatment in this world, animals deserve our compassion all the more.

Whatever position these writers held on the question of animal souls and eternal life, they agreed that beasts are unable to anticipate the future and thus cannot foresee their deaths. Even if they do have immortal souls, they cannot know that eternal bliss awaits them: they live as if this were their only life, which makes their awareness of the present—including present suffering—particularly acute. Rather than disqualifying animals from our concern, their inability to conceive the future makes it all the more necessary that we protect them in the here and now.

Among the reasons that Primatt's book was so popular in the eighteenth and nineteenth centuries was that he devoted much of it to finding scriptural authority for his argument. (His citations from the Hebrew Bible outnumber those from the New Testament, according to Richard Ryder, by about five to one.) He probably continues to be cited and read among animal activists today not only because his writing is often deeply stirring, but also because he makes the groundbreaking claim that animals have a *right* to happiness. What gives them this right, said Primatt, is a matter not of understanding or language, but of feeling: their ability to suffer.

Primatt was the one of the first major English writers to make a claim for animal rights, which, he believed, lay at least partially in the limitation of the rights of humans to abuse them. While Primatt accepted that animals are different in kind and degree from people and therefore subordinate to us, he argued that, nonetheless, "pain is pain, whether it be inflicted on man or on beast." To suffer pain is to suffer evil, and it is "cruelty and injustice in him that occasions it." While we do have God's permission to eat the flesh of some animals, this "cannot authorize us to put them to *unnecessary* pain, or *lingering* death." Since, for a beast, present pain and present happiness are all, "therefore, whilst he lives he has a right to happiness." Unlike us, an animal cannot care whether he dies today or tomorrow. "But if he is to die tomorrow, it is not right to put him in pain today. He has a right to happiness, at least I have no right to make him miserable." God's covenant after the Flood is a covenant of "peace, harmony, and love," and it extends to all.

But does "all" include only warm-blooded animals, who bleed and cry as we do? What about cold-blooded creatures, who seem, at least to us, to be mute, even unfeeling? If beasts and humans are all created in accordance with the same divine plan, must we extend the same degree of compassion to all the rest of animal creation—not just to horses and sheep, but to fish and insects, too?

An anonymous clergyman made this point in a Shrovetide sermon attacking cockthrowing, published in 1761 under the title "Clemency to Brutes." Animals who can moan and cry do speak "forcibly for themselves to the hearts of their persecutors." But mute beasts are fellow creatures, too.

> Did not the same Hand which made them make us? Are they not formed with equal thought and accuracy? Are they not, considering the difference of their natures, as bountifully provided for? Have they not impressed on them as vehement a desire of continuing their kinds? Appear they not, when bruised or wounded, or otherwise evil-treated, to seem equally sensible of pain?—Yes, considered in all these respects, the very meanest worm is our sister.

The anonymous clergyman was echoing a passage from the book of Job: "I have said to corruption, Thou art my father: to the worm, Thou art my mother, and my sister" (17:14). But whereas the biblical passage refers to human death and the grave, he turned it into a lesson intended to govern the conduct of the living, and represented the worm as a sentient being whose own pain and death have meaning, too. Shakespeare had given voice to a similar feeling in *Measure for Measure*:

> And the poor beetle, that we tread upon,
> In corporal sufferance finds a pang as great
> As when a giant dies.

These eloquent words were much quoted by eighteenth- and nineteenth-century reformers.

Among them was Thomas Young, the rector of East Gillings in Yorkshire. In his *Essay on Humanity to Animals* (1798), he pleaded with people not to step on worms and snails, citing Shakespeare's lines. Young also condemned the common practices of eating live oysters, skinning live eels, and boiling live lobsters. Following Primatt, he argued for the *rights* of animals. Beasts, he said, have natural rights that can be deduced even independently of Scripture by paying attention to what nature gives them: the ability to experience pleasure and pain, and the earth's abundant provision for their needs. Similar arguments were made by some moralists for the natural rights of mankind, and they apply also to animals, he maintained.

Killing animals for food (then as now) was a particularly vexed issue among animal welfare proponents (and will be taken up at greater length in the following chapter). Most of these clergymen agreed that humans had the divinely sanctioned right to kill and eat animals: God explicitly permitted meat-eating in his covenant with Noah after the Flood. (The small number of Christians who expressed qualms about meat-eating asked whether it was not more desirable for us to try to imitate the human condition *before* the Fall, when we were vegetarians, than to rest content in our carnivorous fallen state.) Some defenders of meat-eating, like Primatt, considered that in the same covenant God promised animals, too, a type of happiness peculiar to themselves: to be fed, to have rest, and to be treated with kindness. So, while we are allowed to kill animals for food, it is our divinely imposed duty to do this quickly and compassionately. And while the animals live, it is our duty to ensure that their lives are free of suffering.

The clergyman James Plumptre took this responsibility considerably further than most when he published a book entitled *The Experienced Butcher,* which combined a historical survey of the profession and a discussion of the laws relative to it with a manual about how to butcher honorably and compassionately. Plumptre directed his work to general readers as well as to butchers themselves, for his message was as much a call to compassion as a defense of slaughtering. His purpose, expressed on the title page, was to defend the "respectability and usefulness" of the butcher's "calling" (using this word made clear Plumptre's acceptance that the killing of animals was sanctioned by God). On his title page, Plumptre also juxtaposed two biblical passages: "Thou makest man to have dominion of the works of thy hands; thou hast put all things in subjection under his feet; all sheep and oxen; yea, and the beasts of the field" (Psalms 8:6–7) is followed by "Blessed are the merciful, for they shall attain mercy" (Matthew 5:7).

Making their arguments within a specifically Christian tradition of biblical teachings, allusions, and exegesis, these clergymen made common cause with other Christian and non-Christian philosophical, scientific, and political thinkers. The philosopher David Hume argued that animals and humans engage in the same process of reasoning and similarly experience emotion, and that animals are capable of feeling sympathy for one another. The natural historian Erasmus Darwin (grandfather of Charles) observed, as did other scientists, the many structural similarities between animal and human bodies; the analogy suggested to him that we might share other functions and faculties as well.

The atheist philosopher Jeremy Bentham, writing in 1781, questioned the basis upon which animals were tormented as slaves. Surely, he said, a grown horse or dog was more rational than a newborn infant. As David Perkins, writing on animals in Romantic poetry, points out, Bentham's utilitarian philosophy stresses two premises of particular importance to animal welfare: that pain is an evil, and that to behave ethically requires that we seek the greatest happiness of all of those affected by our acts— including animals. (This position underlies some current animal rights arguments: Peter Singer, the world's best-known animal rights ethicist, is a modern-day utilitarian.)

Many of the clergymen who wrote on cruelty were also schoolmasters who paid particular attention to encouraging kindness in children. Like Hogarth, they believed that cruelty is progressive. The cruel child grows up to become a cruel adult; cruelty to animals develops into cruelty to humans. So it is crucial to instill principles of benevolence and compassion in children, not just for animals' sake, but also for the sake of human society. Christopher Smart thought this, too: unlike the suffering cats in *The Four Stages of Cruelty,* his Jeoffry, he wrote, "is an instrument for the children to learn benevolence upon." The idea that (in Wordsworth's phrase) "the child is father of the man" was repeated frequently, by clergymen, schoolteachers, philosophers, and poets: later, it would be echoed by politicians as well.

The philosopher John Locke, whose writing on education had a profound influence on thinking about child development and schooling in the eighteenth century, emphasized the connection between childhood cruelty to animals and adult cruelty to humans, saying that children should be brought up to abhor the idea of tormenting or killing an animal, except in some "nobler" cause. Cruelty in itself is not innately pleasurable, he believed: children learn from the example of adults to enjoy inflicting pain on other creatures. So it is incumbent upon parents to instill proper values of benevolence and to guard against the unnatural, cruel pleasures that the world can teach a child. Locke approved of the mother who always allowed her daughters to have whatever animals they wanted as long as they took good care of them; if one of them failed to do so, she was rebuked and might even have to give up her pet. Thus, these girls "were early taught diligence and good nature. And indeed, I think people should be accustomed, from their cradles, to be tender to all sensible creatures," wrote Locke.

This theme was reiterated many times, with increasing urgency, in the years after Locke. In her writing for children, the feminist Mary Woll-stonecraft deplored cruelty to animals, and the Scots poet Joanna Baillie exhorted girls to exercise a humanizing influence upon their brothers—for cruelty, so often assigned a class position, had also acquired a gender. Though many reformers were certainly conscious that everyone was capable of cruelty, the lower classes and men—and especially lower-class men—were considered particularly prone to it. Women and girls were much more likely to identify with the suffering animal. In a painting illustrating a home demonstration—part education, part entertainment—using an air pump to drain the air from a bell jar containing a white cockatoo, Joseph Wright of Derby revealed a great deal through how each person responds to the pet bird's struggles for life.

This painting is thought to represent a gathering of some members of the Lunar Society, an informal group of scientifically inclined men (including Erasmus Darwin and Joseph Priestley, a preacher, chemist, and radical). Some critics have argued that this painting alludes to the last scene of Hogarth's *Stages of Cruelty,* with a group of spectators gathered around a scene of scientific cruelty. Here, the onlookers react in different, revealing ways. Two of the adult men beside the experimenter are engaged with it; one tries to exhort one of the girls to pay attention while the other holds a watch to time the cockatoo's struggles. A third man, however, looks downward, perhaps frowning in disapproval at the cruelty. The young courting couple have eyes only for each other, while a boy looks on with interest.

On the right, a servant is doing something near the window. Is he lowering the birdcage because the pet will survive to be put back into it, or is he simply removing it because the bird is going to die? Or is he drawing the curtain to cast "lunar" light onto the experiment, or is the moon itself retreating behind the clouds in order to darken this shameful nighttime scene? These questions are debatable, but other messages in the painting are clearer. Of all the people present, our eyes are most immediately drawn to the two illuminated girls who stand at the center of the painting. Significantly, they have no mother figure to comfort them: the only other female in this masculine circle is the young woman

Demonstrations of the air pump were sometimes offered in private homes as a kind of educational entertainment for the whole family, although not everyone paid attention, nor did everyone approve. Joseph Wright of Derby, *An Experiment on a Bird in the Air Pump,* 1768. (The National Gallery, London)

who is interested solely in her lover. One girl looks up at the bird in pity and sadness, while the older girl hides her eyes. These girls feel the lesson of humanity to which most of the males seem indifferent.

IT IS CLEAR that the ranks of clergymen who, like Young and Primatt, published essays and preached sermons on the treatment of animals were growing in the eighteenth century, and that more and more secular writers were expressing similar concerns. Less clear is the extent of their effect on the public at large. Changes in attitudes were indeed taking place, throughout the kingdom, in both urban and rural areas. The preponderance of these were happening among the "middling sort," particularly the educated, professional classes, and among the aristocracy and gentry (at least, as long as their own pastimes of hunting and shooting were not attacked). The subscription list published at the front of Richard Dean's book contains nearly five hundred names, many of them belonging to clergymen, aristocrats, gentry, and professional men; women's names appear on it, too. To be sure, subscriptions were taken in advance of publication (and often in advance of writing), so the number of subscribers indicates only that Dean was well connected. But it also suggests that, at least in his case, there was a reading public receptive to the topic of his book and willing to support its publication, if not necessarily in agreement with all the sentiments it expressed in its final published form.

However, Dean's attitudes were very far from universally held, both among these privileged social groups and among those who ranked lower on the social scale. Humphrey Primatt recognized that by writing his book he would be courting the ridicule and abuse heaped upon anyone who attempted to defy "prejudice" and "long received customs":

> To make a *comparison* between a man and a brute, is *abominable*: To talk of a man's *duty* to his horse or his ox, is *absurd*; To suppose it a sin to chase a stag, to hunt a fox, or to course a hare, is *unpolite*; To esteem it *barbarous* to throw at a cock, to bait a bull, to roast a lobster, or to crimp a fish, is *ridiculous*.

The derision he expected obviously came from his social circle: not the "lower orders" who would become the first, most obvious targets of the nineteenth-century anticruelty campaigns, but the literate classes for whom these polemics were written, and at whose thinking and behavior they were also directed.

When, in the fall of 1772, the Reverend James Granger preached to his parishioners in Shiplake, Oxfordshire, on the text "A righteous man regardeth the life of his beast," he provoked an uproar. His sermon, he remarked when he published it, "gave almost universal disgust to two considerable congregations." Granger's sermon was not particularly radical: he accepted the idea of man's dominion, but preached that it must be a merciful one, that humans are accountable to the beasts that serve us. We are God's viceroys, not tyrants, he said: necessity compels us to kill animals for food, and we have the right to do so. But until that point, they have as much right to the enjoyment of their lives as we do, and their deaths should come without suffering. Granger attacked bullbaiting, observed that dogs are taught to be cruel by humans, and charged that horses, those docile, generous, and useful animals, were treated more barbarously in England than anywhere else in the world. This country, he declared, was indeed the proverbial "Hell of Horses."

Granger's words shocked and offended the Shiplake congregations. Talking about dogs and horses in a sermon, he noted wryly in a post-script, was denounced by his parishioners as a "prostitution of the dignity of the pulpit," giving proof of their parson's "growing insanity." So outraged was his flock that the bishop had to pay a personal visit to the parish to calm them down. When, apparently undaunted by the furor, Granger published the sermon as "An Apology for the Brute Creation," it was reviewed favorably and was well spoken of in London. But it sold fewer than one hundred copies. As James Turner has observed, by this point in the eighteenth century, while there were many people who had come to *believe,* in some vague way, in kindness to animals, there were still very few who genuinely *cared* about it. For those who did care, however, advocacy for animals was inextricably intertwined with other outcries against the status quo that arose in the revolutionary period of the later eighteenth century. Those outcries included challenges not just to British institutions but to the very food Britons ate. England's vaunted identity as a nation of beef-eaters was not a source of pride, radicals argued, but rather a source of sickness and oppression.

CHAPTER 9

THROW DOWN THE BUTCHER'S KNIFE

✳   ✳   ✳

A T THE time of his nervous breakdown, Dr. George Cheyne weighed nearly four hundred fifty pounds: he was, he claimed, the fattest man in Europe. As a young man in Scotland, Cheyne had lived in a constant state of internal warfare as his self-control fought losing battles against his love of food and drink. When in 1701, at age twenty-nine, he moved to London, one of the consumer capitals of the world, the sheer array of delectable temptations available at the shops, at the taverns, and in the homes of his friends overcame the last shreds of his resistance. He fell into a company of high-living young men, drinking so heavily and dining so sumptuously that, he said, "I grew excessively fat, short-breath'd, lethargic and listless."

As his body ballooned to the point of immobility, Dr. Cheyne was plagued with fever, dizziness, and headaches, accompanied by deepening anxiety, depression, and self-loathing. His friends dropped him, and he retired to the country, where he lived in isolation, dosing himself with heavy medication, including mercury and laudanum, which caused chronic vomiting. These dangerous remedies resulted in his enormous body "melting away like a snow-ball in summer," but this was no answer to what ailed him. Dejected, Cheyne began a course of spiritual reading that improved his spirits, and he moved to Bath to take the waters—but when he started to feel better and began once again to eat meat and drink alcohol, his physical and emotional illnesses returned. Hearing of a doctor who had cured himself of epilepsy by consuming nothing but milk, Cheyne sought him out, and discovered his solution—and with it, a path to fame and fortune.

His return to health was not without relapses, but eventually he came to eschew rich food and wine altogether, and found that the less meat he ate, the better he felt. Meat, he realized, was a toxic substance. With his own personal success story—today we would call it a recovery narrative—and the prescription for health he formulated, consisting of a simple diet of vegetables and milk, George Cheyne became a celebrity doctor. He also became eighteenth-century England's most famous vegetarian—though he did not call himself that, for the word did not enter common usage until the founding of the Vegetarian Society in 1847. Dr. Cheyne acquired famous patients (including John Wesley, Alexander Pope, and the best-selling novelist Samuel Richardson, as well as numerous aristocrats), published popular tracts on diet, health, and longevity, and established his practice in Bath, England's most fashionable spa. His name appeared often in the media—newspapers and magazines, prints and poems; people talked about him; he had fans. He was an eighteenth-century Nathan Pritikin, Dean Ornish, and Andrew Weil, all rolled up in one.

Cheyne certainly had his critics. Vegetarians, especially proselytizing ones, then as now provoked intense hostility and ridicule among carnivores—hostility that was particularly acute in a society for which the song "The Roast Beef of Old England" (written by Henry Fielding, the author of *Tom Jones*) was virtually a national anthem.

> *When mighty Roast Beef*
> *Was the Englishman's food,*
> *It ennobled our brains*
> *And enriched our blood.*
> *Our soldiers were brave*
> *And our courtiers were good*
> *Oh the Roast Beef of old England*
> *And old English Roast Beef.*

Roast beef was the emblem of good old simple English virtues (particularly when compared with the fussy "made dishes" concocted by those decadent and dangerous frog-eaters across the Channel). Furthermore, meat was considered a necessary part of the human diet. Going without meat was widely believed to lead to sickliness, even death. To the objection that, according to the Bible, humans had done perfectly well without meat before the Flood, it was argued that vegetables had been more nutritious in those days, but that when the waters inundated all the vegetable life on earth they leached it of its nutritional value—and that was why, after the waters receded, God gave Noah and the rest of us permission to begin eating animals.

It is not surprising, given these views, that Cheyne was often mocked or satirized. Such was the price of fame, unconventionality, and the apparent contradiction between his continuing bulk and his dietary strictures—for, as his ridiculers often pointed out, despite his vegetarian diet he remained obese all his life. Concerned with the quality of what he and others ate, the doctor, at least in his own case, was less stringent about quantity. Even his friends made fun of him. Lord Bolingbroke told of a breakfast he and Alexander Pope had with Cheyne, where they listened to the doctor go on about "the enormous immorality of using exercise to promote an appetite" while watching him tuck into his meal of "a gallon of milk coffee and five pounds of biscuit." Another friend, the poet Edward Young, wrote, "Who damns our trash, with so much trash replete? / As, three ells round, huge Cheyne rails at meat?" (Three ells equal one hundred and thirty-five inches.) His size did not seem to hurt his popularity or his authority with his patients, however. The fact that Cheyne lived to the advanced age of seventy-three certainly enhanced his credibility.

Cheyne advocated a diet of vegetables, grains, seeds, fruits, and milk: the last, as a processed form of the grass eaten by cows, was believed to *be* a vegetable. That this logic could extend to the cow itself had occurred to John Evelyn, who thought that animals that ate only vegetables essentially *were* vegetables. (Obviously this notion could have played havoc with the idea of a vegetarian diet as something distinct from a carnivorous one, if consuming only vegetable eaters—as most people did, since in the West carnivorous animals usually were, and still are, considered inedible—was essentially the same as consuming only vegetables.) To us today, perhaps barring his ideas about milk, Cheyne's diet seems strikingly modern (although in reality it is quite ancient). Even the good doctor's enthusiasm for bleeding and "vomit pills" to purge the system sounds familiar enough in our age of cleansing fasts and colonic irrigation. (Telling his friend Samuel Richardson that his short neck made him an ideal candidate for a "vomit now and then," Cheyne prescribed seasonal purges: "You have bled already, and a puke would do well to introduce winter.")

Cheyne may have turned vegetarianism into a cult of celebrity, but he was far from the first or only prominent vegetarian in England. The radical Protestant sects that flourished around the time of the Revolution in the middle of the seventeenth century produced a number of radical vegetarians, as Tristram Stuart details in *Bloodless Revolution,* a fascinating history of the influence of India and Hinduism on English thinking about meat-eating. Even if the groups themselves did not doctrinally impose vegetarianism, there were members of the Shakers, the Levellers, the Diggers, and the Quakers, among others, who embraced the purity of a meat-abstinent diet as a way of preparing the soul for God, of acknowledging animals as fellow members of God's creation, and of making a political attack upon the sinfulness, decadence, and inequality of English society. Specifically vegetarian sects existed, too, such as the Rationals, founded by the religious radical Roger Crab.

Thomas Tryon, a religious Dissenter, hatmaker, and prolific writer who was strongly influenced by Hinduism, made arguments about animal capacity similar to those of Margaret Cavendish (however little else the Puritan radical and the royalist duchess had in common). Tyron spoke of animals as "fellow citizens of the world." Interest in a vegetable diet was not associated only with religious and political radicals, however: the royalist John Evelyn, though not a vegetarian for most of his life, argued for both compassion to animals and the healthfulness of a nonmeat diet. An avid gardener, he wrote a book on "sallets" (salads) that was credited with bringing these dishes some degree of popularity.

Even René Descartes endorsed the healthful properties of a vegetarian diet. Believing, like Dr. Cheyne, that the human body was not well adapted to eat meat, Descartes lived primarily on vegetables and grains, with an occasional egg, and proselytized his regimen among his friends. He had no moral objection to killing animals, of course, but for the sake of prolonging his own life he avoided eating them. A vegetarian diet, he and his followers believed, could enable humans to live for centuries (although, unfortunately for the reputation of his theory, he died at the age of fifty-four).

Dr. Cheyne based his own signature diet upon a combination of ancient pagan and Christian practices and modern science. His concern was individual health; to forswear animal flesh suited the human body, he argued. This healthful diet promoted good sleep, well-being, and a long life. Cheyne was also motivated by concern for the natural world and the suffering of animals; he thought that our nervous systems naturally predispose us to sympathize with animals, and that this God-given human attribute outweighs the biblical permission to eat meat. For fear of being labeled a fanatic, however, he withheld this aspect of his belief system until late in his career, instead stressing the welfare of the *human* animal.

Later vegetarians following in Cheyne's footsteps were more explicit about their chosen diet's connection to animal suffering. Some, such as the poet Percy Bysshe Shelley, saw a carnivorous diet as not only unhealthy but unnatural; humans, Shelley believed, did not possess the appropriate teeth and digestive tract to eat flesh. He argued that meat (and alcohol) degraded our physical as well as our mental health: our carnivorous, alcohol-sodden diet not only makes us sick, it also turns us into murderers, robbers, and madmen; it lies at the root of human wretchedness. True, he acknowledged, some animals were obligate carnivores. Nature was indeed, as the poet Tennyson would later say, "red in tooth and claw." But even in carnivorous nature one does not find the refinements of torture that we inflict upon the animals we eat: castration,

mutilation, imprisonment, the slow bleeding to death of calves, the boiling of live lobsters. "What beast of prey," asked Shelley (echoing, although probably not deliberately, John Wesley), "compels its victim to
undergo such protracted, such severe and such degrading torments?"

For those predecessors from whom eighteenth-century vegetarians
often drew their inspiration, the status of beasts was a central point.
The ancient Western traditions of vegetarianism—as well as the non-
Western traditions that were becoming better known as more English
came into contact with the societies and religions of the Middle East
and Asia—certainly acknowledged the physical and mental benefits of
a nonmeat diet. But they were also often based upon a belief in human
responsibility to animals and kinship with them. These traditions, both
Eastern and Western, saw animals as kindred spirits—sometimes literally so. One of the most influential figures was a Greek philosopher of
the sixth century B.C.E., Pythagoras.

In her poignant, delightful poem "The Mouse's Petition," the celebrated poet Anna Laetitia Barbauld spoke in the voice of a trapped
mouse about to be used in an experiment by the clergyman-scientist
Joseph Priestley, the discoverer of oxygen. Mrs. Barbauld's poem left
the nature of the experiment unspecified, but very likely it involved an
air pump, or perhaps electricity, another of Priestley's interests. Speaking in simple balladlike lines—just the sort of verse we imagine a poetically inclined mouse would utter—the "guiltless" mouse likens himself
to an unjustly condemned prisoner facing execution, and pleads for
mercy. Among the several arguments the mouse makes for compassion
is this caution about killing:

> Beware, lest in the worm you crush
> A brother's soul you find;
> And tremble lest thy luckless hand
> Dislodge a kindred mind.

The mouse is speaking as a Pythagorean.

Pythagoras, who abstained from eating animal flesh, was the first in the Western philosophical tradition to systematize the idea of metempsychosis, or reincarnation: the transmigration of souls. According to his doctrine, our souls are immortal, and after our bodies die they enter other bodies. While there was some dispute among Pythagoras's followers about whether souls migrate among species or restrict themselves to humankind, many believed that human souls can enter animal bodies. So the worm we crush underfoot might contain a soul that belonged to another human being, perhaps even our own brother. Animals could indeed be our kin, quite literally.

Stories about Pythagoras handed down through the ages cast him as something of an ancient Greek animal whisperer. A common story recounted that he once convinced a bull found munching his way through a bean field to stop eating the plants by murmuring something into the beast's ear. (For somewhat obscure reasons, beans, like meat, were proscribed in the Pythagorean diet; he may have disliked them because they caused flatulence, which perhaps invoked the smell of decaying bodies.) In any event, whatever Pythagoras said, it convinced the bull never to eat another bean: he was rewarded by living to a ripe old age, and everyone called him Pythagoras's holy bull. Pythagoras also tamed a rampaging she-bear, whom he converted to a diet of barley and acorns, making her such a peaceable plant-eater that she never again attacked other animals or anything else. As for his doctrine of metempsychosis, the ancient historian Xenophon told the story (mockingly) that Pythagoras once "stopped a man beating a dog because he recognized in the dog's cries the voice of an old friend." With the barrier between humans and animals utterly breached by the notion that the same souls inhabit all bodies, that a deceased friend or relative might live on in a pig or cow, abusing an animal becomes a crime against people, too, and meat-eating becomes cannibalism.

The philosopher Empedocles once gave a Pythagorean account of animal sacrifice as practiced by the ancient Greeks. He imagined a scenario in which a man is about to sacrifice an animal that now possesses the soul of his deceased son, transforming the sacrificial act into murder: "The father lifts up his own son in a different shape and, praying, slaughters him, in his great madness, as he cries piteously beseeching his sacrificer; but he, deaf to his pleas, slaughters and prepares in his halls an evil feast. Just so does son take father, and children mother: they tear out their life and devour their dear flesh." Greek mythology is filled with hellish dinner parties in which children are vengefully fed to parents, and the idea recurs in the English literary canon: Shakespeare's *Titus Andronicus* culminates in just such a horrific (and nauseating) act of cannibalism.

The concept of devouring a family member strikes such a nerve that it seems to be a deeply rooted anxiety across history: imagine the repulsive power of the idea that the slab of old English roast beef lying on your plate might have been a member of your family. Even beyond literal kinship taboos, the idea of eating our own kind has a terrible force; cannibalism, real or imagined, is one of the demarcations that "civilized" societies use to separate themselves from "barbaric" ones. Think of Robinson Crusoe's horror when he comes across the footprint that indicates the presence of cannibals on "his" island, and later spies on them during their grisly feast: Crusoe fears for his life, but he is also almost crazed by moral revulsion. (Of course, as Montaigne coolly pointed out, such moral revulsion is a highly arbitrary, artificial, self-interested, and bigoted position, given all the savagery the so-called civilized societies take for granted when they themselves commit it. The Greek root of "barbarian," *barbaros,* simply and tellingly means "non-Greek.") Even among non-Pythagoreans, the notion that humans have even a metaphorical kinship with the food we eat has motivated vegetarians from ancient times to the present day—and has been simply repressed by many meat eaters.

The doctrine of metempsychosis, understood through both its Hindu and Pythagorean manifestations, was far from a mainstream belief in eighteenth-century Britain. (The common name for a vegetarian or vegan was "Pythagorean"—usually applied derogatorily.) But metempsychosis did have English Christian defenders, who were attracted to it as a model of the immortality and preexistence of the soul. These included the seventeenth-century school of philosopher-theologians known as the

Cambridge Platonists. Dr. Cheyne himself had, as a young man, developed his own idiosyncratic theology that involved a form of reincarnation, though he did not publicly acknowledge this until late in his life. At a time when claims of human uniqueness and exclusive possession of reason were being challenged and undermined, the idea of transmigration of souls could be a compelling critique of orthodoxy. If souls live by turns in humans and beasts alike, one modern scholar points out, then there is a connection and continuity among all living things, the great chain of being is a great circle instead, and the line separating human from animal is nonexistent.

As a concept, metempsychosis also might have some practical advantages. John Zephaniah Holwell was a former colonial governor in India who became one of England's most respected authorities on Hinduism, and scandalized many of his countrymen when it later became apparent that he had become, in essence, a Hindu himself. A vegetarian who believed that Hinduism was the foundation of Judeo-Christianity (and that Moses was a reincarnation of the Hindu god Brahma), Holwell wrote that to accept the idea of the transmigration of souls would particularly benefit women, allowing them to imagine that "the spirits which now animate their favorite lap-dogs, cats, parrots, squirrels, monkeys &c. heretofore animated the form of a beloved friend, tender parent, husband, brother, child, lover &c. and their extravagant (and now irrational) fondness for these animals will then appear to be founded on principle." In other words, metempsychosis would finally give women a *good* reason for loving their pets. Moved by the ladies' example, Holwell explained, the rest of mankind would start to care for animals, no longer killing them to eat them or for any other reason.

Holwell probably considered women potentially receptive to the idea of transmigration of souls because in his day they were widely considered to be inherently more sympathetic to animals than men were— for women were more like animals themselves. By the commonplace patriarchalism of the eighteenth century, men were more intellectual, women more physical; men in greater part mind and spirit, women, who bear and nurse children, more body and, therefore, more animal.

Though this idea rationalized women's subordination to men on many fronts—legal, economic, political—some women writers found ways to turn the liability into a strength by embracing their supposed kinship with beasts, both as a way of expressing compassion for animals and as a way of figuratively critiquing their own status. In particular, certain admired eighteenth-century female poets, including Mrs. Barbauld, drew upon a Pythagorean model in their work (though not consistently or exclusively), creating a body of verse that in some ways was a female counterpart to the writings of Anglican clergymen such as John Hildrop and Richard Dean. Speaking as women, these writers identified with beasts against the "tyrant Man" (by which noun they meant not human but male), in the name of "breaking down the barrier" between the human and animal worlds.

Certainly the Pythagorean motif could be used conservatively, in the way of traditional Christian moralists, to ascribe beastly qualities to human weaknesses and sins, as we have seen—"as lecherous as a goat," for instance, or "as gluttonous as a hog." In *The Merchant of Venice*, Gratiano sneers that Shylock's "currish spirit" must once have inhabited a wolf that had been hanged for killing humans, "for thy desires / Are wolfish, bloody, starved and ravenous." The clergyman Richard Dean said semifacetiously that the ancients' "witty invention" of transmigration of souls allowed a true poetic justice: when the souls of people who abuse animals transmigrate into animals, they learn firsthand what it's like to be a carthorse or a spaniel. Dr. Johnson's acquaintance the poet Anna Seward (who, dubbed "the Swan of Lichfield," apparently possessed some beastlike characteristics herself, though nice ones) wrote an "Ode on the Pythagorean System" in which she imagined the soul of a lecher ending up in the body of a goat, and other such moralistic migrations: the link to animals as a punishment for human frailties. In poems she wrote later, however, her view of animals became both more profound and more moving.

In her playful yet sensitive poem, "An Old Cat's Dying Soliloquy," Seward invoked a more traditional Christian view of heaven—except that this is a cat's heaven. Selima the elderly cat dreams of her encroaching death, imagining an afterlife that—like the idyllic human version, where rivers flow with milk and honey and fruit falls from the tree into one's hand—is a perpetual feline smorgasbord of wingless birds carelessly hopping within reach, fat mice waddling about, fish obligingly jumping out of the streams onto land, wells brimming with cream, and gardens bursting with catnip. The only thing old Selima regrets is that her human companion will not be there with her, for this paradise is exclusively for cats.

In a related if more serious vein, Seward's "On the Future Existence of Brutes" argues that a just God would bar animals from an afterlife only if their lives here on earth were happy. But animals' lives are obviously far from happy, thanks to man. Would God deny beasts recompense for their great suffering at man's hands, she asks? No, she answers—not if he were a just God. How could we imagine that a dog, in so many ways as intelligent, sensitive, and educable as a human, does not have an afterlife? To think that the dog's purer spirit sinks downward while the human spirit soars to heaven is arrogance indeed.

The Pythagorean concept of kinship could be used imaginatively to mount a critique of the barrier set between humans and animals by both mainstream Christianity and the habits of human society. When poets such as Seward and Barbauld used this idea, it was not that they were committed Pythagoreans in the sense that they believed in the transmigration of souls; it was that they found in the concept a way to talk about the connection between humans and animals. Neither Barbauld nor Seward was a vegetarian, whether influenced by Pythagoras or by Dr. Cheyne. Indeed, Barbauld was disturbed when "The Mouse's Petition" was claimed by antivivisectionists; she was not opposed to animal experiments, she said, and Dr. Priestley had been her teacher and friend. But these women did use the concepts of the transmigration of souls and the immortality of animal souls as literary devices allowing them, as women, to address poetically the bond that all humans share with beasts, and that most humans deny, ignore, and violate.

Pythagorean ideas, whether used by diet doctors or by poets, offered a challenge to reigning attitudes and habits, and a critique of them. In the poems, this critique is sometimes expressed in language that invokes the politics of the period. When Anna Seward referred to animals as the wretched subjects of a tyrant's sway (the tyrant being man), and when Mrs. Barbauld had her mouse sigh for liberty, they were using a vocabulary that was being heard more and more frequently in the later eighteenth century: the vocabulary of liberty and of rights. The English mouse pleads to his captor:

> *If e'er thy breast with freedom glow'd,*
> *And spurn'd a tyrant's chain,*
> *Let not thy strong oppressive force*
> *A free-born mouse detain.*

"Freedom," "tyrant's chain," "oppressive force," "free-born," "detain": these words and ideas were politically charged. They lay behind some of the most important reform efforts of the day, especially abolition; they underlay revolution, too, in particular the American Revolution in 1776 and the French Revolution of 1789. The same idealism that inspired many in England to make common cause with the revolutionaries in France, especially in the early years of their revolution, could also be combined with radical vegetarianism and turned to the cause of animals. The eighteenth century's most powerful assault on humans' use of animals combined vegetarianism and animal rights in a revolutionary manifesto that left concern with souls, migratory or otherwise, out of the picture.

IN 1779, A young Scots poet named John Oswald joined the British army, enlisting in the newly created 2nd Battalion of the Royal Highland Regiment, known as the Black Watch. Instead of being sent to join the 1st Battalion fighting General Washington's rebels in the American colonies, the 2nd Battalion was sent to defend British colonial interests in India against incursions by the French and their Indian allies. When he arrived as a young officer in Bombay en route to Madras in the spring of 1782, Oswald was around twenty-two years old. Having grown up in Scotland, which harbored strong pro-American and republican sentiments, he had already been exposed to radical ideas. His experience in India made him a revolutionary. It also made him a vegetarian.

What Oswald saw of the British soldiers' greed for plunder, their massacres and rapes of Indian people, made him resign his commission. Before returning home—a journey he would make primarily on foot—he headed out on a walking tour of India, where he practiced Hinduism and associated with Indian people. According to one of his contemporaries, Oswald "imitated the Gentoos [Hindus], abstained from animal food, and regularly performed the usual ablutions."

Returning to England, Oswald involved himself in radical political circles and, like many British intellectuals and idealists, embraced the cause of the French Revolution as it began in 1789. He wrote tracts in defense of government by the people, an alarming idea to the political establishment in London, to which revolutionary France constituted a grave threat. Indeed, England, along with much of the rest of Europe, would go to war with the new French republic within a few years, and the repressive political atmosphere that resulted was hostile not just to revolutionaries abroad but also to radicals at home, as well as to reformers of all stripes. When the revolutionary wars segued into the Napoleonic Wars, this state of affairs would continue, setting back the causes of both abolition and animal welfare.

Early in the revolution, Oswald, like many British sympathizers, went to France. In Paris, he encountered William Wordsworth, who later wrote two poetic recollections of Oswald the revolutionary, one sympathetic, the other not. He may also have encountered the Irish politician and landowner Richard Martin and a friend of Martin's who would also play a large role in the animal protection movement: Thomas Erskine, a radical Scots barrister. Both of them were in Paris watching developments at first hand.

Oswald, however, did not intend to be an observer but a participant. He was the first British citizen to become a member of the Jacobin Club, and he became an officer in the Republican army. There, he championed the widespread use of the "people's weapon," the pike—that fearsome emblem of the revolution—and commanded a pike corps. Oswald would give his life in the service of the French republic, falling in battle against counterrevolutionaries in the Vendée in 1793. Before his death, he published one of the greatest polemics ever written in defense of vegetarianism and against cruelty to animals: *The Cry of Nature; or, An Appeal to Mercy and to Justice, on behalf of the Persecuted Animals.*

Vegetarians were by no means necessarily radical. Dr. Cheyne, for instance, thought that only the elite possessed the sensitivity to suffer from nervous disorders and therefore require a vegetable diet. The crude, healthy common folk—as he saw them—were not his concern. But a refusal to eat meat could lend itself to a radical critique of a status quo in which some beings held life-and-death power over others, whom they exploited and whose existences they made wretched. Various types of power relationships, apparent both in the outposts of England's growing empire and at home, were analogous to one another: colonial rulers to colonized subjects, masters to slaves, the upper classes to the lower classes, humans to animals. One did not need a belief in metempsychosis to grasp these connections, and animals did not need to possess human souls to claim a moral kinship with us. Indeed, Oswald, an atheist, rejected the religious arguments for a vegetable diet, and said that, however much he admired the Hindus, he did not believe in reincarnation. For him, the eating of animals was one form of the oppression arising when one group holds power over another.

The Cry of Nature makes the connection between revolution and the cause of animals. Oswald writes that although his own vegetarian diet may be considered an "irregularity" now, he hopes that, after the reader sees "the barbarous governments of Europe giving way to a better system of things," the day will come when "the wide circle of benevolence" will also embrace "the lower orders of life." Invoking the Hindu vegetarians as exemplars of mercy, Oswald argues that eating flesh is not only unhealthy and unnatural but also cruel.

Oswald's defense of animals held up the "civilized" mercy of Eastern societies in stark contrast to the barbarism of the British; he thus inverted the way in which most English and Europeans thought of non-Western cultures and peoples, and challenged a common rationale for British imperialism. He also argued along class lines: meat-eating, as something only the rich could afford, was another symptom of the inequalities by which the ruling classes oppress the poor. And he echoed the argument, illustrated by Hogarth, that linked all forms of violence: "From the practice of slaughtering an innocent animal, to the murder of man himself, the steps are neither many nor remote."

For Oswald, taking his cue from the French Enlightenment philosopher Jean-Jacques Rousseau, human history has followed a bloody trajectory away from our earlier, better natural state to a false and corrupt "civilization." Gradually accustoming ourselves to eating flesh in order to pacify imagined gods whose worship demanded animal sacrifice, early man was placed by his religion into an unnaturally violent relationship with animals; that relationship continued to degrade as human society grew further from a state of nature, and our relationship with animals became crueler. Now, our appetites, our religion, and our science all collude in merciless exploitation of innocent animals. Their instrument is the butcher's knife.

Oswald attacks men of science, who "with ruffian violence interrogate trembling nature, who plunge into her maternal bosom the butcher's knife." He calls vivisectionists "barbarians." And in a strikingly modern-sounding passage, Oswald argues that we distance ourselves from the cruelty of our dietary habits by having others slaughter and butcher animals for us. For most of us, he says, the horrors that our diets actually involve are kept at a convenient distance: here he anticipates those who point out how our supermarkets detach their plastic-wrapped meat from its origin in a living animal, and how our slaughterhouses conceal from our view what goes on inside. We are able to feed on animals without remorse, Oswald wrote, "because the dying struggles of the butchered creature are secluded from our sight; because his cries pierce not our ear, because his agonizing shrieks sink not into our soul." If we personally had to murder the animals we eat, far fewer of us would eat them: "Were we forced, with our own hands, to assassinate the animals whom we devour, who is there among us that would not throw down, with detestation, the knife?"

Oswald's abstention from meat was widely known among his contemporaries, as was the simplicity of the way he lived: he was said to drink with his meals no more than half a dozen glasses of wine, moderation indeed in an era when many judged their drinking by the bottle rather than the glass. His example as well as his writing influenced those who later also wrote about animals' welfare and about vegetarianism, among them George Nicholson, who wrote *On the Primeval Diet of Man* (1801), and Joseph Ritson, in his *Essay upon the Abstinence from Animal Food* (1802). Both men were, like Oswald, radicals. Ritson knew Oswald only by reputation and (unlike Nicholson) did not know of *The Cry of Nature,* but in his book he similarly praises the Hindus (while distancing himself from the idea of transmigration of souls), attacks blood sports, connects the exploitation of animals with the exploitation of slaves, makes a connection between human rights and animal rights, and argues the unhealthfulness of a carnivorous diet.

But most people of the day were affronted and threatened by both the radicals' political agenda—particularly after the French Republic turned to the guillotine and declared war on England—and the claims they made for animals. The well-known Platonist Thomas Taylor indirectly acknowledged this in his mock-serious *Vindication of the Rights of Brutes,* where he parodied Mary Wollstonecraft's radical writings on the rights of men and women by means of a *reductio ad absurdum:* applying the language of rights to animals. When they spoke of animal *rights,* and linked them to the rights of man, radicals aligned the cause of animals with claims on behalf of humans aimed at destroying entrenched structures of power and privilege. As a result, radical notions of animal rights were met with particularly vehement mockery. Henry Redhead Yorke, Esq., for instance, who knew Oswald in Paris in the early years of the revolution (and later recanted his own youthful radicalism), referred to him as "the mad Colonel Oswald, who had written several insane publications in behalf of what he called his fellow creatures, the brutes." Oswald's time with the Brahmins, Yorke scoffed, had "turned his head."

Yorke used to get into political arguments with Oswald, when Oswald would attack representative democracy in favor of true participatory democracy, in which people would meet together to make their own laws. Yorke ridiculed this idea by connecting it to Oswald's "insane" position on animals: "I have often endeavoured to persuade him, that his plan was not sufficiently extensive, as he had excluded from this grand assembly of the animal world the most populous portion of his fellow-creatures, namely cats, dogs, horses, chickens, &c."

His wholehearted participation in the French Revolution also earned Oswald his reputation as a hypocrite, who abstained from animal blood but was nonetheless thirsty for that of humans. When Louis XVI was executed, the pike brigade commanded by Oswald guarded the guillotine. After the king's head was cut off, according to one report, Oswald joined the crowd dancing joyously around the scaffold. Subsequent vegetarians and animal welfare proponents unsurprisingly had difficulty dealing with this image; Ritson omitted it from his admiring account of Oswald's life. Oswald presented the kind of contradiction that enemies of animal welfare and vegetarianism—not to mention of republican radicalism—delighted in pointing out.

Pythagoras's ancient biographer, Iamblichus, said of that philosopher that he abstained from eating animals because it was "conducive to peace." People who abominate the killing of other animals, Pythagoras believed, will consider it an even greater wrong to kill another human or go to war. Oswald himself held that cruelty to animals led to cruelty to humans. But he would have seen nothing inconsistent in participating in the execution of a king, whether he actually danced in Louis's blood or not. The king represented an entrenched social system whose elite had long fattened themselves by the miserable exploitation of the common people, who were the human equivalent of oppressed animals. In a just society, Oswald believed, the knife would be laid down—but first it must be turned against the butcher.

It would not be Oswald, fallen on the battlefield, who transformed the lot of animals in British society, and in so doing helped transform the society as a whole. There would be no sudden revolutionary change. Rather, more pragmatic, often much more conservative reformers would take the first steps on that long, slow road. Yet these reformers were not unlike Oswald, in that they were trying to change an entrenched system—a system whose defenders sometimes seemed to consider them almost as radical a threat to the social fabric as those who had beheaded a king. Twenty years of legislative battles went by before their efforts began to bear fruit. The man who was ultimately most responsible for making British law recognize cruelty to animals was neither a vegetarian nor a revolutionary like John Oswald. But Richard Martin was, in his own way, just as much of a firebrand.

CHAPTER 10

HAIR-TRIGGER MARTIN AND
THE WOLFHOUND

✳   ✳   ✳

IN 1784, as John Oswald was learning from the Brahmins in India,
two other men met to fight a duel in Ireland. Their chosen place was
the saw pit in the barracks yard of the British army garrison at Castlebar,
County Mayo. Eighteenth-century Ireland was notoriously inflamed
with a passion for dueling, an inclination reputed to be as natural to
Irishmen as breathing, or as drinking themselves into a stupor. Although
both duels and drunkenness were as common in England as they were
on the other side of the Irish Sea, Ireland had gained a reputation as
a culture that virtually required men to "blaze" forth at the slightest
provocation.

Even by such standards, this particular duel was a clash of titans.
George Robert Fitzgerald, dubbed Fighting Fitzgerald, the son of an
aristocratic Mayo family, was answering a challenge delivered to him by
Richard Martin of Connemara in neighboring County Galway. In 1784,
thirty-year-old Richard Martin, the heir to Ireland's largest estate, had
not yet acquired the nickname Humanity Martin (later, the more familiar "Humanity Dick") that would be given to him by his friend King
George IV. Rather the contrary: at this point in his life, he was widely
known by the bloodier epithet "Hair-Trigger Martin." The occasion for
this particular duel was as appropriate to Dick Martin's later moniker
as to his current one, however. The man who would become renowned
for fighting in Parliament on behalf of animals, who would give his

name to the world's first animal protection legislation, was about to risk his life to avenge a cold-blooded murder—of a dog.

The victim was a gentle, beloved wolfhound belonging to Martin's friends the Brownes, the family of the second earl of Altamont. Fitzgerald, who held a grudge against the earl's brother, had appeared at their door requesting to see the dog, and, when the servant brought the wolfhound out onto the steps, had put a pistol to the animal's head and fired. Fitzgerald then declared, with his characteristically bizarre arrogance, that wolfhounds ate the scraps of meat that should go to the poor, so he would no longer permit the Brownes to own such animals. He did leave a note, however, in which he magnanimously gave each of the women of the family permission to keep her lapdog.

Fighting Fitzgerald lived a life punctuated by duels—indeed, he had once been trepanned to remove a bullet from his brain. Perhaps, people said, it was this hole in his head that accounted for his extreme viciousness, although apparently he had been violent even before the surgeon cut into his skull. Fitzgerald was said to carry a cudgel with him in readiness for impromptu street fights, and would go to great lengths to provoke a duel, planting himself in the middle of a pedestrian path next to a muddy road so that, when jostled by a passerby trying to avoid the muck, he could take offense and challenge him. He once stabbed a man who accidentally stepped on his dog, and he kept a tame bear that he liked to dress in a gentleman's cloak, with a scarf covering his head. He also enjoyed shooting dogs: the wolfhound Prime Serjeant was not the only pet of an acquaintance he killed. (One owner of a dog he shot retaliated by killing four of Fitzgerald's own spaniels.)

Dick Martin was already known in western Ireland for his love of animals, and he had been particularly fond of Prime Serjeant. Fitzgerald's act outraged him. In the eighteenth century, such an insult and injury were more than enough to justify a duel. Since Prime Serjeant had not been Martin's dog, however, it was not his place to take offense: the code of honor governing such matters was strict. But when the Brownes' attempts to exact revenge upon Fitzgerald were stymied,

Martin bided his time, waiting for a reason to challenge Fitzgerald himself, and he eventually found one. Though enrolled as a member of the bar (a step on his way to a political career), Martin had never tried a case; when the opportunity arose to act as prosecutor in a case against Fitzgerald (who was accused of unlawfully imprisoning his own father, whom he apparently shackled to his bear), Martin accepted willingly. During this trial, the only one he would ever participate in as a barrister, Martin's badgering succeeded in inflaming Fitzgerald's resentment against him, so it was only a matter of time until the latter delivered the welcome insult that would allow him to respond with a challenge.

At the age of thirty, Dick Martin was one of Ireland's most celebrated "fire-eaters" (the popular term for duelists). Though rumor inflated the number of the duels he had fought and won, his was nonetheless an impressive record. His reputation as a fearless fire-eater stayed with him his entire life, not least because he was known to punctuate an argument by ripping his shirt open to display the bullet scars on his chest. Martin had killed his own cousin, to whom he had once been close, in a duel that he had tried unsuccessfully to avoid. (Martin had deliberately fired low, into the man's leg, but the wound became infected and, in this era before antibiotics, the cousin died a week later.) Though tormented by guilt and remorse, Martin did not lose his fire-eating fervor. A much-circulated anecdote from later in his life reported that, on the eve of a general election, Martin was asked which candidate would win the election, himself or his opponent. He replied, "Why the survivor, to be sure." This reply was not necessarily facetious. In 1803, when Martin's countryman Richard Brinsley Sheridan stood for election, one of his fellow Whig candidates was killed in a duel by his Tory opponent, who both won the election and was acquitted of murder.

On the day of their duel, Martin and Fitzgerald assumed their positions, standing at such close range that when they extended their arms to take aim, the barrels of their pistols nearly touched. They fired their first shots simultaneously. Even at that close range, Fitzgerald's shot missed. (Had eighteenth-century flintlock pistols been nearly as accurate and powerful as modern handguns, and had duelists always been sober when fighting, the ranks of fire-eaters would have been much thinner, and the animal protection law might have had to await a later day.) Fitzgerald's second shot did strike Martin in the chest, while Martin succeeded in wounding him twice. Martin's injury left him with the scar he later enjoyed showing off, but Fighting Fitzgerald turned out to be unscathed, for he had secretly worn armor under his clothes.*

The duel with Fighting Fitzgerald may have been the first actual battle that Richard Martin fought on behalf of animals, but it would not be the last, although he later confined himself to using words (with occasional recourse to fists) rather than guns. Some forty years after the duel, this flamboyant man would battle to force the world's first national animal protection law through Parliament. (To someone who asked why he was so concerned for animals, Martin is said to have replied: "Sir, an ox cannot hold a pistol!") His efforts on behalf of animals, said the Victorian journalist Samuel Carter Hall, would "shed a halo round the name and consecrate the memory of Richard Martin," making the Irish MP one of the "benefactors of his country and all other countries, of the Old World and the New."

Many of the qualities that made Dick Martin a successful benefactor of animals, and humans, too, had been honed in his upbringing in the rugged countryside of western Ireland. As a young man, he cut a dashing, romantic figure, and in his later years and after his death, he would achieve near-mythic stature in his native country. Another of his nicknames was equally revealing: he was the "King of Connemara." For Richard Martin was son and heir to a family whose vast landholdings in Ireland's wild west, the ancient home of the Celts, made them a defiant near-sovereignty. The Martins were one of the

---

*Martin later tried to renew the duel but Fitzgerald refused to fight. Prime Serjeant and the many people injured by this psychopath were finally avenged by the law. Despite the aristocratic protectors who had saved him from the hangman in the past, Fitzgerald was convicted of the assassination of a human, and was executed.

fourteen "tribes" of County Galway—so dubbed by Cromwell for their apparent savagery—whose Norman ancestors had settled in the region after the Conquest. Their estate, over 190,000 acres of rough, wild country, encompassed a third of the county. In Connemara, it was not that the Martins took the law into their own hands—they *were* the law.

The Anglo-Irish novelist Maria Edgeworth recalled having heard her father talk of Richard Martin, the fabeled King of Connemara,

> and his way of ruling over his people with almost absolute power, with laws of his own, and setting all other laws at defiance. Smugglers and caves and murders and mermaids and duels and banshees and faeries, were all mingled together in my early association with Connemara and Dick Martin, "Hair-Trigger Dick."

On the one occasion when she met Dick Martin, not long before his death, Edgeworth said, "my blood crept slow and my breath was held when he first came into the room." Even though she found the elderly Martin surprisingly smaller than the larger-than-life image she had conjured out of these stories, she was still awed by his aura of glamour and danger.

Dick Martin's Connemara was, and still is, a remote, desolate, breathtakingly beautiful terrain of mountains, moors, and bogland, populated by wild animals—including Ireland's only native horses, the "Connemara ponies"—and a few humans, who in the eighteenth century would have been almost wild too. Lacking roads, seamed only by faint, narrow tracks, eighteenth-century Connemara was virtually inaccessible except by sea. The seas off Connemara had once been the haunts of Grace O'Malley, the legendary pirate queen, and in Martin's time fierce bands of smugglers, whom his family profited from and protected, plied their trade among the hundreds of coves and inlets engraved into its eighty long, lonely miles of coast.

Richard Martin was born in Galway in 1754, the first child of Robert and Bridget Martin. He spent much of his childhood in the Connemara wilderness, learning to handle gun and sword, to ride great horses and sail a boat through the rough waters of loch and ocean. Like most of the Irish gentry (and quite unlike the English landowners), Martin was at ease with the local fisherman, farmers, miners, and smugglers—and they were at ease with him. But his parents also wintered in Dublin, where young Dick's manners got considerable polishing among that sophisticated city's elite. It would be remarked of him in later life that, for all his raucous humor, his buffoonery, and his heavy Irish brogue, Martin was also an urbane gentleman, capable of speaking with a correct English accent when he chose and as comfortable charming the ladies in fashionable drawing rooms as he was galloping his horse along the lochs and mountains. "His observation was acute," wrote the journalist William Jerdan, "and his conversation agreeable, polite, and entertaining."

His father, Robert, instilled in Dick a lifelong mission: to free Ireland's majority Catholic population from English Protestant repression. Both the gentry and, even more, the impoverished peasantry suffered greatly under English Protestant rule that discriminated against Catholics at home and abroad and that ruthlessly exploited Ireland as a colony. The law dictated that no British monarch could be a Catholic or marry one; Catholics were ineligible to serve in Parliament, hold government office, or vote; they were not permitted to attend university, to bequeath land holdings to a single heir (the point of this ban was to break up the big estates), to lease land for longer than thirty-one years, to possess or carry a gun, or to own a horse worth more than five pounds. The protectionist English government placed crippling tariffs on Irish and European trade, as well (thus enabling the booming criminal economy of smuggling).

Later in the eighteenth century, some of these laws were eliminated or modified, and many of them were ignored, especially in the far west. But everyone from aristocrats to tenant farmers felt the weight of oppression, and on the poor it sat with particular heaviness. Protestant landowners despised their tenant farmers as savages—or as animals. Lord Chesterfield, for a short time lord lieutenant of Ireland, wrote that the Irish Catholic peasants "were worse used than Negroes by their Lords and Masters."

As a Norman-Irish family, the Martin family was Catholic, but like many of the Irish gentry, Richard's father had nominally declared allegiance to the Anglican church in order to maintain control over his property. But Robert Martin had greater plans for his eldest son: he raised and educated him as a Protestant, so that Richard would be able to enter the Irish Parliament to fight for Catholic emancipation. From an early age, therefore, Richard Martin was imbued not only with loyalty to his people and with the physical courage to duel over an affront, but also with the passion to fight in the public and political arena for a just cause. Martin would fulfill his father's vision in a political career that took him first as a legislator to Dublin and then, upon the Act of Union that made Ireland part of the new United Kingdom, to London. There, the Catholics of Ireland would not be the only politically voiceless beings for whose welfare he fought.

From his mother, Bridget, Richard Martin gained elite connections with some of the principal aristocratic families of western Ireland. As a child, he spent much time in the houses of the Irish aristocracy, especially on the estate of his uncle Lord Trimlestown. From his mother and her family, Richard also received a legacy that would propel him into the other great political mission of his adult life, the one for which he is remembered today: he learned to love animals. An avid horseman and hunter, Richard undoubtedly was deeply attached to his horses and hounds (if slower to consider the hares and foxes they hunted). But Dick also grew up surrounded by pets. Bridget and her sisters filled their houses with dogs, cats, and canaries, talked about them and traded them around, his biographer says, like so many picture postcards. There were other, more rarefied beasts in Dick's childhood as well. When he visited his uncle, he could enjoy the menagerie of exotic animals that the baron, like many aristocrats of his day, kept on his estate.

To pursue his goal of educating Richard for a parliamentary career, Robert Martin sent him, aged seven, to be educated in England. In so doing, he took one more step in creating an activist in the cause of animals. Dick had the good fortune to be at Harrow when, in his later years there, a new young schoolmaster, Dr. Samuel Parr, joined the school. Parr, like most of his contemporaries, did not spare the rod, but he was also a kind man and much beloved by the boys. He was an enlightened, reformist thinker—his radical sympathies would later earn him the nickname "the Jacobinical parson"—who nourished in his students a love of justice and a compassion for animals. Dr. Parr gave Dick's native attachment to animals intellectual refinement, and placed his love of his own pets and horses within the larger context of humans' God-given duty to care for all the members of his brute creation.

Samuel Parr, like his contemporary Humphrey Primatt, preached that our humanity is at stake in the way we treat animals. Like Hogarth, Parr believed that cruelty is progressive, that the child schooled in viciousness will grow into a vicious adult. The schoolmaster saw it as his duty to teach his pupils not only to respect beasts but also to *feel* for them. Cruelty, he taught, destroys the best part of human character, our compassion, and replaces it with what is most detestable in us, tyranny. "He that can look with rapture upon the agonies of an unoffending and unresisting animal will soon learn to view the sufferings of a fellow-creature with indifference," Parr preached. Once children's hearts are "familiarized to spectacles of distress," it is very difficult to teach them mercy. Cruelty must be nipped in the bud by parents, teachers, and society at large. In teaching this lesson, Parr probably found in young Dick Martin a particularly attentive pupil.

After his years at Harrow, Martin went on to Trinity College, Cambridge, where he also enjoyed access to London high society. He left Cambridge after two years (a common practice among gentlemen not bound for a profession such as the Church), and was admitted to the bar at Lincoln's Inn. Along with his cousin James Jordan (the one who later died of wounds suffered in a duel with him), Richard embarked upon the grand tour of Europe. After the usual travels through France and Italy, the young Irishmen added an unusual detour, sailing for the

West Indies. In Jamaica, Dick got a firsthand look at the slave system, and could see how the condition of Irish Catholic laborers resembled (and did not resemble) that of the African slaves who were the linchpins of the colony's prosperity, producing the sugar that England craved. One thing the African slaves had in common with the Irish poor would have been quite obvious: their colonial masters treated them as animals. Perhaps Martin saw slaves being sold at the block; certainly he would have seen them being driven like beasts in the fields.

After Jamaica, Martin and Jordan traveled to another unconventional destination: England's seething North American colonies, where revolutionary fever was reaching its height. There Martin, identifying, as an Irishman, with the colonists' grievances against English rule, breathed in the heady air of sedition and rebellion. He was in New England on April 19, 1775, when the first shot of the American Revolutionary War was fired. Soon after that, he and Jordan sailed back to Ireland. Exciting as it might have been for Martin to witness the revolution firsthand, there were pressing reasons to return home: Ireland had its own liberation battles to fight. Dick would now embark upon the career his father had set for him in his childhood: politics.

British rule of Ireland was embodied in a lord lieutenant, answerable to London, but the country had its own parliament in Dublin, consisting of elite, dominantly Anglo-Irish Protestants. (Catholics were given the vote in 1793, but would not be permitted to enter Parliament until 1829.) In June 1776, Martin took a seat in Parliament by a method not unusual then: being defeated for election in Galway, he simply bought a seat for Jamestown in County Leitrim. Later, he was also elected to command the Galway Volunteers, an Irish militia, and given the title of colonel, which, by adding a bit of military dash to his public image, suited him.

In Parliament, Martin, short and stocky, made his mark as a pointed, pithy speaker who exuded determined energy. He could handily turn a phrase and he skillfully used robust humor—often at his own expense—to disarm his opponents. A hallmark of his political career, in fact, would be the way he cultivated a reputation for eccentricity and drollery that would often lead people to underestimate him. The journalist William Jerdan commented that "his sterling qualities were so embossed with wild humour and fun, that it was no easy matter to form a correct judgment upon his real character." Martin's first immersion in the rough-and-tumble of Irish politics lasted until 1783, when he was defeated for reelection; he would return to the Irish Parliament in 1798.

At about the time that he took up his political career, Richard fell in love with and married Elizabeth Vesey, a lively young woman with aristocratic connections. During his time in Dublin, they threw themselves into the social life of that fashionable city, taking a particular interest in its flourishing theater and developing a taste for amateur theatricals themselves. They had three surviving children. But strains developed in the marriage. Money worries were a constant source of tension, and Dick was often away from home on politics or business, leaving Elizabeth to fend for herself. One of the ways in which she fended for herself was to have an affair with their children's young tutor, Wolfe Tone. (Tone later became an Irish revolutionary; convicted of treason by the British government, he committed suicide in his cell before his scheduled hanging.) The Martins' daughter Laetitia was probably fathered by Tone. Elizabeth's restlessness was apparent to many people, especially the servants, but her husband remained oblivious.

When the French Revolution began, the Martins were in Paris, where they had settled for an extended visit earlier that summer. In witnessing his second revolution, Richard mingled with other British and Irish visitors and expatriates, many of whom were stirred by the great experiment unfolding before their eyes, for it had not yet turned to the guillotine and pan-European war. Among those the Martins met in Paris was a young Scots barrister named Thomas Erskine, who had already made a name for himself back in England as a great courtroom orator with radical sympathies. Erskine had been defending counsel against several high-profile government prosecutions. Though his successful defense of George Gordon, indicted for inciting the violent anti-Catholic riots that had destroyed lives and property in London in 1780, might not have endeared him to Martin—Erskine had not shied from playing upon anti-Catholic sentiment in his client's defense—they had in common their interest in the happenings in France, and their love of animals.

When Erskine's and Martin's paths crossed again in London, how-ever, they were at odds with each other over a matter more personal than the Gordon case. In France, the problems of the Martin marriage had flared into open confrontation. Elizabeth had begun an affair with a very wealthy man named Petrie, and when they returned to England in 1791, she left Martin for him. After his appeals asking Elizabeth to re-turn did not succeed, Martin both sued her for divorce on grounds of adultery—in those days, to divorce required an act of Parliament, which he got—and sued Petrie for "criminal conversation," that is, for violating Martin's rights to his wife. To defend himself, Petrie employed Erskine. But even his fabled eloquence could not prevail, for Petrie's guilt was obvious: Elizabeth was openly living with him. Martin won damages of ten thousand pounds. Disdaining to profit from his wife's infidelity, he converted the money into coin and had his coachman scat-ter it from the coach as he rode out of town.

What he felt for Erskine at that point could not have been positive. But over thirty years later, long after Elizabeth Martin had died, after Richard had happily remarried (in 1796, to Harriet Evans Hesketh, a novelist, with whom he would have four children), and after Erskine had been appointed lord chancellor and ascended to the House of Lords, the two would become allies in a cause close to the hearts of both of them: animal protection.

In 1794, Robert Martin died and Dick assumed the proprietorship of the vast, beautiful, and financially encumbered estate in Connemara. He established his home in Ballynahinch Castle on the shore of a lake of the same name, across from the island where the romantic ruins of Grace O'Malley's castle brooded. Martin once told his friend the prince of Wales that the approach to his Ballynahinch Castle from the gatehouse of the property was thirty miles long. So remote and inaccessible, so distant from the reach of British law, was Connemara, that Martin, like his father and uncle before him, ruled it as a little kingdom.

As King of Connemara, Martin wielded his power without hesitation, as, essentially, a feudal lord. Assuming the Martins' hereditary right to establish their own court, he served as prosecutor, judge, and jury. He also served as jailer, for he possessed his own prison in the pirate queen's castle. Having banned cruelty to animals on his own estate—for example, he enforced the Irish statute against the widespread practice of tying the plow to the horse's tail—Martin would sentence those he convicted of abuse to a term in the ruins, reputedly rowing them there himself and, after a short imprisonment during which they presumably contemplated the error of their ways, rowing them back again. By all accounts, such imprisonment was brief and not physically harsh, and Martin's behavior was well within the bounds traditional to his feudal position. He was a man of his time, who exercised the prerogatives and power of his class. Even outside his Connemara kingdom, he could behave like one accustomed to taking the law into his own hands. But as a parliamentarian he also dedicated himself to enacting laws and trying to ensure that they were enforced by the proper authorities. And he was never cruel to other humans, any more than he was to beasts. As Carter Hall commented, "I believe Dick Martin had as warm and sound a heart as ever beat in human bosom."

For all his life, indeed, Dick Martin had a reputation as a kind and benevolent landlord, providing needy tenants with food and shelter even though his own finances were always precarious, protecting rebels from the reach of British law, and advising youths who were at odds with their families. In return, his people gave him love and fierce loyalty. Commenting that Martin was "almost idolized" by the people he ruled in Connemara, Hall related an anecdote about the time a ship from England, on which Martin was thought to be a passenger, foundered in the Irish Sea. The members of his Ballynahinch household were distraught about his probable death. But one old woman was heard to say: "No one need be afeared for the master; for if he was in the midst of a raging sea the prayers of widows and orphans would keep his head above water."

Despite his enormous landholdings and wealthy family connections, Martin was never a rich man: far from it. His estate was largely an expanse of unprofitable wilderness that had come to him already greatly encumbered with his ancestors' debt, which he only increased. His reckless, generous, high-living improvidence was part of Martin's legend: in the words of a Victorian historian, he was "renowned for hospitality in a land of hospitality." Unfortunately, what he possessed in generosity was not matched by financial acumen. None of the many schemes he tried in his life to repair his fortunes, such as undertaking operations in a promising copper mine that was discovered on his land, ever succeeded. Martin lived plagued by debt, creditors, and unsuccessful or short-term attempts to milk political patronage to secure posts that would bring in an income. Hall remarked, with probably only some exaggeration, that for much of his adult life, the King of Connemara scarcely had one hundred pounds to call his own.

Martin was returned to the Irish Parliament in 1798, just two years before it would cease to exist. In the late eighteenth century, Irish nationalism was on the rise, and agitation for both Irish independence and Catholic emancipation was increasing. A powerful mood of nationalist fervor and nascent revolution permeated the country, inspired by the U.S. and French examples. The English colonial rulers, the Anglo-Irish Protestants who dominated Parliament, and the Irish Catholics all had different agendas, often directly conflicting, but sentiment for independence among the two latter groups was strong. After this sentiment erupted into the Irish Rebellion of 1798, the English government pushed to bring Ireland into the fold by uniting the two kingdoms, secretly promising the Catholics that it would support emancipation and secretly promising the Protestants the opposite. (English politicians were divided on the issue of Catholic emancipation, some supporting it out of principle and/or policy, while others

Colonel Richard "Humanity Dick" Martin (Courtesy of the Royal Society for the Prevention of Cruelty to Animals, Horsham, West Sussex, U.K.)

aligned themselves with King George III, who was vehemently anti-Catholic.)

Martin exerted himself to support the union, believing that the cause of both Ireland and Catholics would be better served by a united legislature in London than by a Irish one in Dublin controlled by Protestants. This was a judgment he would later come to regret, as he became aware of the ministry's duplicity, but it set the stage for his work on behalf of animals. In 1800–1801, the Act of Union passed, creating a new political entity (the United Kingdom), a new flag (the Union Jack, combining the Irish cross of St. Patrick with the national flags of Scotland and England), and a newly expanded Parliament, as the Irish legislators abandoned the old Dublin statehouse and moved to London. Richard Martin, elected a representative for County Galway, was among them.

THE HOUSES OF Parliament that Martin entered in 1801 sat, as they do now, on the north bank of the Thames in the Palace of Westminster. However, the palace of 1821 was not the soaring example of Victorian neo-Gothic with its beloved clock tower that we know today, but instead a ramshackle hodgepodge of cramped medieval buildings. (Most of these old buildings would burn down in 1834, clearing the way for the present landmark.) The Commons had been meeting in St. Stephen's Chapel since the sixteenth century, when the Protestant Reformation turned formerly Roman Catholic ecclesiastical buildings to secular use.

The MPs were an elite group, for only men of substantial wealth could vote or be elected. (The extension of the franchise further into the ranks of middle-class and, eventually, working-class men was still more than a decade away; women would not gain the vote until another century had passed.) They customarily met at night, sometimes not adjourning until after dawn. A great chandelier of candles blazed overhead and more candles burned in sconces along the walls, adding to the thickness of the air. The atmosphere was sometimes somnolent, sometimes rambunctious, for sessions took place after the members had dined, and at their leisurely late-afternoon dinners the politicians could easily consume several bottles of claret—several bottles per person, that is. If the House of Commons was not an institution known for decorousness—and it certainly was not (any more than it is today)—this reputation must have been greatly enhanced by the advanced state of inebriation in which some members, including some of Parliament's leading lights, attended to the nation's business.

Here, in the early years of the nineteenth century, the world's first legislative battles on behalf of animals would be fought, eventuating in the victories of 1821–22 that would, as Hall said, "consecrate the memory of Richard Martin" and give him his enduring nickname, Humanity Dick. But Martin did not act alone, nor was he the first to act: others had begun this work twenty years before. The history of the first animal protection legislation is one of fits and starts, where years go by between each parliamentary battle. Those years were not fallow ones, however, for while the legislature was quiet the animal protection movement was rising in the arena of public opinion, preparing the ground for the next bout in Parliament. When Humanity Dick Martin finally succeeded with his own groundbreaking legislation, the way had been paved for him by the determined efforts of people both in and out of Parliament during those two decades before.

PART THREE

Speaking for Animals

CHAPTER 11

TAKING THE BULL BY
THE HORNS

❋   ❋   ❋

O N THE face of it, Sir William Pulteney seemed an unlikely champion of animals, quite different from dashing Dick Martin. An unprepossessing, independent-minded native Scotsman of seventy-six, Sir William had probably never fought a duel. Restrained and cautious rather than outgoing and improvident, he dressed modestly and lived frugally. Few would have guessed, to see him, that he was one of the richest men in Britain; but, courtesy of an unexpected series of deaths, his wife had inherited the enormous fortune left by her uncle the earl of Bath, and Pulteney managed it judiciously. As the MP for Shrewsbury, Pulteney specialized in trade, fisheries, agriculture, and transport, and was well respected for his expertise in economic and constitutional matters. Outside of Parliament, he busied himself with property development at home and abroad. So little is his memory connected with the history of animal protection that his entry in the *Oxford Dictionary of National Biography* does not even mention the event that earned this unpretentious, business-minded baronet a place in our story—when, on April 2, 1800, Sir William rose in the Commons to propose the first animal protection bill ever to be introduced in a national legislature. It was a bill to end the "savage custom," as he called it, of bullbaiting.

Bullbaiting, Sir William told his colleagues, was a "cruel and inhuman" sport that attracted "idle and disorderly persons," taking workingmen away from the occupations that supported their families and setting bad examples of "profligacy and cruelty" for the masses. He urged Parliament to ban it. Immediately, another parliamentary baronet, Sir Richard Hill, rose to support the measure. The MPs often heard Hill speaking on issues of social morality. He had been the first Evangelical Christian ever elected to Parliament, although by now he had been joined by several other "Saints." Hill was particularly known for larding his speeches with quotations from Scripture, a rhetorical technique not calculated to move the hearts of those of his fellow legislators who viewed Evangelicals as hypocritical killjoys and often greeted his fervent appeals with laughter. No one raised any opposition, though, and Pulteney and Hill were instructed to prepare the bill.

When it came up for debate on April 18, however, an MP who had not been present in the earlier session rose to his feet. William Windham, the secretary at war in Prime Minister William Pitt's government, was a slender man of fifty, with an aquiline nose, dark, hooded eyes, and a generous expanse of brow. Windham was considered by many to be one of the most intellectually gifted men of his generation. Urbane and scholarly, he was an old friend of Dr. Johnson's, at whose funeral he had been a pallbearer, and a skilled linguist who had written treatises on mathematics. He was an avid sportsman, too. Plagued by nerves before parliamentary speeches, Windham nonetheless spoke impressively and often. He had a gift for using homely (some said vulgar) examples to drive his point home, and he ranked as one of the greatest orators in a legislature that also boasted the rhetorical talents of George Canning, Richard Brinsley Sheridan, William Pitt the Younger, and William Wilberforce.

Although many MPs found the bullbaiting bill trivial, even funny, Windham confronted it with all his powers of persuasion, speaking long and eloquently to defeat it. Did the honorable members realize what they were doing, Windham asked his colleagues? Bullbaiting was an ancient custom that had existed for more than a thousand years without any evil effects: why had his fellow members now, all of a sudden, become so alarmed by it? It was not increasing in frequency; it did not harm people. He himself had seen two bullbaitings as a boy, and they had not damaged him. Indeed, such sports increased the vigor and manhood of Englishmen; furthermore, England had long been famed for its bulldogs, a valiant breed that was shamefully degenerating.

Pulteney's bill, Windham charged, was sanctimonious, interfering, and a dangerous precedent. Its supporters were petty tyrants who would strip common folk of one of their few pleasures. Of course, the poor were not there to speak for themselves, but Windham would speak for them, and here is what they would say:

> "Why interfere with the few sports that we have, while you leave to yourselves and the rich so great a variety? You have your carriages, your town-houses, and your country-houses; your balls, your plays, your operas, your masquerades, your card-parties, your books, your dogs, and your horses to amuse you—On yourselves you lay no restraint—But from us you wish to take the little we have?"

If the bill's supporters were worried about the sport's cruelty, Windham went on, they were hypocrites. What about the upper-class people who shot ineptly at birds and left them to die slowly of their wounds, or who enjoyed running horses into the ground in order to see a hare or stag have its entrails ripped out? Were these sports any less cruel than bullbaiting? he asked. (Windham knew that among his colleagues there were quite a few who greatly enjoyed these activities.) Parliament would be guilty of pure class discrimination if it banned the people's sport of animal baiting without also banning the gentry's pleasures of coursing, hunting, shooting, and cockfighting, he declared. This was the first time that this all-or-nothing argument was used against an animal protection bill, but it would not be the last.

Windham's "class warfare" argument was both true and disingenuous. Everyone knew that the foxhunters and grouse shooters who occupied both houses of Parliament would never pass legislation curtailing their own pleasures. In fact, hunting was becoming more widespread at this time (although so, too, were the attacks on it). Some of the bill's proponents did believe that bullbaiting was different from hunting and shooting, arguing that its entire purpose was cruelty, whereas in the other sports cruelty was, as it were, a by-product. But for most of the MPs genuinely concerned about animal abuse, the primary issue was strategic. It would have been utterly self-defeating to begin a campaign against cruelty by trying to outlaw upper-class sports. (The truth of this is obvious when we consider that Parliament did not ban foxhunting until 2005, and that the ban, recently upheld by the Law Lords, is still bitterly opposed by some people.) An incremental approach offered a way to begin the process of reform. This had been the strategy of the abolitionists, who first focused on ending the slave *trade* as a more manageable goal than attacking slavery itself.

Windham had another objection to the legislation. This bill, he said, was the pernicious result of a "busy meddling spirit" to legislate on matters that were none of Parliament's business. Morality, he believed, was a matter of the individual heart, not the law's enforcement. Once one started legislating this kind of thing, there would be no end to government's interference with the individual liberties that made Britain great. Windham was correct in his accusation that the bill would abridge certain freedoms and property rights, for it would limit English citizen's rights to treat however they wished the animals they viewed as private property.

To Windham, such a "petty, personal, and local" issue was beneath the dignity of the House, distracting it from truly important matters. Furthermore, it risked stirring up the masses, a frightening prospect in these dangerous times. None of his hearers needed to be reminded what the masses had been doing for the last decade on the other side of the Channel. The specter of the guillotine, years of war, and the rise of an ambitious general named Napoleon Bonaparte were never far from British minds in 1800.

Faced with such an onslaught of reasoned argument, indignant resistance, and ridicule, the proponents of the bill tried to fight back. Pulteney retorted that contrary to enhancing the vigor of the English people, bullbaiting actually led to their decline. It was particularly pernicious for the laboring poor, he repeated, returning to a recurrent theme among some of the bill's supporters, for it made them drop their work for a week at a time to attend baitings, where they gambled away the money that should go to their families.

George Canning, one of the founders of the conservative periodical the *Anti-Jacobin* ("Jacobin" here referred to radical English supporters of the French Revolution), rose to defend the secretary at war. A young man, Canning had been in Parliament for seven years and was establishing his own reputation as an orator, a reputation enhanced by his tall, upright figure. Elaborating upon the argument that this bill would punish the poor while the rich continued to be indulged, he repeated that there should be no end to bullbaiting unless they also put a stop to hunting and shooting. Furthermore, he said, picking up another of Windham's arguments, animal baiting bred heroic spirit and courage, nobility of sentiment and elevation of mind in those who practiced it—and England, at war with France, needed all the heroism and manliness it could muster. Never before, he pronounced, "was so absurd a question brought before Parliament."

The most forceful rebuttal to these arguments was made by Parliament's (literally) most theatrical member, Richard Brinsley Sheridan. Born in Dublin, the son of an actor and a novelist, Sheridan had been a schoolboy at Harrow with Richard Martin. He was now a famous playwright, author of some of English literature's funniest plays (including *The School for Scandal* and *The Rivals*). Though he had retired from playwriting, he remained the manager of the Theatre Royal, Drury Lane. Introducing a bit of playhouse insouciance into Parliament, the hard-drinking, gregarious, and witty Irishman was another of the House's great orators. He had established his reputation for rhetorical brilliance in the trial of the former governor of the Indian colonies, Warren Hastings, when he had flayed Hastings in a famous speech that continued over several days. Finishing that oration with the words "My lords, I have done," Sheridan had collapsed, as if overcome with exhaustion and emotion—a nicely staged melodramatic finale.

Now Sheridan wondered aloud: Why, if the bill was really so absurd, did Windham and Canning expend so much of their breath opposing it? First, he addressed their sudden concern for the well-being of the lower classes. If, in any other context, someone had showed such desire to eliminate the differences between rich and poor as they apparently felt, he would be denounced as a radical. Furthermore, Sheridan exclaimed, there was nothing noble or sporting about baiting at all. Any fight among animals in which one of them was tied to a stake was "cruel, disgraceful, and beastly." And why all this praise for such "sullen, stubborn, and treacherous" creatures as bulldogs? Once they took hold, these beasts never let go—rather like certain political appointees, he added, getting a laugh from the members. In fact, Sheridan pronounced, this bill did not go far enough. An honorable friend of his intended to introduce a bill "for preventing inhumanity to animals in general"—and it would particularly apply to horses, who were subjected to the "most vicious and unmerited cruelty" every day in the streets.

Those who, like Sheridan, wanted to ban bullbaiting often professed great sympathy for the bull, which they commonly referred to as innocent and gentle, and a notable lack of sympathy for the dogs, although they, too, were injured and often killed. It was the idea of a one-sided battle that particularly disturbed people: the image of a single bull, tied to a stake, fighting off waves of attacking dogs. This emotion may have been enhanced by the fact that the figure of "John Bull" had evolved from its original role as a satiric caricature of the stereotypical beef-eating Englishman into an affectionate symbol of English national identity itself. But to the sport's defenders, it was the *bulldog* that embodied the admirable English fighting spirit, symbolized the country's martial valor, and provided a nostalgic connection to the traditions of a rural world that was fast disappearing before the onslaught of industrialization. While those against bullbaiting spoke of the unsporting torture of the bull, those in favor of it spoke of the heroism, courage, and pedigree of the dogs.

The evening wore on in heated debate, punctuated by boisterous calls of *"Hear, hear,"* laughter, and applause. Opponents ridiculed the sorts of people whom they imagined to be distressed by the sport. Windham sneered that the bill had probably been instigated by some small-time country squire "whose hedges have been damaged, or whose wife might have been frightened at seeing a bull-bait." Why didn't she complain when she heard the baying of the hounds at a hunt? Canning argued that if it were the business of legislatures to protect all individuals from potential harm, they would never stop making laws. He himself had recently seen an overdriven ox gore "a poor little old woman in a red cloak." How would the House have reacted, he asked his snickering colleagues, if he had promptly introduced a bill to outlaw the goring of little old women in red cloaks? Yet overdriving oxen did more damage in one year than bullbaiting did in twenty. (Later, in an open letter rebutting these arguments, John Lamb, the brother of the writers Charles and Mary Lamb, remarked that if this red-cloaked woman had been well-to-do and young, sentimental tears would have been shed on her behalf—it was her poverty and her age that allowed the MPs to find her "misery so diverting.")

When the vote was finally called, the bill lost by only two votes, 41–43. Its supporters immediately declared that they would introduce it again in the next session. *The Times,* whose far from impartial coverage of the debate quoted the opponents' arguments at much greater length than the proponents', crowed its approval of the outcome. "It should be written in letters of gold that a Government cannot interfere too little with the people," the paper editorialized. Laws should not interfere with people's pastimes or their property. If Parliament were to head in this direction, it predicted ominously, free will would vanish: "We must eat, drink, and play and sleep by act of Parliament." Mr. Windham must intervene with his "manly language" whenever Parliament threatened to interfere with private life.

A bit of doggerel that circulated around town celebrated the victory in another way.

> *For dogs and hares*
> *And bulls and bears*
> *Let Pultenay still make laws,*
> *For sure I be*

That none but he
So well can plead their cause.
Of all the House,
Of man and mouse,
No one stands him before,
To represent
In Parliament
The brutes, for he's a boar [bore].

ONE MP IN particular professed himself "greatly hurt" by the bill's failure. William Wilberforce was all the more disappointed by the outcome
because he had been prevented from voting. He wrote in his diary that
he and some other supporters who had not been on the floor when the
vote was called had not received the usual summons, and therefore had
missed it. Had he and two of his allies been there, the bill would have
passed. It is not clear from Wilberforce's comment whether he thought
that this was an oversight or deliberate sabotage. (In any event, this was
not the near miss that it might seem, since the bill also would have had
to pass in the House of Lords, where its opponents would certainly
have argued that upper-class blood sports would have to be outlawed as
well and would thereby have guaranteed its defeat.)

Wilberforce had had a particular interest in the bullbaiting bill, dating from earlier that year. A group of men had come to London from
the provinces with the purpose of finding a legislator who would sponsor a ban on the pastime. Of course, they had turned first to Wilberforce, whose fame as a reformer had spread throughout the kingdom.

The son of a wealthy merchant in the Yorkshire port city of Hull,
Wilberforce had been a member of Parliament for nearly twenty years,
having been first elected when he was only twenty-one. His unusually
sweet and melodic voice, distinguished both in singing and in oratory,
had earned him the sobriquet the Nightingale of the House of Commons. Fifteen years had passed since he had seen the light of Evangelical Christianity and had dedicated his life to the service of God, yet

unlike some of his stricter brethren, he retained much of the wit and charm that had made him so popular as a young man.

Wilberforce was Parliament's greatest reformer and one of its greatest orators. Many who admired him likened him to an angel, for his devout religious belief and for his unworldly air, which sometimes seemed at odds with the real-world politics that were his life's work—a contradiction that underlay the charges of hypocrisy often leveled against him by his opponents. Wilberforce's speeches were fast-paced, yet almost conversational: he shunned the showy conventional elegance of the oratory practiced by some of his colleagues. James Boswell, who once heard Wilberforce give a speech, was unimpressed by the little "shrimp"—until he began to speak. Boswell, temperamentally averse to Evangelicals, was struck almost against his will by the power of Wilberforce's eloquence. With each word Wilberforce uttered, Boswell marveled, "he grew, and grew, until the shrimp became a whale."

For more than ten years, Wilberforce had been engaged in his life's mission: leading the parliamentary fight to abolish England's highly lucrative slave trade. The previous summer he had suffered a crushing blow when the House of Lords, succumbing to politicians who represented the powerful slave traders in Bristol and Liverpool and the sugar planters in the West Indies, had defeated his Slave Limitation Bill, which he had finally forced through the Commons. He was a man who took his losses to heart, and never before, he said, had he been "so disappointed and grieved by any defeat."

The parliamentary battle to abolish the slave trade was Wilberforce's greatest cause, the one we remember him for today. But in his own day his name was linked to a staggering number of the reform movements that had begun to spring up in the later eighteenth century. "Good causes," says one of his biographers, "attached themselves to Wilberforce like pins to a magnet." In addition to his frustrating and still fruitless efforts against the slave trade, Wilberforce worked for prison reform, medical aid to the poor, public education, agriculture reform, poor relief, child labor reform, the establishment of Sunday as a day of rest for the laboring classes, and a national program of smallpox inoculation—to name just a few. (That the inoculation was made from cowpox, a related virus, provoked the journalist William Cobbett to attack him for wishing to impregnate children's veins "with the disease of a beast.") Wilberforce believed, he said, that "God Almighty has set before me two great objects, the suppression of the slave trade and the reformation of manners." By manners, he meant what we would call morals: social behaviors such as drunkenness, dueling, prostitution, adultery, and cruelty.

Evangelical Anglicans, like Methodists and Quakers, often made a point of opposing cruelty to animals, and were particularly critical of the blood sports that seemed to them particularly degrading and "barbarous." It was because of this, and because of his reputation as both a reformer and an animal lover, that the provincial delegation chose to approach Wilberforce. When they came face to face with the famous MP, they found a slight, frail-looking man, whose face, with its long, turned-up nose and nearsighted yet still fervent eyes, was drawn with exhaustion and pain. The long, frustrating fight against the slave trade had taken an enormous toll, and Wilberforce was not a healthy man in the first place. He suffered chronic stomach pain, probably from inflammatory bowel disease, exacerbated by stress, for which he found relief only through opium pills.

Wilberforce's illness had been so severe in the year before the animal welfare proponents approached him that his doctors had recommended, futilely, that he retire for a year. He told the delegation that while he would certainly support a ban on bullbaiting, he wished they would find another sponsor. If they could not convince another MP to take up the cause, he promised, then he would lead this battle, too— though he considered himself, as he told his friend and fellow Evangelical reformer Hannah More, to be only a "common hack" (that is, a drudge, like a hired horse) in such matters. As it happened, the country delegation found another sympathetic ear in Pulteney. Perhaps this added to Wilberforce's regrets, however. For he, the experienced parliamentary strategist, was particularly disgusted with the terms on which its sponsor had defended his bill.

Pulteney "argued it like a parish officer," Wilberforce complained, "and never once mentioned the cruelty." During the debate, Pulteney actually had called the sport "cruel, brutal, and inhuman," saying that the practice of baiting an animal tied to a stake was a "refinement of torture." But both his and Hill's arguments did seem particularly to focus on the perceived "barbarity" of the common folk as the evil, implying that bullbaiting was more objectionable because of the license it permitted to the drunken, vulgar mob—taking workingmen away from their labors for extended periods—than because of what it inflicted upon animals. This complaint, though accurate, played directly into the hands of clever opponents such as Windham, for it gave considerable weight to his argument that the proposed ban reflected little more than class bias, less a concern for bulls or dogs than a desire to "civilize" the lower orders according to middle-class standards, leaving the privileged free to indulge their own bloody pleasures.

After the bill was lost, Wilberforce confronted Windham and Canning, showing them graphic accounts of the cruelties of animal baiting that he had received from some country magistrates. Windham, he said disgustedly, read them "coldly." Canning responded differently, however: reading the magistrates' accounts made him feel ashamed of the role he had played in the bill's defeat. He told Wilberforce that "he had no idea of the real nature of the practice he had been defending."

DESPITE PLANS TO reintroduce the bill in the following session, only in 1802 did the bill make its reappearance. During the intervening year, its advocates' sense of urgency was renewed by an appalling incident that occurred in the old market town of Bury St. Edmunds in Surrey.

On the morning of November 5, 1801, a group of men led a bull into the street. It was Guy Fawkes Day, named after one of the conspirators in the failed 1605 Gunpowder Plot to assassinate King James I and blow up Parliament. That evening, people all over England would gather around bonfires to cheer as the flames devoured "guys," effigies of Fawkes, but other entertainments that preceded the fires varied according to local custom. Bury's long-standing tradition was a bullbaiting. But the particular bull available that year was unlikely to provide much of a spectacle against the dogs, for he was known for his gentleness. What nature had not done for the bull, therefore, the men had to do themselves: they had to transform him into a vicious beast.

Bullbaiters had developed a number of creative techniques to guarantee that an enraged animal, or at least a terrified one, faced the dogs. They might blow hot pepper into his nose, or spread gunpowder over his body and set it alight; they might cut off his horns or his tail and ears and pour caustic liquid into the wounds. Firecrackers were always popular, thrilling the spectators with the explosions while at the same time they sent the animal into a frenzy. The men in Bury chose a simpler technique, which was to goad the bull by jabbing him with knives and pitchforks until he was maddened with the pain. Knowing that they had a gentle animal to work on, they must have undertaken this torture with some gusto.

Stabbing the bull certainly succeeded in enraging him, but what happened next departed from the plan. The bull suddenly burst free of his tethers and stormed into the center of town, where he rampaged through the streets. Pedestrians ran for their lives while shopkeepers slammed shut their doors and threw the bolts. The would-be baiters ran after the crazed bull, trying to snare him with ropes before he gored someone to death. (This had happened just two months earlier in Eccles, near Manchester, when a drunken man was killed by a goaded bull.) Finally they entangled the beast and dragged him into the bullring.

The bull was now more than primed for baiting. But before they released the dogs, the men added a refinement. Their motives for what they did next are not recorded in the reports of what transpired that day: perhaps they were furious with the beast for the trouble he had caused, or worked up into a frenzy of sadistic excitement; perhaps they simply wanted to make sure he did not escape again. Whatever their reason, they cut off all four of the bull's hooves. Then they released the dogs. The *Bury Post* described with outrage the pathetic spectacle of the maimed bull trying to defend himself against the dogs, "feebly supporting himself on his mangled bleeding stumps!"

To disable an animal by cutting off its hooves or severing its tendons was not unheard of: the practice was called houghing. Drovers and slaughterhouse workers were reported sometimes to abuse in this way the cows, sheep, pigs, and even horses in their charge, apparently out of frustration with a recalcitrant animal, or as a sadistic amusement. The horse authority John Lawrence reported that in 1793 two Manchester butchers cut off the feet of some sheep and drove them through the town. (They were fined twenty shillings each, because the sheep did not belong to them; had the sheep been theirs, Lawrence commented, they could have burned them alive with impunity.)

In any context, the deed done in Bury was one of extreme cruelty, and to many who otherwise defended bullbaiting, an unsporting one. Others, however, thought that its excess only revealed the savage inhumanity inherent in the sport itself. The incident became notorious: the local newspaper's account was reprinted (without additional comment) in the London *Times* a few days later. The *Times* left out, however, the *Post*'s additional commentary: "Good God! in what age, in what country, do we live?" We claim to be civilized, but "the beast is tortured merely for the diversion of savages; and yet there are men professed champions of Christianity and social order, who can stand up and vindicate such amusements." The target of these remarks was clearly Windham.

The following spring, Sir Richard Hill read the account of the Bury baiting aloud in the Commons as a stark example of "the barbarous custom of bullbaiting in its true light." If Parliament had passed the ban on bullbaiting two years before, this incident might never have happened, he implied. Now, partially motivated by this atrocity (and reports of other cruelties associated with the sport) and partially by more protests against its savagery from around the country, the bill was back. This time its sponsor was John Dent, MP for Lancaster—a slave-trading port.

An example of the strange bedfellows created by the issue of animal welfare, this bill united Wilberforce, Parliament's leading abolitionist, with Dent, the slave trade's staunch supporter.

Dent had earlier attempted to impose a tax on dogs, whose population, he reported, was increasing alarmingly, leading to a rise in sheep killing and hydrophobia (rabies). Furthermore, dogs consumed too much of the flour, oatmeal, offal, and table scraps that should go to the poor, he said, and a tax would produce revenue for the government. More than one member detected an anticanine prejudice in this bill: Sheridan wondered whether Dent was a Pythagorean who had taken a dislike to dogs in some former existence as another animal. (Perhaps he had in mind a hare or a bull.) The bill eventually passed, in an amended form, but stuck its sponsor forever with an irresistible nickname, "Dog Dent." (Much fun could be had with this: sometimes Dent was elevated in rank to Sir Dogby, other times simply known as the Dog; his wife, naturally, became Mrs. Dog.)

As the debate began, Sir Richard Hill was once again among the first to speak, beginning: "Sir, I rise in behalf of a race of poor friendless beings who certainly cannot speak for themselves." Hill referred to some things that had changed since the previous bill. Now, many supporting letters and petitions had flooded in, signed by members of the peerage, clergy, tradesmen, mayors, and magistrates. Parliament was now larger, since the new Irish members of the Commons had taken their seats early in 1801, and Hill was pleased to call upon his Irish colleagues to join the ranks of supporters.

Other components of Hill's speech had not changed, however. Again, he didactically cited Scripture, this time Solomon's declaration that, in Hill's words, "the merciful man regarded the life of his beast, but that the tender mercies of the wicked were cruel." He reminded everyone of the story of Balaam's ass, to whom an angel had given the power of speech so he could rebuke his master for cruelty. Hill suggested that it would not be amiss in a "Christian assembly" to take seriously such angelic visitations on behalf of animals.

Once again, Hill also cast aspersions upon the character and class of those who enjoyed such barbarous sports. The preamble of the printed bill complained of the sport's encouragement of "idleness, drunkenness and rioting," and the "great corruption of morals" of the common people, but said nothing specific about cruelty to animals. Asserting that "the amiable sex"—that is, women—were generally in favor of the bill, Hill admitted that there were exceptions: the sorts of women one found staggering out of a gin shop in the slum of St. Giles, for example, or "riding in a cinder-cart." Wilberforce, who had made certain to be present that day, must have felt his heart sink as he listened to his fellow Saint's "foolish speech," as he later called it. For Hill once again invited attack on the bill's supporters as sanctimonious meddlers hostile to the pleasures of their social inferiors and indifferent to their welfare. But as it turned out, not Hill but Wilberforce himself bore the brunt of their opponents' sarcasm.

Windham once again led the opposition. This time he lacked his primary ally, for Canning was absent. Those graphic accounts of baiting had made him less eager to defend the practice, and he was also influenced by some fellow MPs who were supporting the bill in response to pressure from their constituents. Although Canning had not come around to Wilberforce's side—he still felt that bullbaiting was not a serious issue, and had assured Windham in a letter that he remained an ally, referring jocularly to bulls as "butcher's meat"—he had decided to abstain from voting this time.

Windham might have lost his major ally, but many others continued to support him. He opened with a long speech, making the same arguments he had used two years ago—though now he made them more explicitly, and, this time, he engaged in personal attack. Wilberforce felt, he later said, that his opponent's words were "aimed expressly at me, though I had not [yet] spoken." Windham returned to his theme that the bill threatened national security, but this time he was more specific about the nature of the threat, which, he implied, included Wilberforce and his ilk. Opposition to bullbaiting, he warned his colleagues, aligned two dangerous factions, the Jacobins and the Methodists (a relatively new Evangelical sect). One would not think that, on the face of it, these two groups had much in common, he admitted, the former being atheistic political fanatics and the latter being Christian religious fanatics. However, they were both extremist groups and in this matter their interests coincided. The abolition of bullbaiting was part of their insidious radical agenda to undermine British institutions.

Methodists, Windham pronounced, wanted to deny the working classes pleasures out of a puritanical wish to control their behavior, while Jacobins would deny them pleasures in order to radicalize them by making them aware of their oppression. His ad hominem attack on Wilberforce was (deliberately) inaccurate, for the abolitionist was not a Methodist: Windham meant to slur all types of Evangelicals as fanatics. And, as the devout, essentially conservative friend, and usually also the ally, of the Tory prime minister, William Pitt, Wilberforce was an enemy of the Jacobins. Now Windham was accusing him and his supporters of working against the stability of Great Britain by pressing for reform during a perilous time, when any kind of change could undermine the existing order, already under attack from forces both foreign and domestic.

Britain had been at war with revolutionary France for nearly a decade, but very recently the powers had signed a treaty. (The Peace of Amiens would prove to be short-lived, however.) The mood of conservatism and backlash that had settled over the country during wartime persisted even after the peace, which many people in and out of Parliament, including Windham, opposed. Windham supported some liberal causes such as abolition and Catholic relief. (The year before he had resigned as secretary at war over the king's opposition to Catholic emancipation.) Having supported the French Revolution early on, he had since turned against it and become the leader of the group in Parliament called the alarmists, for whom the political situation required avoidance of anything that might weaken the English state—even reform of the egregiously corrupt methods by which members of Parliament were elected. Windham was one of the chief opponents of election reform, declaring that no one in his right mind would begin repairing a house during hurricane season.

If one wanted to experience the destructive effect the response to the French Revolution had on Britain, wrote Sir Samuel Romilly, one should take up the cause of humanitarian reform. Romilly was a distinguished lawyer, MP, abolitionist, legal reformer, cat lover, and supporter of anticruelty bills, who also wrote a tract on humane methods of slaughtering cattle. He discovered through his own reformist efforts that the reaction to France had produced "a stupid dread of innovation" and a "savage spirit." For instance, when Romilly introduced a bill to repeal the law that made pickpocketing a capital crime, a young nobleman told him that treating thieves with compassion just made them worse, declaring, "I am for hanging all." As the government cracked down on British revolutionaries and republicans, suspending habeas corpus and arresting radicals, all types of reform became suspect as threats to old British values and its systems of privilege. Just as the "stupid dread of innovation" greatly hampered attempts to end the slave trade, so, too, it hindered other reforms.

It may seem preposterous to think that a bill outlawing bullbaiting might be a threat to national security. But those who argued this believed that in such a time of crisis, there should be no breaking with long-sanctioned customs, and certainly no extensions of the law into new territory. The radical animal-rights views espoused by some revolutionaries, vegetarians, and anti-imperialists probably also colored the issue of animal welfare in Parliament. Furthermore, the guillotine cast a long shadow across the Channel into England, where the fear of the mob became palpable. Implied in Windham's defense of bullbaiting was a "bread and circuses" argument: the masses must be allowed their bloody distractions so that they could turn their propensity for violence against the bodies of animals instead of rising against their social superiors.

Windham's attack on Methodists also expressed both his fear of the masses—Methodism appealed to the laboring classes—and his hostility to the reformist sentiment that underlay Evangelicalism in general, which had arisen as a reform movement within the Anglican church. England, the Saints thought, was a cesspool of corruption, degradation, and sin, where prostitution and sexual deviance were rampant, the morals of the upper classes depraved, the church rotting from within, and drunkenness habitual from the aristocrats downing their multiple bottles of claret to the poor people lying in the streets in gin-induced stupors. Evangelical Christians sought nothing less than a sweeping conversion of British society.

In actuality, most Evangelicals were deeply conservative in many ways, fearing social upheaval as much as any government minister or Tory squire, and seeking alliances with the establishment. Their concerns were moral rather than political, and their interests lay more in the spread of true religion than in any political ideology. But Anglican Evangelicals such as Wilberforce did preach submission to authority and often supported repressive government measures against individual freedom, such as the suspension of habeas corpus, the banning of public meetings, and a strengthening of the power of magistrates. The Saints founded the Society for the Suppression of Vice, an organization dedicated to stamping out moral offenses of many sorts, such as swearing, drinking, gaming, atheism, lewd books, debauchery, adultery, blasphemy, Sunday commerce, and cruelty. These efforts often appeared to be (and indeed often were) impositions of their puritanical beliefs upon the behavior of others. Evangelicals were prone, their opponents often charged, to self-righteous "cant" and hypocrisy.

Yet, genuinely coercive as the Evangelicals' agenda could be, the reality was more complicated. In Wilberforce's mind, the effort to stamp out vice, for instance, was the best way to achieve a truly humanitarian end, which was to decrease the great numbers of Britons who languished and died in the pestilent prisons, who were shipped, at peril to their lives, to Australian penal colonies, or who were simply hanged. Similarly, though his efforts to ban Sunday commerce were often seen as the sanctimonious imposition of a pleasure-hating regimen hostile to everything but Bible-reading on that day, Wilberforce well knew that Sunday, the holiday of the rich, came at the expense of the poor who served them. Their servants, coach drivers, watermen, and waiters had no day of rest at all.

The Victorian historian Thomas Macaulay famously quipped that the seventeenth-century Puritans wanted to ban bearbaiting not because of the pain it gave the bear but because of the pleasure it gave the spectators. This sentiment was often heard with respect to the reform efforts of the Evangelicals, too; but in both cases, the condemnation was too easy and too sweeping. Although they certainly were concerned with social control, the Evangelicals' efforts against bullbaiting and other forms of cruelty also emerged from genuine concern both about the lives and souls of the poor, and about the great suffering of animals visible everywhere one went. Many Evangelicals genuinely believed in extending Christian charity to beasts for their own sake.

Furthermore, as Windham knew perfectly well, Evangelicals were not the only people who found bullbaiting unacceptably cruel. The anti-Evangelical horse expert John Lawrence implicitly drew a comparison with slavery when he referred to animal baiting as "chaining and staking down wretched captives" to torture them. Such "useless barbarity," he wrote, "is absolutely unlawful, contrary to the light of reason, and the dictates of humanity, the foul disgrace of common sense, and never ought to be tolerated for a moment." And it would have taken a long stretch of the imagination to view Richard Brinsley Sheridan as a Saint.

When Windham finally came to the end of his long speech in the Commons that evening, Wilberforce had to respond to his attack. After all, Windham had essentially accused him of subversion, misrepresentation, unpatriotism, and even of unmanliness, for he had implied that the bill's advocates were dominated by the emotions of their wives. Wilberforce had lost his prepared notes and, perhaps in his anger at the personal attack on him, forgot some of what he intended to say. But, as his friends later told him, he spoke well. Bullbaiting, he said, "fostered every bad and barbarous principle of our nature." The cruelty to the bull, that "honest, harmless, useful animal," was terrible: Wilberforce cited the cutting off of horns. At this, some of the other members cried, *"Never,"* but Wilberforce had received detailed information from country magistrates. He told of an instance in which people trying to enrage a bull sawed off his horns and poured a caustic liquid into the wounds. "Wretched indeed must be the condition of the people of England," Wilberforce cried, "if their whole happiness consist[s] in the practice of such barbarity!"

Emotions ran high as other members spoke on both sides. The debate followed the lines of the first one: against the ban were adduced tradition, the happiness of the lower orders, the valor of men and dogs, its class bias, and the dangerous precedent of such social legislation. For the ban were cited the sport's savage cruelty, its disorder, its immorality, and its deleterious effects on national character. Some of the bill's supporters emphasized the cruelty to the animal, others the barbarism of the spectators. Sheridan bluntly accused Windham of missing war and carnage so much that he was displacing his love of bloodshed onto fights between beasts. Cruelty to animals was a moral crime, he said, no matter under what circumstances it was done, and gave graphic examples of owners horribly mutilating their bulldogs in order to display their tenacity. He also observed that Windham's apparent concern for the poor was nothing but cynical opportunism—the "mask of friendship for the people."

But the arguments of Windham and his allies carried the day. The bill was defeated again, by a larger margin than before: 51–64. The bull-baiting bill, having failed twice, was now dead. Some of its supporters rushed into print to attack the outcome. Percival Stockdale, for instance, deplored "the protracted torture of a strong and powerful, yet captive and helpless animal" as "the most hideous moral deformity of the human species." For their part, the bill's opponents took to the streets in celebration.

AFTER PULTENEY'S FIRST anti-bullbaiting bill had been defeated, the *Times* had expressed certainty that the issue was dead forever. "All hopes of success in a future Parliament for the bullbaiting bill must vanish," it predicted confidently, "as it cannot be supposed that the minority will increase by the introduction of so many Irish members [after the Act of Union]." The newspaper's certainty depended on the stereotype of the violent Irishman, while Hill had called upon these same Irish members to support the bill. In the short run the *Times* writer was correct, though not for the reasons he gave. In fact, because the Irish and English election cycles were not yet synchronized, most of the Irish members were back in Ireland electioneering when the debate was held.

So Richard Martin, who almost certainly would have supported the bill (and did attempt later to reintroduce it), was in Galway at the time. Two decades were still to pass before he would throw himself into the battle to protect animals. Seven years would pass before the next animal protection bill was brought before Parliament (although when it was, concern for the welfare of beasts would be the explicit focus). In the interim, magazine articles would continue to be published castigating abuse, and sermons would exhort parishioners to think of the lives of their beasts. Famous writers would place animals at the center of their work more frequently than ever before, artists would paint them, and sentimental depictions of them would tug heartstrings, playing upon emotions and prompting people to identify with their fellow creatures. Public opinion, stirred by other reform movements of the day, was gradually turning in favor of animal protection, too.

In the aftermath of the 1802 defeat, however, proponents of bullbaiting flaunted their victory. Stamford, home of the country's best-known bullrunning, had submitted two petitions in favor of the bill, signed by the mayor, aldermen, and justices of the peace, as well as other citizens. However, Stamford had also submitted the only petition to oppose it, signed by other householders and burgesses who defended the long tradition as a custom begun in medieval times that was central to the town's identity and the pleasure of its residents. The victorious opponents had rung the town's bells joyously when the second

bill was defeated. Two local candidates for Parliament had invited citizens to a celebratory public dinner—to be preceded by a bullbaiting.
Throughout England in subsequent years, bulls led to the ring were
decked with ribbons and placards reading: SANCTIONED BY WINDHAM
AND PARLIAMENT.

CHAPTER 12

THE UNFORTUNATE TOURIST'S DOG

❉   ❉   ❉

IN JULY 1805, a shepherd leading his flock to pasture on Mount Helvellyn in the English Lake District heard an eerie sound: the howling of a dog. Dogs did not usually wander alone through that remote area, where wild animals roamed and the last drifts of the previous winter's snow had only recently receded. So the shepherd traced the sound to its source. Near a cluster of rocks underneath a high cliff, he discovered a small terrier, skittish and lame, who backed off as the man approached but seemed unwilling to go far. Near where the dog had been, the shepherd noticed what looked like a pile of rags. But as he moved closer, he realized that the rags were a tattered suit of clothes, and that they encased a decayed, headless human body.

The subsequent investigation identified the remains, whose skull was found nearby, as those of a young Manchester Quaker named Charles Gough, who visited the Lake District regularly to sketch its beautiful scenery. Gough had disappeared that spring after leaving his inn for a walk over Helvellyn, accompanied by his little terrier named Foxey. Gough, the coroner concluded, had died when he fell from the cliff above, probably as a result of losing his way in the fog. Foxey had remained by her master's corpse for three months, somehow managing to survive.

It did not take long before the poignant story of the faithful dog who had braved the elements in order to watch over her master's body spread widely throughout Britain. The story was told and retold in various ways. First circulated through gossip and newspapers, in subsequent months and years it was depicted by poets and painters. Most famously, among the several poets to treat of it, two major Romantic writers took it up. William Wordsworth's poem "Fidelity" celebrated the dog's "love sublime" and "strength of feeling, great / Above all human estimate!" Sir Walter Scott, Britain's literary lion of the day, imagined the feelings of the dog as she waited patiently beside her master's body:

> *How long didst thou think that his silence was slumber?*
> *When the wind waved his garment, how oft didst thou start?*
> *How many long days and long nights didst thou number*
> *Ere he faded before thee, the friend of thy heart?*

The painter Francis Danby, a member of the Royal Academy, portrayed a frightening scene in *The Precipice,* where the man's body lies splayed against the rocks as the dog looks up in helpless despair, dwarfed by the jagged mountain towering over them. Edwin Henry Landseer, a popular painter noted for his sentimental portrayals of animals (he was also the sculptor of the Trafalgar Square lions), struck a poignant note in line with Scott's poem: the little dog rests her paws on the chest of her fallen master, gazing down at him intently as if trying to will him back to life. Landseer entitled his painting *Attachment.*

The story of Charles Gough and his faithful Foxey became the day's favorite dog fidelity story. From then on, tales about dogs who guarded their masters' bodies, dogs who returned to their dead masters' haunts, dogs who refused to leave their masters' graves, and dogs who traveled long distances to be reunited with their masters have never lost their appeal. Foxey's reign in the public imagination would not be eclipsed until fifty years later, when Edinburgh's Greyfriars Bobby, who guarded his master's grave for fourteen years, became a celebrity visited by people from all around. In the years after the discovery of Gough's body, many variations of the Unfortunate Tourist story were told and retold, most emphasizing the dog's noble sacrifice and devoted love. Some accounts added that the dog had given birth to puppies, which did not survive because she devoted herself to watching over her master—showing that

Foxey guarding her master's body. Sir Edwin Henry Landseer, *Attachment,* 1829. (St. Louis Art Museum, gift of Mrs. Eugene A. Perry in memory of her mother, Mrs. Claude Kilpatrick, by exchange)

her love for the man was so great that it overcame her canine maternal instincts. At the top of Mount Helvellyn, a monument was erected to commemorate Foxey's fidelity.

From the moment that Gough's body was discovered, however, other stories suggested a darker version of events. Most accounts described the dog as emaciated when she was found, having kept herself barely alive, or so people conjectured, by catching small animals or eating sheep that had died. However, other accounts suggested that Foxey had not been ill and thin when she was discovered, but suspiciously healthy and plump. Furthermore, the damage to Gough's body was usually ascribed to ravens, but, some people muttered and some newspapers reported, perhaps the culprit was Foxey herself. Hadn't the dog really survived by eating her master's flesh? Rather than sacrificing herself to guard her master's body, the rumor went, Foxey had saved herself by feasting upon it.

This idea was shocking and repellent to those who responded emotionally to this story, for it violated the common understanding of the nature of dogs, as well as the principles underlying humans' relationship to all pets. It was as if a tacit contract had been broken. If pets, by definition, are the domestic animals that we do not eat, the implicit quid pro quo is that we are the animals that pets do not eat. Pets hold their privileged status by implicitly surrendering some part of their animal nature into the control of their masters. (When they do turn against humans or human property of their own accord, they are executed.) Animals living as dependents and helpmeets of humans are expected to take on human virtues, such as restraint. And no domesticated animal has occupied a more privileged position than the dog.

The cynical (or just realistic) counterstory was largely squelched by the sentimental one.* The tale of Charles Gough and his faithful Foxey was just one of many touching depictions of animals expressing

---

*H. D. Rawnsley, a clergyman, poet, and chronicler of the Lake District, who was one of those responsible for erecting the monument to "Fidelity," investigated this story in the late nineteenth century and published a pamphlet about it in 1892. Rawnsley surveyed all the accounts, interviewed local residents, including shepherds, and tracked down an elderly man who had been alive at the time it happened. He concluded that Gough had two dogs, a spaniel and a terrier, and that it was the terrier Foxey that had accompanied him that day. He believed that Foxey had not eaten her master's flesh, both because most accounts said she had not, and because he had testimony from local shepherds that such a dog would never do that kind of thing: it would be like a child feeding on its dead parent, one old shepherd said. It is obvious that Rawnsley himself wished to believe this.

Britons' increasing attachment to their pets. Landseer would make a career painting dogs in noble and affecting contexts. His painting *Saved*, for instance, depicts a black-and-white Newfoundland dog who lies panting on the shore, with an unconscious little girl, whom he has just saved from drowning, lying draped over his front paws. (So often did he paint black-and-white Newfoundlands that this color variation of the breed is now officially known as "landseer.") Didactic children's literature—with titles such as *Julia and the Pet-Lamb; or, Good-Temper and Compassion Rewarded* (published in 1813) and *The Sin of Cruelty* (a tiny chapbook published after 1799 by the Religious Tract Society)— used similar examples to encourage children to be kind to animals. Sarah Trimmer wrote many children's books, such as *The History of the Robins*, that used animals to teach that compassion and discipline went hand in hand. But these depictions were not limited to popular and children's literature; as the examples of Wordsworth and Scott show, they became mainstays of adult writing, too, particularly during the vogue for sentimentality that began in the mid-eighteenth century and had thoroughly permeated both literature and society by the nineteenth.

The ability to sympathize with a being in distress—human or animal—became the sign of a morally superior person who possessed a refined intellect and tender heart. A large genre of artistic productions sprang up to give people the opportunity to enjoy plangent emotions and display their sensitivity by weeping pleasurably at heart-rending scenes. Laurence Sterne's *A Sentimental Journey* featured a caged starling who moaned, "I can't get out." The most appealing character in his novel *Tristram Shandy* is the comically sentimental Uncle Toby, who releases a fly with the words "Why should I hurt thee?— This world surely is wide enough to hold both thee and me." Byron gave his hero Don Juan a soft heart for cats and birds. The Evangelical poet William Cowper wrote affectingly about the hares he saved from the hounds and kept as pets. Animals are God's creations, and it is a hard heart that is not swelled by the "sight of animals enjoying life," he wrote in Book 6 of *The Task*. In "Auguries of Innocence," the radical mystical poet William Blake wrote, "The Bleat, the Bark, Bellow & Roar / Are Waves that Beat on Heaven's Shore."

Sentimentality obviously had limited ability to affect human behavior, when compassion conflicted with custom, convenience, and appetite: Oliver Goldsmith's fictional Chinese visitor puzzled about the English attitudes toward animals, observing that "they pity and they eat the object of their compassion." But animals played an increasing role in literature that joined sentimentalism with more specifically political ideas. In Robert Burns's famous "To a Mouse," the plowman who speaks the poem recognizes the affinity between Mousie's vulnerability to the plow that has just torn apart her nest and his own vulnerability as a poor rural laborer. Blake wrote perhaps the most powerful political poem about animals of the time, "Auguries of Innocence," which begins "A Robin Red breast in a Cage / Puts all Heaven in a Rage." Humans' cruelty to animals not only angers heaven, but also destroys our humanity.

> A Horse misus'd upon the Road
> Calls to Heaven for Human blood.
> Each outcry of the hunted Hare
> A fibre from the Brain does tear.

Samuel Taylor Coleridge applied the principles of the French Revolution to human relationships with animals in his "To a Young Ass," calling the animal "brother" (not in the Pythagorean sense but in the revolutionary sense of "liberté, égalité, fraternité"). This language of sentimentalism, brotherhood, and liberty was also among the common currency that, for at least some reformers, united the plight of animals with that of human slaves.

Later eighteenth-century arguments against cruelty to animals had drawn from both radical and conservative abolitionist rhetoric that to some degree had also been heard in the bullbaiting debates. From different political positions, Humphrey Primatt, John Oswald, and George Nicholson all made a connection between oppressed humans and oppressed beasts. Jeremy Bentham wrote that slaves had been, and in places still were, treated as animals were treated in England, and that this was both an indictment of slavery and an indictment of attitudes toward the brute creation. "The day *may* come," he wrote, "when the rest of the animal creation may acquire those rights which never could have been withholden from them but by the hand of tyranny." Elsewhere he asked, "Why should the law refuse its protection to any sensitive being?" Now that we have started to pay attention to the plight of slaves, he predicted, "we shall finish by softening that of all the animals which assist our labours or supply our wants."

IN 1807, TWO years before Parliament would again confront animal cruelty, Wilberforce and his allies won abolition's first major victory: they finally passed a bill that ended England's slave trade. It had been a long struggle, but the abolitionists had first begun to succeed in changing British "hearts and minds," and then changed British law. They found a powerful tool in the language of sentiment, particularly its emphasis upon the "sympathetic imagination": our ability to imagine that we are someone we are not, to put ourselves in another's place. Abolitionists asked their white British audience, few of whom had ever seen a slave plantation, a slave ship, or perhaps even a slave, to use their powers of imagination and feeling to put themselves into the place of their fellow human beings as they were forcibly seized from their African homelands, endured great suffering on slave-trading ships, and then were brutally abused on the plantations. Black slaves were to be imagined as human beings, rather than "things" and commodities, endowed with equal claims to humanity. The abolitionist slogan "Am I not a man and a brother?" embedded traces of the radical notion of human brotherhood within a sentimental appeal to the sympathetic imagination of all Britons.

Many who argued for animal protection drew upon the idea of sympathy as it was used in the antislavery movement—although the sympathetic imagination had its limitations when applied to beasts, since humans cannot imagine what it is like to be an animal. Still, like their human counterparts, animal slaves were relegated to "thing" status, and suffered. Furthermore, abolitionists frequently argued that slavery was evil not only for what it did to the slaves but what it did to the owners, too: that the brutal domination of nonwhites as if they were animals actually turned the ostensibly civilized white masters into brutes themselves. Many who argued for animal protection echoed these ideas. Just as the existence of slavery corrupted society, they said, so, too, did various forms of brutality to animals, which made humans more brutal than actual brutes. When opponents of bullbaiting spoke of the "gentle bull," for instance, they contrasted the animal with the "savage" baiters. (The fact that the word "gentle" also designated upper-class status played a role in this contrast, too.)

Both the wealthy West Indies planter and the laboring-class bullbaiter or abusive carter, for all the world of difference between them, were brutes who had to be reformed by the standards of enlightened thinking or true religion. Percival Stockdale collapsed class distinctions further when, deploring Parliament's failure to ban bullbaiting, he argued that the poor were actually much *less* accountable for their brutality than were their social superiors who encouraged them to such "deeds of moral violence." Stockdale made the specific connection between slaveholders' abuse of the human rights of African slaves and Britons' cruelty to animals.

With the outlawing of the slave trade, abolitionists' thoughts turned to outlawing slavery itself in British territories—another long, protracted battle. Reformers also felt the time had come to revive the issue of animal protection, since public sentiment had been evidencing more concern for animals in the seven years that had passed since the bullbaiting defeat. One legislator in particular, who had been talking for the past twenty years about wishing to introduce a bill that would explicitly and specifically outlaw cruelty to animals, now felt the time might be right. This was a former lord chancellor, Thomas Erskine.

In the winter of 1808, Lord Erskine hosted a dinner party at his house for a group of distinguished guests, many of them fellow members of Parliament. Those present included Sir Samuel Romilly, who left an account of the lively conversation. Erskine had "always expressed great sympathy for animals," Romilly said, and that evening he entertained his guests with an account of two of his favorite pets, who happened to be leeches. Home and Cline (named after celebrated surgeons) lived in a glass in his library, and Erskine himself gave them fresh water every day. Home and Cline had very different personalities, he explained, but they had worked together to save his life when he had been ill, and, following the practice of the day, they had been used to bleed him.

After his recovery Erskine adopted his faithful leeches, and felt that he had formed a friendship with them. He was certain, he told his guests, that they recognized him when he approached them and that they felt grateful to him for saving them. In fact, exclaimed Erskine, he would introduce them right now—and brought them to the table. (It is much to be regretted that Romilly did not report the expressions of the other guests at these new additions to their party.) Romilly did comment, in his sober, understated way, that "it is impossible . . . without the vivacity, the tones, the details, and the gestures of Lord Erskine, to give an adequate account of this singular scene."

Erskine was a high-spirited man of great wit, intelligence, humor, and sociability. He was the son of a financially strapped Edinburgh aristocratic family and had made his career as a struggling young barrister with radical sensibilities by defending the accused in some of the British government's most notorious criminal trials. He successfully defended the former sea captain Thomas Baille against a government charge of libel when the latter, an eighteenth-century whistleblower, published an exposé of corruption at the Royal Hospital for Seamen. His eloquence kept George Gordon out of prison when Gordon was accused of treason for fomenting the violent anti-Catholic riots that had raged through London in 1780. He had saved the Irish nationalist Horne Tooke from the gallows, and had unsuccessfully defended the

American radical Tom Paine when he was tried in absentia for libel. In 1800, when the first bullbaiting bill was being debated, Erskine was defending a man on the charge of attempting to assassinate the king.

An early sympathizer with the French Revolution, Erskine had spent time in Paris in 1790, where he had met Richard Martin (and then later defended Martin's wife's lover in his criminal conversation case). His extraordinary, emotion-filled courtroom oratory earned him the sobriquet "the British Cicero" (though he was by no means the only English orator to be so called). He was popular with the people, who regarded him as a hero of the common man, if much less popular with the judges, who distrusted the way in which his successful prosecutions were based upon his sometimes open appeal to emotion rather than upon sound legal reasoning.

From a struggling young lawyer concerned about feeding his children, Erskine rose to become the best-paid barrister in Britain, a king's counsel, and a friend of the prince of Wales, whom he served for a time as attorney general. From there it was a short step to Parliament, where he was elected to the Commons for Portsmouth and aligned himself with the prominent Whigs Charles James Fox and Sheridan. And in 1806, he was appointed lord chancellor. He served in this capacity for only a year and was widely considered not to have been well suited for the position. But the office gave him a life peerage, the baronetcy of Restormel, and a seat in the House of Lords. When he created his coat of arms, he took as his motto "Trial by Jury."

Lady Morgan, the Irish novelist, had been thrilled at the opportunity to meet Erskine, whom she idolized from having read his speeches. Inevitably, she was a little disappointed to find that most of the time he "spoke like other persons," and that rather than the godlike being of her imagination, he was in fact was "a thin, middle-aged gentleman, and wore a brown wig." But they got to be friends, and she found him, if vain and egotistical (as those who disliked him charged), also "delightful, always amusing, frequently incoherent—and, I thought, sometimes affectedly wild, at least paradoxical." The Scots barrister took some pains to cultivate his reputation for eccentricity.

Thomas Erskine, first baron Erskine—radical barrister, lord chancellor, and parliamentary animal welfare crusader—was known for his many pets, including a pair of leeches. (Charles Turner, after Sir Thomas Lawrence, 1806, courtesy National Portrait Gallery, London)

Erskine had other pets besides Home and Cline, including a dog named Toss whom clients might see in chambers sitting upright at a table, a legal tome resting between his paws. He had another beloved dog whom he had rescued from being killed in the street by some boys. His other pets included a goose that followed him wherever he went, and a macaw. All of his friends had their favorite anecdotes about Erskine and his pets, and knew of his love for all animals. His friends also had undoubtedly heard him talk, as Romilly said he had done for years, about "a bill he was to bring into Parliament to prevent cruelty to them." He wanted to end the scenes of cruelty he so often witnessed.

One day in London, Erskine had happened upon a wretched horse pulling a heavily overloaded greengrocer's cart. The animal was a living skeleton. Blood ran down its sides from the open sores worn on its back by the harness, and its fetlock was broken so that with every step, the bone protruded. When Erskine accosted the driver, he responded that if the gentleman was so concerned with the state of this horse, would he give him another one in its place? Erskine offered him a guinea for the animal, at which the owner scoffed that he could work the horse for three more weeks and then sell him to a slaughterhouse, for which he would make four or five pounds. So Erskine bought the horse at that price. As he later said to his colleagues in the House of Lords, such an individual act of kindness might rescue one horse but did nothing to prevent "the sufferings of animals, which meet our eye almost every day, and in almost every street of this metropolis." Laws were needed.

Erskine finally introduced his bill, entitled "An Act to prevent malicious and wanton Cruelty to Animals," on May 5, 1809. Though he was generally considered to be a much less forceful speaker in Parliament than in the courtroom, Erskine's eloquence was in full display as he pleaded the case of British animals almost as if they were innocent defendants unjustly accused. The cart horse, and thousands of other beasts like it, seemed never far from his mind.

When debate began on the bill, Erskine told the Lords that this subject had long occupied his attention, being "very near my heart." He read aloud the bill's preamble, which he had written:

Whereas it has pleased Almighty God to subdue to the dominion, use, and comfort of man, the strength and faculties of many useful animals, and to provide others for his food; and whereas the abuse of that dominion by cruel and oppressive treatment of such animals, is not only highly unjust and immoral, but most pernicious in its example, having an evident tendency to harden the heart against the natural feelings of humanity.

Erskine acknowledged that this was rather solemn language, but, he told the Lords, he knew that his bill was necessarily imperfect and would not alleviate all cruelty, or even most—so perhaps the solemn language would influence some people to govern their own treatment of animals beyond the letter of the law. With that, he launched into one of the greatest pieces of oratory ever delivered on behalf of animals; it is known to this day in animal protection circles as "Lord Erskine's speech."

Neither in his bill nor in his speech did Erskine express ideas that had not been articulated before, nor did his bill suggest that killing animals for food was wrong. God did give man dominion over animals, he argued, but by this he meant a form of stewardship over the brute members of God's creation, and recognition of their right to exist. We may make use of them, but our responsibilities to God require their compassionate treatment, including the recognition of their being and purpose unto themselves. "Animals," he declared, "are considered as property only: to destroy or to abuse them, from malice to the proprietor, or with an intention injurious to his interest in them, is criminal; but the animals themselves are without protection; the law regards them not substantively; they have no rights!"

Unlike the bullbaiting bill, Erskine's expressly took as its purpose the protection of animals—not as a kind of by-product of banning a sport, but as the specific goal of the bill. In a real sense, then, this was the first actual animal protection legislation, the first whose stated aim was to give animals protection *in themselves* from "willful and wanton cruelty." The bill was particularly directed at their treatment as they were being driven to market and in the slaughtering yards. Learning from experience, Erskine avoided explicit mention of bullbaiting: when asked whether it fell within the category of "willful and wanton cruelty," he responded that it would be up to the magistrates to decide.

Attempting to avoid some of the other pitfalls and inequalities of the bullbaiting bills, Erskine proposed a law that would apply to the perpetrators of the cruelty, whether owners themselves or owners' employees; if an employee could show that he treated the animal cruelly as a result of his master's orders, the prosecution would fall upon the master. As to the lower orders of humans so often held responsible for abuses, Erskine said, this was the effect not of nature but of ignorance.

A side benefit of his bill would be to instill into the greater British society the principles of mercy and justice.

Erskine's bill was intended to cover all domesticated animals, but
much of his emphasis fell upon horses, on whose behalf he spoke with
great passion. Drivers were at fault when they beat their horses, he
said, but cruelty could be indirect as well as direct, and thus be perpetrated by the higher social ranks. Every time a gentleman or gentle-
woman insisted that coach drivers whip the horses to get them to town
faster, they were responsible for the consequences in animal suffering:

> Horses panting—what do I say! literally dying under the scourge,
> when on looking into the chaises, we see them carrying to and
> from London men and women, to whom or to others it can be
> of no possible signification whether they arrive one day sooner
> or later, and sometimes indeed whether they ever arrive at all.

This law, by punishing the innkeeper who owned the horses, would
give him justification for refusing to sacrifice them to the whims of his
social superiors when they insisted upon galloping over the roads for
no good reason except to fill up their dreary existences. "I can see no
reason," Erskine exclaimed, "why all such travelers should not endeavour to overcome the *ennui* of their lives, without killing poor animals,
more innocent and more useful than themselves."

Erskine described how people would buy up old, ill, and broken
horses with the intention of overloading them, working them until
they collapsed, and then selling them to the slaughterhouse, where
they were left to die slowly of starvation. Sometimes, the magistrates
had told him, the horses gnawed on each other's manes in their an-
guish. Anticipating the objection that the concept of "willful and wanton cruelty" would be difficult to enforce, he countered by observing
that this was the sort of determination magistrates made every day in
regard to humans, as they decided cases of assault and injury.

The *Times,* which had reversed its earlier position, reprinted extracts from Erskine's speech, editorializing in the bill's support: "Of the necessity of such a measure, no one who walks our streets or travels our roads, if he has the proper feelings of human nature about him, can entertain the least doubt." Such a bill, the newspaper continued, was eminently worthy of its sponsor: he who had put his great talents to the service of defending wrongly accused humans was now laying the foundation to do the same "even for the mute and unconscious part of the creation."

In subsequent debates, several of Erskine's colleagues proposed amendments narrowing the scope of the bill. The earl of Liverpool observed that applying it to all domestic or tame animals would be "ludicrous," so the bill was limited to beasts of burden. Erskine was willing to make any amendments that would allow unanimity, for, he thought, it would give the bill a particular authority and make it less likely to provoke opposition in the Commons. On June 9, the Lords passed the bill unanimously, and sent it on to the Commons—and Willliam Windham.

In his speech, Erskine had made a point of professing respect and admiration for Windham, whom he praised as a humane man. The sponsors of the bullbaiting bill had been sincere, but their emphasis upon the human bullbaiters had obscured the real principle of animal protection. As a result, Windham had opposed the bill because, said Erskine, "it was never fairly presented to his heart, and his intellect had got a wrong bias upon the subject."

When Erskine presented his bill to the Commons, however, he found that Windham's heart remained unmoved. Just as he had opposed the bullbaiting bill, now Windham brought his eloquence to bear on defeating this one. He again delivered the longest speech in opposition, a series of counterarguments amply interspersed with ridicule that elicited boisterous laughter and cries of *"Hear! hear!"* from the assembled members. Some of his arguments were familiar. This bill was partial, he said, and only touched upon certain abuses, leaving out those that members of Parliament were complicitous in themselves: hunting, horse racing, and so on. This bill attempted once again to enforce morals, he also argued, which remained an inappropriate goal of legislation.

In this speech, Windham also struck some new notes. This time, he acknowledged the suffering of animals and said he regretted it. But no other country had ever attempted to legislate how humans treated animals, he observed. Lord Erskine had proclaimed that this bill would represent a "new era in legislation." Yes, indeed: and that was exactly why it needed to be resisted; new eras in legislation should be considered warily, not rushed into. He suspected, he said, that the sponsors of this legislation were motivated by mere glory and ambition (an accusation to which Erskine's reputation for vanity and egotism made him vulnerable). Certainly, being the first to champion the "rights of brutes" was a distinction—though, Windham sneered, not a particularly proud one.

Windham said that he did not object to individuals trying to lessen the suffering of animals, but if the legislature paid too much attention to all the suffering in the world, it would be overwhelmed. How can you legislate compassion? Would a rich man be held accountable because a poor man died in a neighboring street? Our duties to animals fall into the category of "imperfect obligations"—of those acts, such as charity, that cannot be legislated. Furthermore, contrary to Erskine's argument, man's dominion did not logically mean that man should treat animals humanely. If this were true, he asked, where would this end? The logical extension of this bill would be to outlaw the killing of animals for any purpose, including eating them. But then, he pointed out scathingly, "the bill does not recommend that degree of humanity."

Against Windham's speech other MPs spoke heatedly. One pointed out that the old argument that the bill did not go far enough could be made with respect to every criminal law ever passed. Wilberforce agreed, arguing strongly in favor of the bill. When one of Windham's supporters objected that a driver had told him that some horses needed to be beaten to make them obey and that this did not hurt them, another MP suggested that unless he had somehow been metamorphosed into a horse, he could not know it did not hurt them. Romilly spoke at length in favor of his friend's bill, observing that laws against cruelty to humans were routinely left up to magistrates to interpret; why not so for animals? Could anyone doubt, he asked, that if someone were to keep a group of horses and starve them so that they began to eat one another, this was "wanton and malicious" abuse? This elicited shouts of *"Hear, hear!"* from many members, the *Times* reported. The debate went on until three o'clock the next morning, at which point, there being only eighteen legislators still present, the house adjourned. When the vote was finally taken at a subsequent meeting, however, the bill lost, 27–37.

Just as with the bullbaiting bill, the defeat of Erskine's bill did generate some outcry, most eloquently an open letter to Windham, probably written by John Lamb, that refuted his arguments point by point and argued the need to legislate justice and compassion to all creatures. John Lawrence compared the debate on the bill, where the cruelties to horses were glossed over, to earlier slave trade debates, where the "horrors of the middle passage, the murders and cruelties committed upon the negroes, and that compendium of all the crimes that hell itself can instigate, the African Slave Trade, were extenuated—defended."

The following spring, Erskine reintroduced the bill in the House of Lords, having amended it in response to one of Windham's objections. He hoped that its unanimous passage by the Lords the year before meant that it would pass there again, and that his amendment would get it through the Commons. But he was wrong. Perhaps the earlier opposition had been weak because some of the members believed that the bill would never clear the Commons. Now, peers who had been acquiescent before spoke up in opposition. They worried that such a law would be troublesome and potentially open to abuse, and debated its specific wording. Objections also mounted along the lines of Windham's the year before: this matter was not fit for Parliament to legislate upon, being concerned with animals, not humans. It set a dangerous precedent.

Erskine, forced to defend his bill, said that he "received more letters than would fill three trunks as that on their lordship's table, from all parts of the country; detailing the most horrid acts of cruelty." He told of an instance in which a man had killed two mares by thrusting a whip handle into their bodies. The man was not held liable, because it could not be proved that he acted out of malice against the mares' owner. As always, the infliction of injury on the mares themselves was not a criminal offense.

The opponents remained intransigent, however, raising more objections. Erskine expressed surprise at this sudden opposition, when everyone had been silent the previous year and the bill had passed unanimously. Now, saying that he did not want to proceed without unanimity, he reluctantly withdrew the bill. The second round of attempts to legally safeguard animals from cruelty, like the first, had ended in failure.

ON JUNE 4 of that year, William Windham died, probably from delayed complications of an operation he had undergone to remove a tumor from his hip. (To subject oneself to surgery took much courage in those days before anesthetics.) As one admirer remarked, after a long, complex career, Windham had the bad fortune to go down in history primarily as the parliamentary advocate of bullbaiting. The radical journalist Leigh Hunt wrote that while one could understand Windham's opposition to Erskine's bill as a legalistic difference of opinion, there was no possible defense of his position on such a cruel sport as bullbaiting, which was "a mere enjoyment of torture, for which I think there could hardly have been found another regular advocate, besides Mr. Windham, unless they had sent to the Inquisition for one of its familiars."

While clergymen outside of Parliament continued to preach on the need for kindness to beasts, poets continued to give animals a large place in their poems, and all sorts of people lavished their love on pets in unprecedented numbers, the legislative cause of animal protection would languish for more than a decade. That decade was a momentous one. King George III, who in 1810 commemorated fifty years on the throne, was more frequently succumbing to his recurrent fits of "madness" (now thought to have been a genetic disorder of metabolism, porphyria). In 1811, he was finally pronounced incapable of governing and his son appointed prince regent, bringing the Whigs to power and inaugurating the period known as the Regency. England continued to fight for its empire against Napoleon, defeating him once and for all at Waterloo in 1815. The abolitionists, having outlawed the slave trade, now labored to end slavery itself throughout the British empire—a long, slow process that would take twenty-three more years.

In the fall of 1809, a few men in Liverpool met to found an organization they called the Society for Preventing Wanton Cruelty to Brute Animals. Probably inspired by Erskine's bill, the founders meant this society to be one of the many "schemes of benevolence" timed to celebrate the king's jubilee. Their purpose was "to meliorate the state of brute animals, by preventing those sufferings which they unnecessarily experience at the hand of man." This they pledged to do both through attempts to educate the public against abuse of animals, and through "the exercise of coercion." By "coercion," they specified, they meant recourse to the law when possible (as, for instance, enforcing a local ordinance against the overloading of cart horses); shame (presumably public humiliation of offenders susceptible to it); and what they called "individual discountenance" (a term that suggests a wide range of possibilities).

The Liverpool group published a twenty-one-page report stating the cause of its founding: that the abuses suffered by animals were incontrovertibly evident, that this constituted "one of the most pressing grievances of the present age," and that animals had not yet experienced the various improvements in civilized life that had benefited various categories of humans. "Oppression of those who cannot complain, and have no means of redress or revenge, has something in it peculiarly abhorrent to the nature of every generous and enlightened mind: inasmuch as it savours strongly of cowardice, and cannot urge in its justification those provocations which excite the enmity of one man against another," they wrote.

Their particular focus, the society's founders determined, would be on the working animals so central to a busy commercial port city such as Liverpool, particularly its draft horses, who were commonly overloaded and abused. Acknowledging that many other sorts of cruelty abounded elsewhere in Britain, they pointedly rejected a major argument against animal protection that had been effectively voiced in Parliament and in opposing newspapers: that because *"all* good cannot be accomplished, we are, therefore, not called upon to exert ourselves for the production of *any* good." As a local organization, they would concentrate on the instances of animal abuse specific to the metropolis of Liverpool.

The Society for Preventing Wanton Cruelty to Brute Animals was the first animal protection group that we know of. It published a detailed mission statement and held two subsequent public meetings. After this promising beginning, however, it vanished, apparently unable to attract enough members and financial support to continue. Whether the place was Liverpool or the Houses of Parliament in London, the necessary confluence of the right people and the right time had not yet occurred.

So—barring individual intervention such as Erskine's—the horses of Liverpool and everywhere else in Britain continued to be overloaded and abused, and coach horses were still driven to death on country roads. A bill to prevent the reckless and immoderate driving of stagecoaches was introduced in Parliament in 1816: it was designed to prevent injury to passengers and did not mention the horses, though it would have lessened the frequency with which they were whipped and overdriven. It passed the Commons but was dropped in the Lords.

Draft donkeys and horses continued to be starved in the slaughtering yards. A betting event that became popular with young Regency bucks was the timed race, a competition to see who could drive his horse one hundred miles in the shortest time. Many a horse died in these events. Stamford continued its bullrunning; the cockpits and dogfights flourished; and country squires rode with gusto to the hounds.

Erskine's oration in defense of his bill was published, to much admiration in certain circles. But the prince regent's rule brought him no return to office. He more or less retired into private life, making an unsuccessful attempt to farm some land he had bought and contracting an equally unsuccessful, and short-lived, second marriage. He returned to radical causes on occasion, however, and restored his place in the public eye as the people's champion, opposing bills suspending habeas corpus and outlawing seditious meetings. In 1817, Erskine published *Armata,* a fictional voyage resembling *Gulliver's Travels,* where, in thinly disguised form, he retold the story of the failure of his animal protection bills. Asking what could account for Windham's opposition, he came up with only one answer: insanity (of a specific, limited type). He attacked the concept of imperfect obligations and exclaimed that the opponents of his bill misrepresented it when they claimed that it was intended to legislate moral duty. For all it might help to foster the habits of noncruelty in the populace, his bills had been designed not to instill a sense of duty in people, but to prevent them from treating animals cruelly. His focus had not been the humans, he said, but the animals.

Erskine's frustration at the failure of his bills was palpable, but he never followed up on his pledge to introduce another bill that might win passage. As the Napoleonic Wars brought many reforms to a standstill, he may have despaired of getting it passed, or simply wished to pass the baton to another. But no one was at hand in the immediate aftermath to take it up.

And what of Richard Martin? He was an elected member of the House of Commons in 1809, when Erskine's bill was debated there, yet his voice had not been heard. It is possible that, as with the bullbaiting debate, he was not in London at the time. Parliamentary records do not report him as having spoken at all during that session. Financial difficulties had prevented his coming to London to take his seat for an earlier session; perhaps the same had happened again. Whatever the reason for his apparent absence in 1809, Martin continued to serve in Parliament until he was defeated for reelection in 1812 (upon which occasion, he challenged the winner to a duel, although it was never fought). In the election of 1818, however, he regained his seat. And in 1821, three years after his return, Martin took up the cause of animals in Parliament. When he did, this Irish fighter brought to the battle all the force of his "indomitable resolution."

CHAPTER 13

HUMANITY DICK

✳   ✳   ✳

W HEN RICHARD MARTIN rose from his seat to address the House
of Commons, his fellow MPs must have stirred expectantly. At
sixty-seven years old, the feisty Irishman was one of Parliament's most
flamboyant characters, with those dueling scars decorating his body,
that rowdy sense of humor, and that tendency to hurl himself passionately into causes. Martin was not one of the great orators of the Commons, not one of those members who could go on for hours and still
keep his audience spellbound, but he often laced his speeches with
jokes that kept his colleagues laughing. And while he may have come
late to the cause of animal protection, once he had embraced it he
threw himself into the fight with all his characteristic fervor and com-
mitment. Though most of his previous legislative activism had been on
behalf of Irish Catholics, he also had supported ending the death
penalty for forgery, and had tried on several occasions to pass legislation that would establish the equivalent of a public defender's office for
poor people accused of capital crimes, who under existing law faced
the gallows with no one to speak for them in court. He was a reformer,
both by both instinct and by experience.

Still possessing the actor's flair that he had honed as a young man in
Dublin's amateur theatricals, Martin could switch his accent as the occasion required from the broad brogue of his native Connemara
wilderness to the refined upper-class English of a genteel London
drawing room. When he was particularly impassioned, he brought the

Irish to the surface. So it was probably in his brogue that he spoke on that evening, and as usual he made a few jokes to enliven his speech. But the topic he addressed was no joking matter, at least not to him. To many of the other members, however, the occasion for his speech was nothing but a joke, which they greeted with hilarity or indignation, or both. For Dick Martin's purpose was to resurrect the issue of preventing cruelty to animals.

It was June 1, 1821, a year after the death of old, "mad" King George III brought an official end to the Regency period by allowing his estranged son, the former prince regent, finally to take the throne as George IV (although he had not yet been crowned). Martin was speaking in defense of legislation he had introduced, a "Bill to Prevent the Ill-Treatment of Cattle." After a twelve-year hiatus, an animal cruelty bill was once again before the House of Commons. But this time animal protection had a new champion in Hair-Trigger Dick Martin.

This new animal protection bill covered a limited number of species: in its original form, it explicitly addressed cruelty against "any horse, cow, ox, heifer, steer, sheep and other cattle." Under the bill's terms, those who had in their custody any such animals, and who "wantonly and cruelly beat, abuse[d] or ill-treat[ed]" them, could be summoned to appear in the local magistrate's court in the district in which the offense took place if a witness lodged a complaint against them. (Thus, violations were given a status lesser than that of a misdemeanor, a medium-level category of offense that would have sent offenders to the circuit courts where the magistrates had power to impose stiffer punishments.)

Martin had prepared the Ill-Treatment of Cattle Bill with the assistance of Wilberforce and another Evangelical abolitionist, Thomas Fowell Buxton. The Galway MP was far from a Saint, but, as always, political alliances in the name of animals joined disparate people. As he worked on his bill, Martin also sought out the opinions of various authorities. He interviewed magistrates and talked with clergymen, one of whom might well have been his old schoolmaster Dr. Parr, and another of whom was probably an Anglican priest named Arthur Broome, who in recent years had been trying to interest people in forming a society dedicated to animal protection. Martin also consulted John Lawrence, the sober-minded horse expert who had written against cruelty to horses and other animals in his books on horse care and in letters to the *Monthly Magazine* and the *Sporting Magazine*. (Though Lawrence, as befitted his association with the latter magazine, was a defender of the hunt, his attacks on what he saw as willful, malicious cruelty were heartfelt.) Martin and his allies must also have lobbied members of the Commons.

As the journalist William Jerdan observed, for all Martin's eccentricities and zeal, he "was gifted with an abundant fund of sound common sense." His capacity for compromise and moderation and his ability to work with others guided him on this occasion. The limitations in his bill were strategic, for previous history had clearly showed that a more sweeping measure would stand little chance of passing. Times had changed since Erskine's bills of 1809–10, but they had not changed that much, especially within the Houses of Parliament.

In the Commons, Martin's bill was greeted with the usual storm of laughter, ridicule, and outraged hostility, as its opponents rose to denounce it. Their arguments had not changed since a decade before. Some members objected to the bill's specificity. Nicholas Ridley Colborne, a former ally of Wilberforce's in opposing the slave trade, complained that the measure was wholly unnecessary, or at least inefficient, since, he said, it would punish servants for mistreating the beasts while not touching the stagecoach owners who so often broke their horses down by compelling their drivers to whip them on for long distances at great speeds. Besides, he then declared, Parliament these days was becoming much too inclined to legislate on matters that were none of its business. *"Hear, hear!"* cried his fellow MPs.

Alderman Christopher Smith, a wine merchant and former radical, countered that in his opinion this bill to protect horses did not go far enough. Why should Parliament favor only horses, he asked, when cruelty was so often done to asses, too? The alderman was serious, but so comical did some members find the word "asses" that, as he tried to explain himself further, Smith's voice was drowned by "the noise and laughter which prevailed." The *Times* reporter, squeezed into his dark seat at the back of the visitors' gallery, could scarcely hear him. The laughter grew louder when Smith moved an amendment that would insert the word "asses" after "horses" in the bill, and became even louder still when the chairman solemnly repeated the hilarious word. The addition was agreed to, however, and the bill expanded to include "mare, or gelding, mule or ass."

Mr. Monck exclaimed that the bill was utterly unnecessary and deplored the trend of proposing unnecessary legislation, which could lead to dangerous extremes. What, he declared, in mock horror, might happen if a bill for the protection of horses and asses should pass? He would not be surprised if someone next proposed a bill for the protection of—dogs! "And cats!" hooted another member, to a storm of laughter and calls of *"Hear, hear."* Exactly his point, Monck said: if any member was particularly attached to cats, it would be no time at all before the Commons would have to consider a bill protecting them. Though he did not doubt the good intentions of those interested in the welfare of dumb animals, he concluded, "it would be better to leave them as they now were."

Matthew Wood, another alderman, observed that there were already laws protecting animals driven to market within London. Though they governed damage to animals as property, they were, he said, quite sufficient. Alderman Wood, a Dissenter, did take the opportunity to lobby for a reform favored by many Dissenters and Evangelicals. It might be too much to expect Parliament to pass an act against abuse of horses, he complained, when a "much grosser and more pernicious vice" than cruelty—the English National Lottery—was permitted to flourish with impunity.

Thomas Hamilton, Lord Binning, expressed doubts about the propriety of the bill. Mr. Scarlett, a barrister from a Jamaican planter family who had advised the West Indies slave interests during the slave trade abolition bill, agreed that nothing was crueler than to mistreat "unoffending animals," and nothing more humane than to wish to protect them. But still, he said, this was not an appropriate matter for Parliament to legislate. (*"Hear!"*) "Why should there not be an act of parliament to prevent the horrible criminality of hunting a hare?" he asked. (*Cheers.*) After a hard chase, a hare "felt painful sensations and agitated feelings," yet no one was proposing a law to stop cruelty to her. (*"Hear, hear!"*)

As the evening wore on in animated debate infused with ridicule, scoffing, and general hilarity, more MPs spoke for and against the bill and discussed the amount of the fine it would levy and what possibility for judicial appeal it would contain. Scarlett, invoking the concept of imperfect obligations used by Windham against Erskine's bill, complained that the bill would set "a vast machinery" into place "for doing what would more safely be trusted to the moral feelings of men." (*Cheers.*) David Ricardo, the influential economist, resurrected another old argument, observing that when there was so much cruelty in upper-class sports such as fishing and hunting, the bill should not be passed unless it addressed all possible cruelties. For his part, the attorney general, Robert Gifford, echoing Windham, opposed the bill because it established "a new principle in the criminal law." Others, however, rose to say that they supported the bill, applauded its humanity, and wished Mr. Martin success.

Debate on the bill continued throughout June, as provisions were discussed, and amendments offered and voted upon. Throughout this time, an unprecedented number of petitions in support of the bill flooded in from neighborhoods throughout London and towns all over England—there would ultimately be more than thirty, signed by an assortment of magistrates, clergymen, businessmen, and concerned citizens. Advocates of the bill throughout the country were rousing themselves to lobby in this way—and, clearly, large numbers of constituents wanted their members to act on behalf of animals.

The bill's opponents continued to argue along the same lines that had proved so effective at defeating the bullbaiting ban and Erskine's anticruelty bill, and at various moments, when they thought enough of their supporters were present, offered up measures designed to stall or kill it. At one point they nearly succeeded: a member moved to throw the bill out, and a vote on the motion resulted in a tie. The bill seemed about to be lost; those present looked to the well-respected speaker of the House, Charles Manners-Sutton, whose position it was to break the tie. Manners-Sutton cast his vote against the motion, not because he necessarily supported the bill, but because he thought that it should be discussed fully. So the debate continued. An amendment to add bulls to the list of protected animals was defeated.

At last, at the end of a month of often acrimonious debate and amendments, the final vote was taken on June 29. Perhaps to the astonishment of some (including its supporters), the bill passed—and passed by a surprisingly large margin, 40–16. For the first time in history, the House of Commons had approved an act to protect animals. Martin and his allies must have been elated, if exhausted.

Martin was instructed to present the bill to the Lords, which he accordingly did, along with numerous petitions. When the bill came to the Lords on July 4, however, the earl of Lauderdale rose to state he would oppose it, on the grounds that the matter was unsuitable for legislation. But first he would wait to see whether any other noble lord would come forward as sponsor.

The year before, Lord Erskine had once again endeared himself to the British people by speaking vigorously on behalf of the king's estranged but popular wife, Caroline, during her trial for adultery in the Lords (a trial she had essentially won, although she was never to attain her wish to be crowned queen). And Erskine was on the record as having spoken in the Lords in late May 1821. But he seems not to have been in attendance on July 4 or on the crucial days that followed. At seventy-one, Erskine was just four years older than Martin, but he was looking shockingly old and weary, according to those who saw him then. Perhaps he looked so weary partly because it was at the end of June that his second, unhappy marriage came to an end. It may have been a combination of ill health and family difficulties that kept him away from Parliament.

Whatever the reason for Lord Erskine's absence, it was fatal to the bill. Although two more petitions came in during the next few days, no other peers took it up in the week following its introduction. Then, on July 11, the year's parliamentary session came to an end, and all bills that had not been voted into law by that time were dead. The Bill to Prevent the Ill-Treatment of Cattle had failed. Once again, nothing had been done to alter the prevailing conditions under which horses and other animals in Great Britain lived, worked, suffered, and died.

But Richard Martin had never been a man to shrink from a fight, whether conducted with fists, pistols, or words. And he had with him a group of committed allies. Furthermore, the animal welfare advocates in Parliament knew that they were supported by increasing numbers of men and women outside of it, as all those petitions testified. Between 1809 and 1821, something of a movement had begun to emerge on behalf of animals. So Martin and his allies vowed that they would take up the cause again when Parliament reconvened. Having failed in 1821, they would see what 1822 might bring.

WHY WERE MEN like Richard Martin hopeful that they would, eventually, be able to pass legislation protective of animals? Why did the tide seem to be shifting? Modern historians have plausibly suggested one important contributing factor, which was that, with more people crowding into the cities and with the coming of the industrial revolution, cruelty to animals had gained new visibility: their numbers increased and their abuse—which had been traditional, familiar, and therefore seemingly inevitable—took untraditional, urbanized forms. Too, the horrific plight of the country's work animals and of animals in slaughterhouses was relentlessly on display in urban centers. By 1821 and 1822, these new forms of cruelty were so blatant that every day new people were falling into sympathy with the animal protection cause. Like many of these people, and like Lord Erskine before him, Richard Martin was stirred to action by the condition of the nation's cattle, particularly of its horses.

During the parliamentary debate in 1821, Martin had related an anecdote. One day on Ludgate Hill, the road that sloped down from St. Paul's
Cathedral into Fleet Street, a man had begun to beat his horse. This was
a common enough sight on such a large thoroughfare, and something
the fellow could do with impunity, or so he must have thought. But suddenly two men appeared, dragged the man away from his horse, and
pummeled him instead. Afterward, the horse beater discovered to his
outrage that his assailants had been paid five shillings apiece to thrash
him by an elderly gentleman who had stood nearby, watching with evident satisfaction. The gentleman, of course, was Martin.

Given the difference in social status between them, most people in
the horse beater's position would have slunk angrily away, but this man
was aware of his rights—for while no law forbade him from abusing his
animal, laws did forbid the men from abusing him. So he swore out a
complaint for assault and had Martin summoned before a magistrate.
Martin told the magistrate that he had been infuriated by such abuse
of an innocent animal, but that, choosing on this occasion not to "chastise" the perpetrator himself—he was, after all, sixty-seven—he acknowledged having hired the two thugs to do it for him. The magistrate
advised him to settle the matter by giving the plaintiff the substantial
sum of five pounds, and this Martin promptly did.

Martin was by no means the only animal lover of the time who used
violence to stop a person of lower social status from abusing an animal.
Erskine, for example, had been known to intervene physically himself.
But it was rare that the abuser would turn to the law for satisfaction,
since the law was generally the "respectable" person's instrument.
When Martin told the story of this legal turnabout to his colleagues, he
received the loud laugh he was courting, as his colleagues imagined
fire-eating Dick Martin meekly paying his fine.

But Martin had a larger point to make. The law of the land (at least
on some occasions, if not reliably) might be class-blind enough to allow
a driver or carter to bring in a complaint against a gentleman, but it was
not species-blind. The abused horse had no recourse to the law at all,

and could have been beaten to death without the law taking notice, provided that it belonged to the man who killed it. The animal's suffering still did not exist *as such* in the eyes of the law, for the horse was merely property, to be used as his owner saw fit.

Some of the MPs had probably seen relevant notices in the *Times* during the previous year. One reported a trial in the Durham Assizes in which one William Wilson was charged with maliciously maiming a mare. The witnesses' testimonies, explained the judge to the jury, could not provide a "tittle" of evidence that the prisoner felt any malice against the horse's owner. A juror then told the judge that the jury accepted the argument that Wilson did not hold a grudge against the *man*—but they did believe that he felt malice toward the *mare*. The judge explained that malice against an animal was not a criminal offense. Wilson was acquitted.

More recently there had been the matter of the young man in Plymouth who had fired bullets into his horse's eye and body, causing it great agony without killing it. At one point, the man ran out of bullets and paused, as the horse lay wounded, while his brother ran off to *cast* new ones. The shooter showed no guilt or remorse when bystanders rebuked him. Horrified at the horse's prolonged suffering, the witnesses finally got someone to kill the animal. Some of the townspeople had begun the process of bringing a criminal prosecution against the man, the newspaper reported, "when they were informed, to their surprise and sorrow, that there is no law to punish acts of this description, however barbarous or cruel."

In his anecdote about the horse beater, Martin may have been making another point as well—or, at least, another lesson could have been extracted from his story, whether he intended it or not. Hair-Trigger Martin, the King of Connemara, was accustomed to taking the law into his own hands in duels, and actually to *constituting* the law as prosecutor, judge, and jury in his own domain. But retaliation for cruelty to animals should not be left to impromptu, illegal, and (most significantly) ineffectual private "chastisement." It should be regulated and rationalized as a matter of law and law enforcement—as an aspect of a system operating on behalf of the animal as well as of its owner and abuser.

As his telling of this anecdote illustrated, Martin clearly enjoyed playing into English stereotypes about hot-tempered Irish squires who settled problems with fisticuffs, if not with duels. Actually, his speeches in Parliament often displayed a well-informed mind, political independence from both the government and the opposition, and a principled adherence to the measures he considered best for the Irish people, particularly its Catholics. He was quite capable of thinking and acting strategically on behalf of his causes. But many of his colleagues tended to view Martin as a jokester, even a buffoon—an impression he seemed to encourage. He often acted the wag, cultivating his reputation for eccentricity, making speeches so witty that his colleagues were convulsed in laughter, though it also inclined them to underestimate him.

In one famous instance, Martin, objecting to some colorful typographical liberties the *Morning Post* had taken with his parliamentary speeches, had visited the paper's editor, also an Irishman, named Byrne. Squaring his short, stocky body before the journalist, Martin brandished a copy of the paper and demanded, "Sir, did I ever spake in *Italics?*" At this point, both Byrne and Martin burst out laughing. But apparently, upon hearing this story, some of his colleagues in the House did not comprehend that Martin had been joking. (While genuinely aggrieved at what he felt to be the willful misrepresentation of his words, Martin was far from the literal-minded country bumpkin he was pretending to be.) The journalist Carter Hall, who was obviously very fond of Martin, seems to have fallen into the same trap, for he characterized him after his death as a man who had "blundered into reform." Jerdan was more perceptive than Hall, cautioning against the common misperception that Martin had been little more than a "sheer madcap, a blundering blade without rational aim, conduct, or capacity." This was a "great mistake," Jerdan observed: "No madness ever had more method in it."

One method in Martin's madness would be now, after the experience of 1821, to cultivate more allies in the Lords. Almost certainly he met with Erskine to ensure his active presence and support for the second round. Even if their earlier relationship had been strained by Erskine's defense of Martin's wife's lover, that had been twenty-five years ago. They were allies now.

IN THE SPRING of 1822, one of the most famous athletes in all of England was a monkey. Jacco Macacco was a twelve-pound, ash-colored gibbon with black hands and face. He had begun his fighting career some years earlier, when his owner toured him throughout the country, challenging any dog up to twice the monkey's weight to fight him. Jacco had handily won fight after fight, and his fame spread. The people who bet on him were not gambling on whether he would win or lose, but on whether the dog would last five minutes before the monkey killed him.

Jacco gained such fame in his provincial touring life that the proprietor of the Westminster cockpit bought him, "at great expense." Jacco, billed as "the Italian Monkey," became the pit's star attraction, its undefeated champion. The bills advertising his matches declared that "Jacco has fought many battles with some of the first dogs of the day, and has beat them all, and he hereby offers to fight any dog in England of double his own weight."

Amid a din of hoots and whistles, Jacco would be brought into the pit in a small cage, a chain fastened around his waist, which would then be fixed to a steel stake pounded firmly into the ground. Only when the stake was secured would the gibbon be allowed to leave the cage: presumably his human handlers were as afraid of him as the dogs should have been. (His owner, who stood with him in the ring, kept a steel plate between himself and the monkey for protection.) Then they released the dog. Jacco's strategy was either to curl up until the dog was upon him and then reach up for his neck, ripping the dog's windpipe with his teeth, or to jump on the dog's back and attack his neck from there. Unless the dog's owner interrupted the fight, it was over within three minutes—sometimes as quickly as a minute and a half. The dog

George Cruikshank, *Tom and Jerry sporting their blunt* [**money**] *on the phenomenon Monkey Jacco Macacco at the Westminster-Pit* (circa 1820). Pierce Egan, *Life in London*. (Courtesy of Geisel Library, University of California, San Diego)

would usually asphyxiate or bleed to death soon thereafter. Jacco would be covered with blood, but it was the dog's, not his own. With his thick skin he seldom suffered more than a scratch, and a pail of water thrown over him after a fight was enough to restore him to his former appearance. No dog seemed to stand a chance, but that did not keep owners from pitting their champions against him.

That May, the Westminster pit announced a special event along with the usual fare of cockfights, dogfights, and bear- and badger baiting. "The celebrated monkey" Jacco would fight Tom Crib's white bitch, Puss. Puss herself was a very famous dogfighter and rat-killer, so this was a match to behold. That day, a large, eager crowd converged on the pit, which quickly filled, and many were turned away, to their great disappointment. Puss must have made her fans very happy, for she proved to have extraordinary courage, skill, and stamina. She and the gibbon grappled for a full half hour, during which time the two animals literally tore each other apart. Jacco finally managed to get to Puss's throat and slash her windpipe, but not before the dog had ripped off the monkey's lower jaw. Neither of the animals died immediately—some reports say they lived another half hour, others longer than two hours, before they succumbed.

ON MAY 16, 1822, Martin rose once again to address the House. First he presented a petition from the residents of Camberwell (a country resort south of London, now incorporated into the metropolis) asking the Commons to pass legislation protecting animals from the cruelties so often inflicted on them. Then, he said, he would "horrify the ears of the house" if he told them the stories he had heard recently about cruelty to animals—and one story in particular.

Martin brandished a piece of paper, which turned out to be the bill for the match between Jacco and Puss. The Westminster cockpit, he said, attracted "a set of the greatest vagrants that ever existed." He knew that in previous debates some members of the House had declared that Parliament should not interfere with the pleasures of the lower orders, but those who congregated at the pit were hardly the people. Rather, they were "the lowest miscreants." Then, Martin proceeded to read aloud the announcement of the fight between Jacco and Puss, at which a number of his colleagues laughed. And even as he went on to describe the details of the mortal injuries Jacco and Puss had inflicted upon each other, some of the members, apparently far from horrified, continued to laugh.

The Commons were so used to the Irishman's facetious manner that the chuckles would sometimes start the minute he rose to his feet, even before he uttered a word. But Martin was not in a joking mood. He declared that he had no wish whatsoever to interfere with the people's pleasures, but surely this kind of scene could give pleasure "only to the lowest and the vilest of mankind." At this comment, there were cries of *"Hear, hear!"* from some of the other members—presumably those who had failed to find anything funny in the details of Jacco and Puss's death match.

Martin had spoken that day only to insert into the record his observations about the bloody fight. He was setting the stage for what would come. On May 7, he had received permission to bring his Ill-Treatment of Cattle bill before the House once again. It would be debated later that month.

Among his other preparations for the return of his bill, Martin had visited the Westminster cockpit. He had gone on a Sunday when there was no fighting scheduled, for he did not want to have to witness it. He did see the fifty or sixty badgers caged there, and the bear they kept for baiting. (He also met a met a woman who had recently been hospitalized for six months after being clawed and completely scalped by the bear.) A later account described the way in which, as the time for the baiting approached, the bear would start to moan with fear, which would increase as he was dragged out by ropes to be tethered in the ring. His den was scarred with claw marks from his panicked attempts to escape.

Since the issue of banning animal fighting remained contentious, however, Martin knew that if he had any hope of getting his bill through Parliament, he would have to avoid directly addressing it. But the presence of the Westminster pit and the others scattered all around London would have been another continuing reminder of the kind of suffering inflicted on animals that occasionally burst into wider public attention, as it had with Jacco and Puss.

ON MAY 24, 1822, debate began on Martin's second Ill-Treatment of Cattle bill. The bill stated, "Whereas it is expedient to prevent the cruel and improper Treatment of Horses, Mares, Geldings, Mules, Asses, Cows, Heifers, Steers, Oxen, Sheep, and other Cattle," any person or persons who "wantonly and cruelly beat, abuse[d], or ill-treat[ed]" any of these animals, would, upon the sworn statement of a witness, be summoned before the magistrate. Those convicted would be fined not less than ten shillings and not more than five pounds. If unable or unwilling to pay, the offender would be sent to prison for not longer than three months.

The usual efforts were made by opponents to dismiss the bill, though, perhaps because of the outcome the previous year, they seemed more perfunctory than before. The attorney general tried to stall the bill; Martin accused him of going against "the common sense of the whole nation." Every pulpit in London, he said, had "spoken in a pronounced manner in approbation of it." More surprisingly, other potential obstacles came from his allies. Buxton said that he still had some objections to the bill, and urged Martin to withdraw it in order to introduce an amended measure the following year. Martin refused, however—clearly he felt that he needed to take advantage of the vote the year before. Who knew what further delay might bring? More of the usual arguments were made, pro and con. But this year, as in the year before, the proponents had the votes: the Commons did not disappoint Martin as the Lords had disappointed Erskine in 1810. The bill passed by a substantial voice-vote margin on June 7, 1822.

Now the bill had to go to the Lords—but this time, Lord Erskine was there, ready to take up the cause. On June 10, when the bill was read for the first time, he expressed his satisfaction that it had been passed by the Commons, and presented several petitions in its favor. It was scheduled for discussion a month later. Given its fate the previous year, this must have been an interval of some anxiety. But, with Erskine championing the legislation, the feared opposition did not materialize. Though the peers had the opportunity to suggest amendments that would have sent the bill back to the Commons, they did not do so. Without further amendment, the bill was put into committee on Erskine's motion on July 17, and brought up for final consideration on July 18. Erskine was not in attendance on that final day, but he had done his work. The bill passed easily. It next went to the king, who gave his royal assent on July 22. The Ill-Treatment of Cattle Act, the world's first animal protection law passed by a national legislature, was a reality.

One newspaper wrote: "Lord Erskine tried to deliver the beasts from their bondage, but he completely failed. Mr. Martin's success shows the superiority of genius over learning." (By "genius," the newspaper meant the fortunate combination of particular aptitude and strong inclination for a chosen task.) But, in justice to Erskine, it would have been more accurate to say that the success showed the change in attitudes between 1810 and 1822: Martin had been able to take advantage of twelve additional years of public discourse about the issue. The Scotsman's contributions had been instrumental in paving the way. He could be excused if he felt a pang at seeing someone else's name forever attached to the law he had desired for over thirty years, at the knowledge that he himself would not be the one to receive from posterity the honor given to Humanity Dick Martin. But Lord Erskine had played a vital part, and the history of animal protection has not forgotten him.

Martin's Act was now the law. The next step was to enforce it.

A YEAR AFTER the bill's passage, on a late summer day in 1823, a vegetable hawker named Thomas Worster was weaving through the crowds and traffic of Fleet Street. Beside him plodded his donkey, pulling a small cart heaped with produce. Flicking his long whip over the donkey's back, Worster steered the little animal slowly along the edge of the congested street, trying to squeeze between the people pushing by on the walkway and the coaches and heavy wagons that vied with one another in the center. "Turnips and carrots, ho!" he cried for the thousandth time, straining to force his voice above the clamor.

Suddenly, four large horses pulling a massive stagecoach thundered past. Terrified, the tiny donkey shied and bolted, sending vegetables tumbling into the manure-clogged road. Worster was usually fond of his donkey, whom he fed well, but the creature was so exasperatingly timid, always frightened by the coaches, and the greengrocer was a short-tempered man. He must also have been hot, weary, and footsore after a day spent trudging the streets eking out a difficult living, his throat raw from his incessant cries, his feet and shins caked with muck. Flying into a rage, he pulled out a thick leather strap and began to beat the cowering animal. Again and again the strap's iron buckle cut into the donkey's flesh.

So ferociously did Worster rain blows onto his donkey's back as he drove him along Fleet Street that some passersby paused to stare, disturbed by the sight. Most of them did not think of interfering in this commonplace scene, however. But when Worster lifted his arm to strike yet again, his blow was interrupted by an angry bystander, a stocky gentleman of about seventy who moved with the vigor of someone much younger. A dozen other spectators now sprang to assist the donkey's defender, and Worster, to his astonishment, found his cart pulled up short and his name and license number written down. The outraged gentleman exclaimed in a strong Irish brogue that he had been following the vendor as he thrashed his donkey for nearly a quarter of a mile! If Worster thought that he could beat his animal so brutally with impunity, times had changed: the poor beast now had the law on its side. The costermonger had violated the law that by then had come to be popularly known as Mr. Martin's Act. According to its provisions, Worster would be summoned to bring his donkey to the magistrate's court at the Guildhall. There, the greengrocer would again face his accuser, whose name, he would learn, was Richard Martin. Humanity Dick himself was enforcing his law.

When he appeared with Worster before the magistrate, Martin opened with a brief but impassioned speech; he probably shed his brogue in favor of his cultivated English accent. He described how frequently donkeys were subjected to such cruelty by "monsters upon two legs" such as the defendant, whom he had watched beat his animal in "the most violent and atrocious manner." A thick leather strap like the one Worster used on his donkey, Martin exclaimed, was so dangerous a weapon that, when the French army used to punish its soldiers by flogging them with such belts, most of them died.

His act had established a new "era in legislation," he told the magistrate, because for the first time in history, "it gives rights to brutes— rights against their masters." The new law was highly controversial, however, and its opponents included members of the judiciary. Furthermore, although members of the public now had the right to swear out complaints against animal abusers, and were beginning to do so, they had to be encouraged by the example of successful prosecutions. So Martin, who had assisted attempted prosecutions of abusers prior to the passage of his law, was determined to bring abusers to justice now that there were clear grounds for doing so—whether that meant showing up in court to support others' prosecutions, as he did, or bringing charges himself. Once in the courtroom he would marshal all his considerable force of personality to insist that the magistrate actually apply the law. But Martin's purpose was greater than simply the punishment of individual offenders. Securing convictions, he was convinced, was the only way to spread the word among the populace that such egregious cruelty would no longer be tolerated.

Worster, who arrived at the Guildhall with his wife, admitted that he had beaten his donkey. But, he protested, he really did care for his beast and usually treated him kindly, as the magistrate could see for himself if he would just step into the street where the donkey waited. "Please, your Worship," he told the magistrate, "I always uses the animal well; he's as fat as a mole, your worship, and as good a creature as need be; only he's a little obstinate, and he shies and flies back at the stages, he's so *timorsome*."

"Why, man, you are justifying your conduct," retorted Martin. "I thought you said you was very sorry for what you had done."

Worster insisted that he *was* sorry: "I never beat him but when I'm in a passion," he explained, "and I'm always sorry for it afterwards." If his honor would take pity on him this time, he promised the magistrate, he would never beat his donkey again.

Mollified by Worster's remorse and his promise to reform, Martin asked the magistrate to levy the smallest possible fine, ten shillings. At this, Mrs. Worster exclaimed that even ten shillings were more than poor folk such as they could afford. So when Worster promised the court that in the future he would always lead the donkey instead of driving him with a whip, and that he would tell all his fellow drivers to do the same, Martin pulled out his purse and said he would go halves with him on the fine. Worster paid his share and left the courtroom "seeming very well pleased," according to the *Times*.

Martin must have been satisfied with the outcome, too. Volatile as he was, he was conscious that reform legislation such as Martin's Act could fall harshly upon laboring-class people, especially the donkey and horse drivers who would feel the brunt of the legislation, essential though it was. It was imperative to enforce the act, so in the years after its passage, Martin often patrolled the streets, dragging the worst offenders in front of the magistrates. But when his prosecution was successful and the miscreant seemed to have learned a lesson, he would often pay the fine himself. This was both a testimony to his well-known sympathy for the poor, and another indication that this hotheaded legislator could indeed behave strategically, for too harsh a penalty could generate a public sympathy for the offender.

Most importantly, it was necessary to spread the word. Prosecution was not the real point: the true, necessary goal was prevention. Society must learn to consider cruelty to animals unacceptable; attitudes must change. So Martin must have been gratified when Worster's story spilled from the courtroom and the newspapers into the streets. As people strolled through London, amid the cacophony assaulting their ears they might have caught the strains of a popular song set to a traditional ballad about a man and his donkey. Though the tune was old and familiar, the lyrics had been recently tweaked to bring them up to date.

> If I had a donkey wot wouldn't go,
> D'ye think I'd wallop him? no, no, no!
> But gentle means I'd try, d'ye see,
> Because I hate all cruelty;
> If all had been like me, in fact,
> There'd have been no occasion for Martin's Act.
> Dumb animals to prevent being crack'd,
> On the head.

Passing by a print shop window, they might have stopped to chuckle over several cartoons making fun of the same subject. These referred to a later stanza of "If I had a donkey," in which the animal himself

A donkey appears against his owner, "Bill Burn," under Martin's Act (the paper lying in the left foreground, beside the belt). "Bill Burn" was not a real person, but rather the satirist's opinion of what Parliament should have done with Martin's bill. (The ballad, expressing another point of view, refers to the owner as "Bill Bore.") The caption quotes a stanza from the song: "Bill's donkey was ordered into Court, / In which he caus'd a deal of sport, / He cock'd his ears, and op'd his jaws, / As if he wished to plead his cause." (P. Mathews, engraver, after Charles Hunt, *The Trial of "Bill Burn" under Martin's Act*, courtesy of the Royal Society for the Prevention of Cruelty to Animals, Horsham, West Sussex, U.K.)

enters the courtroom to testify against his abuser. Most of these cartoons satirized Martin and his controversial act, for attitudes were exceedingly slow to change. But the caricatures would have pleased Humanity Dick nonetheless, since they also spread awareness of the law—and of the moral principle behind it.

CHAPTER 14

FOR THE LOVE OF ANIMALS

❋ ❋ ❋

T HE CASE of Thomas Worster and the donkey wot wouldn't go was
not Humanity Dick's first prosecution. By that time, he had been
vigorously pursuing enforcement of his law for a year, having begun
his efforts within days of the king's assent. During the first month he
brought in several prosecutions, all of men who had abused horses.
The newspapers that summer and fall made frequent reference to Martin in the courts, and there were several accounts of other people who
lodged complaints against abusers. Many, though not all, of these prosecutions were successful.

One case, however, sent a different message. A witness brought a
complaint against one William Pocknell, proprietor of an oyster shop in
St. Martin's Lane, whom he had seen deliberately take a large vat of
boiling water used to cook lobsters and pour it over a little dog that was
nearby. The poor animal was badly scalded and ran around crying
piteously; a number of people, appalled, berated Pocknell so heatedly
that he retreated to the back of his shop. The two magistrates who
heard the case, convinced that the act fell under the definition of willful
and wanton cruelty, were about to levy a fine according to the provisions of Martin's Act when, looking over its preamble, they realized that
it did not mention dogs. Furthermore, it was obvious that dogs could
not be construed as falling into the category of "other cattle." Reluctantly, they dismissed the charges. Immediately afterward, another case
was brought before them, against a journeyman poulterer for plucking

a live chicken—a common practice, for the feathers were thought to come off more easily from a living bird. The witness had protested to the journeyman, who replied that he had better get out or he would get his own feathers plucked, and a kick in the arse as well. Once again the magistrates deplored the cruelty, but had to dismiss the case.

The limitations of Martin's Act were already becoming apparent. In some cases, such as those just described, the magistrates wanted to convict but the animals were not covered. In other cases, magistrates who were reluctant to convict found that the language of the act— "wantonly and cruelly beat, abuse, or ill-treat"—allowed them to dismiss charges by saying that the act was not wanton, or that it was not both wanton *and* cruel and that it had to be both; or they held that overloading a wagon, for instance, was not beating, abusing, or ill-treating. In the next session of Parliament, Martin began the work that would occupy the rest of his legislative career: the attempt to pass more legislation, both to amend and strengthen his own act, and to extend protection to other kinds of animals.

For his first attempt, Martin plunged into the most contentious territory of all: he sought leave to introduce a bill to ban bullbaiting and dogfights. Again, he encountered the familiar objection that unless the sports of the upper classes were also banned, none should be. Martin, however, had prepared for this argument, which he called "most absurd." If five hundred people were cast away on a desert island and could not all be saved, he asked, did that mean that none of them should be saved? (Wilberforce, who remained a strong supporter of Martin's efforts, commented that this "most fallacious" class argument "has its root in a contempt for the poor," since those who used it did not actually care about their well-being.) Martin also suggested that if upper-class sports were really as cruel as some of his opponents insisted, then they should use their influence to put an end to them. They could start with the king's own hounds and stags themselves: what an example of benevolence that would be! But he could rally so little support that he was forced to withdraw the bill. When, shortly thereafter, he introduced a bill to strengthen his own act by making malicious cruelty to animals a misdemeanor, it failed. The next year, he was back again with the same amendment. This time it passed the Commons but failed in the Lords. Bills he introduced to ban bearbaiting and regulate the slaughterhouses that session were also derailed.

It had become clear to everyone concerned that the effort to protect animals needed to operate on many fronts. Martin, though he seemed to be everywhere at once, had his limits. And as important as it was to try to get more and better legislation through Parliament, the battle had to be waged elsewhere as well. The law itself, though critical, could only go so far to actually change behavior. It was helpful to have greater numbers of prosecutions brought in, but it was even more necessary to educate people out of habits of cruelty. Society had to stop sanctioning cruelty, and people also had to internalize consideration for animals: the most effective counter to cruelty was for individuals to stop themselves before they raised that whip, cudgel, or knife. The task had three aspects: legislation, law enforcement, and education. To accomplish all three, animal protectionists had to organize, just as abolitionists had so effectively done. They had to unite the efforts of numerous people, not just in Parliament but outside of it, too. They had to become an organized movement.

In earlier decades, especially when legislation such as Erskine's bill had captured momentary public attention, a few people who maintained that individual opinions and efforts were not enough to combat animal abuse had called for founding an organization. One such call had resulted in the Liverpool group, The Society for Preventing Wanton Cruelty to Brute Animals, which was started in 1810 but never entirely got off the ground. In 1820 and 1821, a series of letters on the same theme published in the *Monthly Magazine* generated a larger response. Several correspondents agreed with a writer who said that the "unsupported and desultory attempts" that had been made for animals so far had been ineffectual, and that the only solution was to unite. One correspondent was a clergyman signing himself "Clericus" who proposed calling a meeting and asked others to correspond with him. Clericus, it has been plausibly suggested, was the Reverend

Arthur Broome. This meeting took place in the fall of 1822, when the small group of attendees formed a committee to draft a plan for an organization, and formally thanked Richard Martin for his efforts in passing his act. Nothing more came of this group, however. But, after two years had made apparent the strengths and weakness of Martin's Act, there was new incentive to organize. A genuine movement was rising.

Not a great deal is known about Arthur Broome, who became the founder and first secretary of the Society for the Prevention of Cruelty to Animals, a name he chose himself. As a result, the society's founding has sometimes been inaccurately credited to Martin, but Humanity Dick took pains to acknowledge Broome's indispensable role: "I have nothing at all to do with it," he said a year after its founding; "it is quite a child of Mr. Broome's, and he has acted the part of a good father to it; I must say that." A graduate of Oxford's Balliol College, Broome held curacies in Kent and then became pastor of Bromley, Middlesex, but in 1824 he resigned his clerical position to devote himself to the cause. He must have been in his mid-forties at the time, and he had already published an edition of Humphrey Primatt's *The Duty of Mercy* to which he contributed a preface and additional notes. He dedicated it to Richard Martin, "whose active and unwearied zeal, both in a public and private capacity, in endeavouring to promote a more just and humane treatment of the brute species, bears ample testimony to the benevolence of his heart, and presents an example worthy of imitation." In his second edition of *The Duty of Mercy,* published in 1823, he added a note saying that proceeds from the sale of the book (if there were any) would go to the SPCA—which at that point had not yet been founded. Broome was a hopeful and determined man.

A GREEN PLAQUE now marks the historic site on St. Martin's Lane in Covent Garden, London's formerly raffish theater district, where Old Slaughter's Coffee House once stood. (The coffeehouse's name, ironic under the circumstances, was that of its original proprietor.) On June

16, 1824, Broome called a meeting at the coffeehouse for the purpose of founding an organization dedicated to animal protection.

Twenty-one other men responded to Broome's summons that day. Prominent among them were Martin, Wilberforce, and Buxton, who was now leading the parliamentary battle to abolish slavery throughout British territories. Buxton chaired the meeting. Other MPs present included Sir James Mackintosh, a legal reformer who had collaborated with Martin in a bill to end the death penalty for forgery; James Martin, a City banker (and no relation to Richard); and the liberal politician John Ashley Warre. One notable name was sadly missing from the list of legislators who attended, however: Lord Erskine had died the year before.

Several present, in addition to Broome, were clergymen, including the Calvinist Anglican priest Carus Wilson, a prolific author of cheap religious tracts for the working classes, a founder of charity schools, and, at seven feet four inches tall (in an era in which six feet was quite large for a man), literally a towering figure—he used to amuse people by lighting his cigar at street lamps. Other attendees included Basil Montagu, a barrister, legal reformer, and patron of many Romantic poets; the Tory journalist and writer William Mudford, editor of the newspaper the *Courier;* and Alexander Henderson, a liberal Scots physician and wine connoisseur who surrounded himself with artists and writers.

Also present was Lewis Gompertz, a wealthy Jewish businessman and prolific inventor who, in an age when even vegetarianism was eccentric, was what we today call a vegan (the term did not then exist). Gompertz, politically and personally the most radical of the SPCA's founding fathers, abstained from all animal food and refused to ride in coaches because of the abuse of the horses. Already deeply devoted to the cause of animal welfare, he published that same year his book, *Moral Inquiries on the Situation of Man and of Brutes,* in which he told horrific stories of the routine cruelty to beasts in high life and low, attacked vivisection, defended animal intelligence and emotions, and compared the treatment of animals with that of slaves—and women. (The early feminist Mary Wollstonecraft had said that women were often treated like animals. Gompertz took this analogy one step further.)

It is heartening to imagine these very different, yet all similarly dedicated men seated around a long table in one of the coffeehouse's private rooms, sipping their cups of thick, dark coffee and leaning forward intently to speak. They discussed the impact of the Ill-Treatment of Cattle Act, which, Martin proudly proclaimed, had led to a "revolution in morals." For example, he knew a gentleman who, when a favorite horse that had served him for years went lame, sold it to pull a coal cart in the mines; but now the gentleman had become ashamed of himself and feared that his friends would learn what he had done.

The men agreed that their efforts needed to be directed at the laboring classes, whose habitual abuse of their horses and donkeys, Buxton said, made them more bestial than their animals. They debated how much of their energy should go into prosecution and how much should be spent propagandizing. Broome felt that they should concentrate on publishing tracts and sermons, but Martin expressed doubts about the efficacy of propaganda alone. He knew well the sort of men they were dealing with, he argued, and only the threat of prosecution was forceful enough to change their behavior—although, he cautioned, the society's purpose would be undermined if they become known as nothing more than "a confederacy of prosecutors."

The group agreed to adopt Broome's name for them, the Society for the Prevention of Cruelty to Animals, and appointed him the first honorary secretary. The SPCA's first priorities—this was a compromise—should be multiple: to ensure that Martin's Act was enforced; to educate the public about animal welfare through publications; to investigate the condition of animals in the markets, streets, and slaughterhouses; and to pass stronger laws that would extend greater protection to more kinds of beasts. Mackintosh expressed his wish also to look into humane methods of slaughtering cattle.

Carter Hall, who covered the meeting, wrote that Martin's energy rallied everyone as they assessed the sheer magnitude of the task. When they shook their heads about the likelihood of Parliament's passing more legislation, Martin exclaimed that he would *make* 'em do it." The men divided themselves into two committees. One, whose membership included Wilberforce, Montagu, Gompertz, and Henderson, would be dedicated to publishing tracts and sermons in order to influence public opinion. (The Reverend Broome would also publish an edition of Erskine's speech, whose title page lists several London businesses that would accept donations on behalf of the SPCA. One of them was Mr. Hatchard's Book Shop in Piccadilly, which still sells books there today.) The other, whose mission was to devise methods for better enforcing Martin's Act in the streets, markets, and slaughterhouses, included Buxton, Mackintosh, and, of course, Richard Martin. Following the lead of Broome, who had used his own meager funds to hire a man named Charles Wheeler to monitor Smithfield Market and prosecute offenders, the society subsequently employed its own inspectors.

Within a few years of Martin's Act, reports were coming in that, for all its gaps and weaknesses, the law was nonetheless making a significant difference in the way at least some large animals were being treated. In 1825, Buxton reported to the Commons that Martin's Act had already resulted in seventy-one prosecutions, and convictions had been won in sixty-nine of them. People familiar with Smithfield Market, one of London's principal slaughterhouses, said that "a great revolution" had taken place there. Even some of those connected with that market who had originally opposed the bill had come to support it— and had joined the SPCA, Buxton said.

Since the founding of the SPCA, Martin had accelerated his efforts in Parliament to *"make* 'em do it." Though over seventy years old, he seemed as indefatigable as ever. Martin once said that his political strategy was to throw so much mortar at the wall that some had to stick. Now, embracing that tactic, he rose to introduce bill after bill, braving scorn, ridicule, and ad hominem attacks. True, he still at times played to the laughter, telling jokes on himself, delivering his messages with droll asides, exploiting his reputation as a rough and ready westerner. But he also seemed to register a new urgency that increased as his efforts were stymied one after another. In response, the hostility and impatience of many of his colleagues intensified, and there were always newspaper reporters and satirists eager to take up the task of attacking him. One of his most consistent allies, Wilberforce, retired in 1825.

When the Westminster pit advertised a program of rat catching, dogfighting and badger fighting, and bearbaiting, its advertisement boasted that this would all take place by "the express invitation of several noblemen and gentlemen of the first distinction." Martin read this ad to the Commons as he introduced another bill against bearbaiting. He declared that he had heard too often the accusation from his opponents that he "meddled only with the sports of the poor" and ignored those of the rich. Well, he said, brandishing the ad, here was proof positive that he was "equally anxious to meddle with both, when he found them opposed to the dictates of humanity." Yet when it finally came up for a vote, the bearbaiting bill was once again defeated.

That year, Martin also introduced another bill to strengthen Martin's Act; it lost. Then he introduced a bill to strengthen an earlier act governing the mutilating of cattle; this was defeated as well. In 1826, he introduced another bearbaiting and dogfighting bill, for which he presented fifty-two supporting petitions. Furthermore, he told the members, he was receiving accounts of cruelty from citizens all across the kingdom. When his opponents repeated the accusation that he was standing against the people's will, he could point to all these petitions and letters and ask, "Who, exactly, are 'the people'?" Yet this bill, like the others, lost.

When, that same year, Martin introduced a bill to prevent cruelty to dogs, a member who had been consistently hostile, the Scotsman Joseph Hume, member for Montrose, asked him sarcastically whether he didn't want to protect *cats,* too. Amid the gales of laughter this provoked, Martin said heatedly that surely he would wish to protect them, since cats were subjected to many kinds of cruelty, some of which he named. Hume responded that Martin had trapped himself in a double bind: while introducing a bill that did *not* include cats would be inconsistent, introducing one that *did* include them would be ridiculous. Calls to order filled the House at this point, referring, the *Times* reporter deduced, to "certain odd gesticulations used by the hon. member for Galway, and directed at the hon. member for Montrose."

As Martin barraged the Commons with bill after bill, he often put the discussion on the agenda in the early hours of the morning, in the hopes that as the attendance dwindled, he and his allies who remained would be able to win the vote. When a measure was voted down, he would put up another one quickly—in one instance, during the same evening. But none of them passed.

In fact, many of Martin's fellow MPs had become quite weary of hearing about cruelty to animals from the honorable member from Galway. In a speech given to the SPCA on its first anniversary in 1825, Humanity Dick recounted how his bills "were thrown out actually before they were brought in," and how an "outcry" was raised against him the minute he announced his intention to bring one in. As to the oft-repeated charge of class bias, he declared that he would happily outlaw all cruelties, including those gentlemanly sports he had once enjoyed himself: "But if I can't get 100 per cent, why, then, I must be satisfied to take 50 or 25 per cent," he said. He had to admit, however, that as a member of Parliament he blushed "to be obliged to confess that the great indisposition to put an end to cruelty to animals exists in the Houses of Parliament itself." Why, he said, it seemed that there was more support for cruelty in St. Stephen's Chapel than in the bear garden. He was sure that of the more than six hundred members of the Commons, "there are ten to one against any measure to diminish the sufferings of the brute creation."

Opposition to Martin and his reforms was being expressed not only on the floor of the House, but in print as well. The *Times* reprinted an article from the *Dublin Star* entitled "Mr. Martin of Galway, a Brahmin," which reported facetiously that Martin had become a believer in metempsychosis. The author gleefully wondered how shocked he would be to die and to find himself reincarnated as a water rat, a church mouse, or a watchdog: "Only conceive how Mr. Martin would look if he were transformed into a huge, surly mastiff, chained to a kennel," he sneered.

Martin had other enemies among the press, especially the *Morning Chronicle,* which often mocked him as "the Professor of Humanity." On September 5, 1825, the *Chronicle*'s lead article gleefully quoted at length a diatribe published in *Blackwood's Edinburgh Magazine,* which called Martin an "Irish jackass," a "blustering and blundering blockhead," and an "impertinent and provoking puppy," who weekly "infests" the police offices with his "vulgar and angry gabble." *Blackwood's* also expressed the desire "to see his skull, thick as it is, cracked some day." (The *Chronicle* did not quote, though it alluded to, a subsequent sentence: "Why don't they murder him?") That *Blackwood's* would publish, and the *Chronicle* quote approvingly, such incitement to assault—even to murder—underscores the danger Martin ran with his highly visible prosecutions. (It was not unimaginable that an angry, club-wielding drover or coachman might decide to waylay him in a dark street.) The *Chronicle* followed this up by denouncing Martin for class bias: the writer asserted that there was far greater cruelty to animals perpetrated among the upper and middle classes, including in his friend the king's own stables, than could be found among the lower orders.

The *Courier,* whose editor, William Mudford, was one of the SPCA's founders, defended Martin's character and motives against this "vulgar trash." But the *Chronicle*'s attack clearly upset Martin, who was outraged by the class bias argument and took seriously the call to violence. The next day, he wrote to William Ayrton, the paper's music critic (who was sympathetic to animal protection), complaining that the incessant attacks were setting back their cause. Could Ayrton have a word with the proprietor, William Innell Clement, and ask him "why such a war is kept up to defeat the object of one whose intentions are but to do good—since it cannot render the *Morning Chronicle* popular?" On the following day, prosecuting a cruelty case before a sympathetic Guildhall magistrate, Alderman Bridges, Martin prefaced his testimony with a response to the *Chronicle* writer's charge of class bias: "If he, or any other gentleman whatever, will point out to me any act of cruelty practiced by the highest nobleman or gentleman in the land, be he whom he may, I pledge myself to prefer a prosecution against him." He also initiated a highly publicized lawsuit against Clement and the *Chronicle*'s editor, John Black. For all its unpleasantness, this feud (during which the *Chronicle* began to mock him as "Don Quixote") did generate a considerable degree of public sympathy for Martin and his cause.

WHILE MARTIN WAS fighting on these fronts, the SPCA, after a promising beginning, was entering a very difficult decade. In its first year, the society had engaged in numerous successful prosecutions, having hired two of its own inspectors to patrol the streets and Smithfield Market. Furthermore, it published several tracts on compassion to animals. But problems soon began to loom. While it met regularly during those early months, as its minutes book reveals, often its meetings were very thinly attended. It was derided in the press and in satiric prints as a group of overzealous animal-loving meddlers. The most dangerous threat—as Richard Martin, always in financial difficulties himself, must have appreciated—was debt. The society's inspectors, its publications, and the cost of maintaining an office needed money faster than the donations came in. Broome spent what small income he had on valiantly attempting to preserve the society, for whose expenses he was liable. But in 1826, he went bankrupt and was thrown into debtors' prison. Lewis Gompertz, who became acting secretary during Broome's incarceration, joined with Martin to bail him out, but even so the SPCA, teetering on the edge of collapse, had to suspend operations.

Meanwhile, Martin was confronting his own trials, both old and new. First of all, for all the buckets of mortar he hurled at the legislative wall, he was not able to make any more of it stick. Despite almost superhuman persistence, his confident vow that he would *"make 'em do it"* came to naught. And, after twenty-five years in Parliament, his legislative career followed suit. Once, in a heated exchange with an opposing MP whose constituency was preparing to submit a petition supporting one of his bills, Martin suggested that his opponent would pay a price at the polls for his unpopular position. But it was Martin himself who paid: in 1826, he lost his bid for reelection.

However ridiculous Martin had made himself in some people's eyes by fighting for animal protection, it was not this cause that cost him his seat, but the fraught business of Irish politics. The Galway election of 1826 was even more corrupt, contentious, and violent than usual, and, after the contested election results had unfolded over many months into the spring of 1827, he became its casualty. If the consequences of this defeat for the cause of animal protection were grave, they were equally grave for Martin himself. His financial precariousness had always made him vulnerable; he had accumulated large debts that had long gone unpaid, and had been in court over his obligations more than once. As an MP, however, he had been immune from arrest for debt. Suddenly that immunity was gone.

With his creditors baying at his heels, Martin and his family had to flee the country for France, taking up residence in Boulogne, where they joined the sizable colony of British debtors living just out of reach of the law. There, Martin would spend the rest of his life. A poem dedicated to him spoke of "that dark and dismal day / Which saw thee migrate from Britannia's shore." No longer, mourned the poet, would England benefit from Humanity Dick's "flashes of philanimalian fire." From the other side of the Channel, he watched the fate of the cause to which he had devoted his last years in Britain.

In exile, Martin continued to correspond with members of the SPCA as they attempted to save the organization. During its period of suspension, Broome remained nominal secretary, but in 1828, Gompertz took over in that position and worked to reanimate the society. Broome's own involvement gradually diminished, until in the early 1830s he ceased altogether to attend meetings. (He moved to Birmingham, where he died in 1837.) Under Gompertz's guidance, the SPCA began to rebound. He settled accounts from his own, much deeper pockets, used his business acumen to put the society on a healthier, if still not entirely secure, financial position, and attracted new patrons (including a number of women). He corresponded with Martin on animal protection issues, and embarked upon an ambitious program of publication, prosecutions, and lobbying.

But under Gompertz's stewardship internal dissension plagued the group. In 1830, as Martin watched helplessly from abroad, the SPCA splintered. Some relatively conservative animal protection advocates disapproved of the secretary's leadership, criticizing the use of what they called "paid informers" (the society's inspectors), which Gompertz supported, and deploring what they saw as the misguided zeal with which he (and previously Martin himself) engaged in prosecutions. As would soon become apparent, they also harbored other reservations about the honorary secretary. They founded another organization, the Association for Promoting Rational Humanity Towards the Animal Creation. Despite their policy differences, the two groups worked together on several fronts: education, pamphleteering, legislation, investigation, and, indeed, prosecution, at least of the more extreme cases. So from an early point in the animal protection movement, there was a second organization dedicated to the cause; others would arise soon thereafter.

Policy disagreements were not the movement's only troubles: religious intolerance soon took its toll, and its major victim was the SPCA secretary. The APRHAC began to attack Gompertz for the "Pythagorean principles" they detected in his book, *Moral Inquiries,* and for adopting the vegetarian diet advocated by Porphyry, an ancient opponent of Christianity. Although the SPCA's governing committee nominally supported Gompertz and awarded him a silver medal to honor his service, by 1832 they were considering a merger with the APRHAC. The merger, discussed in a public meeting, was rejected, but the members had undermined Gompertz's authority. Soon thereafter the SPCA voted to endorse a statement similar to one the APRHAC had adopted: it declared that the society was based solely "on the Christian faith, and on Christian principles"—an obvious message to their Jewish secretary. Subsequently, the membership voted to discontinue using inspectors and to devote the society to education.

Gompertz felt forced to resign. He and his supporters formed a third group, the Animals' Friend Society for the Prevention of Cruelty to Animals, which was open to all and, as befitted its founder, more radical in its approach, more willing to criticize upper-class sports, for instance. Now, within the space of a decade, three animal protection organizations had been founded, each vying for limited donations. Trying to raise funds for the AFS, Gompertz observed that for the public "to give their good money merely for suffering animals, appeared to them as so much thrown away" and that "to talk of humanity towards beasts appeared to Englishmen as insanity." Within this climate of limited public support, all three societies for some time continued to work for the same cause, but could not make ends meet. The APRHAC soon dissolved, and its members joined the SPCA. Financial problems and Gompertz's ill health (he died in 1861) brought the AFS to an end by midcentury. Of the earliest organizations, the SPCA alone would continue. (New animal protection groups sprang up in subsequent years.) Meanwhile, with Martin out of the way, Parliament undertook no more action to protect animals.

In 1833, as Richard Martin was nearing the close of his eighth decade, his old friend Jonah Barrington wrote of him: "Mr. Martin still lives and seems to defy, from the strength of his constitution, both time and the destroyer. If ever he should become defunct there is not a bullock, calf, goose or hack, but ought to *go into deep mourning* for him." The bullocks, calves, geese, and hacks lost their champion on January 6, 1834, when Martin died, just a month before his eightieth birthday. His grave was transferred from its original site after the bombing of World War II, but it remains in Boulogne. According to Gompertz, Martin's last words had expressed his concern for the well-being of his family and of his dog. The *Times* briefly noted the passing of "the late eccentric member for Galway." Thomas Hood expressed much more feeling in his "Ode to Richard Martin, Esq.":

> *Thou Wilberforce of hacks!*
> *Of whites as well as blacks,*
> *Pyebald and dapple gray,*
> *Chestnut and bay—*
> *No poet's eulogy thy name adorns!*

But oxen, from the fens,
Sheep—in their pens,
Praise thee, and red cows with their winding horns!

Martin had ended his career in defeat and frustration, and he died without seeing another legislative move for animal protection. But the landmark law he wrote and fought so energetically for lived on—and grew. A year after his death, in 1835, Parliament finally passed an amendment of Martin's Act that extended its provisions to bulls, dogs, and "any other cattle or domestic animal." The law still stipulated that to warrant prosecution the animal had to have been treated "wantonly and cruelly," and the fines levied were lower than those under the first act. But the revisions put an end to bullbaiting. And, ridiculous though some MPs found the idea, even cats now enjoyed a degree of protection.

More bills, extending protection and stiffening penalties, would follow in the decades to come. Writing some thirty years after Martin's death, William Jerdan observed that he could not look around him without seeing Martin's work everywhere, in the "vast amount of miseries" from which the animal world was now protected. For anyone searching for a fitting epitaph by which to remember Humanity Dick Martin, Jerdan offered this one: "He was the most determined enemy to cruelty to animals, and the best friend of the dumb creation that ever lived."

AT THE TIME of Martin's death, the SPCA was still struggling, but it was working to make itself more solvent and respectable (something easier to do now that Gompertz, with his radical ideas, his Jewishness, and his unconventional eating habits, was no longer associated with it). The organization pragmatically sought to secure its survival—and to work most effectively to alleviate animals' suffering—by purging whatever more radical elements it had once contained; it sought to become mainstream and to attract influential patrons. The same year that the amendment to Martin's Act passed, the society added a particularly significant name to its growing list of sponsors. Princess Victoria, the heir to the British throne, had always been an animal lover. She joined the SPCA in 1835, became queen in 1837, and, in 1840, bestowed upon the organization the imprimatur of the Crown. The future of the *Royal Society for the Prevention of Cruelty to Animals* was now secure.

CONCLUSION:
THE LEGACY OF ANIMAL
PROTECTION

※   ※   ※

THE MINUTES of the SPCA's earliest meetings, recorded in Arthur Broome's precise handwriting, are held today in the archives of the RSPCA headquarters in Horsham, West Sussex, a fifty-minute train ride south of London. Turning the age-worn pages of that first minute book, where the inky scrawls of Broome, Gompertz, and others bring the past to life, is a moving experience. Those records make palpable the fierce determination of Richard Martin, still rallying the cause from his French exile; the self-sacrificing leadership of Arthur Broome, painfully noting every new debt; and the unwavering perseverance of Lewis Gompertz, working for animal rights within a hostile society. It is inspiring to relive the society's painful struggles to survive at a time when the future of the cause was in doubt, while all around you, in the RSPCA's modern, airy headquarters, dedicated men and women go about their work and a beloved dog naps under a desk.

Today's bustling headquarters is an indication of how successful the society has been in gaining public recognition and funding—and a similar story may be told in the United States of the American Society for the Prevention of Cruelty to Animals and the Humane Society of the United States, as well as the many other animal rescue and advocacy organizations. Whether they are local shelters like the one at which we adopted our cats Chloe and Graham, or animal welfare lobbying groups that operate nationwide, these organizations can trace their inspiration back to changes in attitudes that began more than three centuries ago.

They can claim descent from the early assortment of people such as Margaret Cavendish, William Hogarth, Humphrey Primatt, and John Oswald, all of whom, in their own ways, set themselves against the status quo of their era. More directly, they can look back to those reformers who forced the law for the first time to become responsive to the plight of animals, and who organized to change the ways beasts lived and died throughout the kingdom and, eventually, much of the world.

The rescued dogs, cats, rabbits, and horses who live with so many of us today ultimately owe their survival to people such as Thomas Erskine, William Wilberforce, Arthur Broome, Lewis Gompertz, and Richard Martin. When Chloe, persevering despite her age-stiffened limbs, clambers onto my shoulders as she first did eighteen years ago; when Maxine unerringly flops onto the very paragraph of the newspaper I am reading; and when Graham claims his rightful place on my lap to gaze entranced at the computer screen, I think of those determined early fighters for the cause of animals with admiration—and with gratitude.

TODAY, IN WESTERN industrialized societies, cruelty to animals is not nearly as visible or, in certain respects, as extensive as it once was, particularly for the animals we consider pets. Cats, dogs, and horses are routinely rescued from abusive owners; people adopt pets from shelters in large numbers; we seem to be paying greater attention to the pressing need to spay and neuter them. Industrialization itself has made obsolete the thousands of beasts of burden who once suffered and died on our streets. Greater numbers of people are choosing to eat only meat that has been certified as humanely raised, or to become vegetarians or vegans altogether. Temple Grandin's groundbreaking work redesigning slaughterhouses has alleviated much animal suffering, and her writing has called widespread attention to the importance and the feasibility of humane animal slaughtering methods. Yet much more remains to be done. Behind the walls of our factory farms, slaughterhouses, corporate laboratories, urban warehouses, and many private homes, animals still suffer.

As Matthew Scully, Eric Schlosser, and Michael Pollan have lately pointed out, our society has arrived at a peculiar, contradictory crossroads, where our attachment to animals seems to be at a level unprecedented in Western history, yet at the same time our postindustrial society inflicts suffering upon animals in vast numbers. However, as demonstrated by the very existence of recent books by these men and Grandin, as well as (to name only a few) Peter Singer, Ingrid Newkirk, Jeffrey Moussaieff Masson, Rod Preece, and Barbara Kingsolver, we seem now to be at a critical moment in our treatment of animals, as more individuals, legislatures, and corporations begin to face more directly what we collectively collude in inflicting upon our fellow creatures.

Today, more attention is being given to the horrific suffering of food animals in our factory farms: the hens confined to tiny battery cages with their beaks cut off, and the sows who, their tails wrenched off with pliers, spend their entire lives in crates only slightly larger than they themselves. While the powerful meat and restaurant industries have been able to stall meaningful legislative action—with the exception of some local bans on foie gras (a minuscule, politically easy target in comparison to chicken, beef, and pork)—public opinion, encouraged by animal advocacy groups, has begun to change, and some individual corporate entities have begun to respond. At this writing, the celebrity chef Wolfgang Puck has just announced that all the restaurants within his empire will serve only humanely raised meat and battery-free eggs; the menus will feature more vegetarian dishes. Burger King has adopted a similar policy, setting a new standard for the fast-food industry.

Individual states have abolished animal fighting and steel-jawed traps; some fast-food chains, responding to pressure from consumers and animal advocacy groups, are trying to ameliorate the gestation crates, battery cages, feedlots, and slaughterhouses behind the vast quantities of meat they serve; we can buy dolphin-friendly tuna at the grocery; and "No Animal Testing" labels appear routinely on our shampoos (though these are often misleading, since the individual ingredients might have been tested on animals, even if the final product has not). Our awareness has been raised about the trauma humans inflict

on highly social, intelligent, long-lived animals, such as the captive elephants performing in circuses or the wild ones slaughtered by poachers, and the laboratory chimpanzees sentenced to sterile lives behind
bars. All these conditions, and many more, have gained new visibility in
recent years, thanks to the efforts of animal protection organizations,
which are complemented and reinforced by the work of environmen-
talists, scientists, lawyers, activists, journalists, and others who have exposed the often quite uncomfortable truths about how abuse of
animals continues to permeate every aspect of our lives.

The legacy of Richard Martin and his allies lives on in the flourishing animal protection movement today—the widely focused groups
such as the RSPCA and its U.S. counterparts, including the ASPCA, the
USHS, and PETA, as well as those with more specific agendas, such as
the Primate Rescue Center, Farm Sanctuary, and the National Wildlife
Federation. There are many, many more, from small local rescue operations to international advocacy organizations, whose politics range
from mainstream to radical. It is heartening to think of the difference
between the struggles of the past and the widespread acceptance of animal protection (and the relative respectability of the once-ludicrous
concept of animal *rights*) today. Yet the very existence of so many organizations, fighting on so many fronts, also reminds us vividly that the
work which needs to be done on behalf of animals is far from over.

THE TEXT OF MARTIN'S ACT

AN ACT TO PREVENT THE CRUEL AND
IMPROPER TREATMENT OF CATTLE.
[22D JULY 1822]

ANNO TERTIO GEORGII IV. REGIS. CAP LXXI.

[Magistrates empowered to inflict a Penalty on Persons convicted of cruel Treatment of Cattle.]

I. Whereas it is expedient to prevent the cruel and improper Treatment of Horses, Mares, Geldings, Mules, Asses, Cows, Heifers, Steers, Oxen, Sheep, and other Cattle: May it therefore please Your Majesty, that it may be enacted; and be it enacted by the King's most excellent Majesty, by and with the Advice and Consent of the Lords Spiritual and Temporal, and Commons, in this present Parliament assembled, and by the Authority of the same, That if any person or persons shall wantonly and cruelly beat, abuse, or ill-treat any Horse, Mare, Gelding, Mule, Ass, Ox, Cow, Heifer, Steer, Sheep, or other Cattle, and Complaint on Oath thereof be made to any Justice of the Peace or other Magistrate within whose Jurisdiction such Offence shall be committed, it shall be lawful for such Justice of the Peace or other Magistrate to issue his Summons or Warrant, at his Discretion, to bring the party or parties so complained of before him, or any other Justice of the Peace or other Magistrate of the County, City, or Place within which such Justice of the Peace or other Magistrate has Jurisdiction, who shall examine upon Oath any Witness or Witnesses who shall appear or be produced to give Information touching such Offence, (which Oath the said Justice of the Peace or other Magistrate is hereby authorized and required to administer); and if the party or parties accused shall be convicted of any such Offence, either by his, her, or their own Confession, or upon such Information as aforesaid, he, she, or they so convicted shall forfeit and pay any Sum not exceeding Five Pounds, nor less than Ten Shillings, to His Majesty, His Heirs and Successors; and if the person or persons so convicted shall refuse or not be able forthwith to pay the Sum forfeited, every such Offender shall, by Warrant under the Hand and Seal of some Justice or Justices of the Peace or other Magistrate within whose Jurisdiction the person offending shall be Convicted, be committed to the House of Correction or some other Prison within the Jurisdiction within which the Offence shall have been committed, there to be kept without Bail or Mainprize for any Time not exceeding Three Months.

[No Persons to be punished, unless Complaint made within Ten Days after the Offence.]

II. Provided always, and be it enacted by the Authority aforesaid, That no Person shall suffer any Punishment for any Offence committed against this Act, unless the Prosecution for the same be commenced within Ten Days after the Offence shall be committed; and that when any Person shall suffer Imprisonment pursuant to this Act, for any Offence contrary thereto, in Default of Payment of any Penalty hereby imposed, such Person shall not be liable afterwards to any such Penalty.

[Proceedings not to be quashed for Want of Form.]

III. Provided also, and be it further enacted, that no Order or Proceedings to be made or had by or before any Justice of the Peace or other Magistrate by virtue of this Act shall be quashed or vacated for want of Form, and that the Order of such Justice or other Magistrate shall be final; and that no proceedings of any such Justice or other Magistrate in pursuance of this Act shall be removeable by Certiorari or otherwise.

[Form of Conviction]

IV. And for the more easy and speedy Conviction of Offenders under this Act, be it further enacted, That all and every the [*sic*] Justice and Justices of the Peace, or other Magistrate or Magistrates, before whom any Person or Persons shall be convicted of any Offence against this Act, shall and may cause the Conviction to be drawn up in the following Form of Words, or in any other Form of Words to the same Effect, as the Case shall happen; (*videlicet*),

"Be it remembered, That on the   Day of   in the Year of our Lord A. B. is convicted before me, One of his Majesty's Justices of the Peace for   or Mayor or other Magistrate of   [*as the case may be*] either by his own Confession, or on the Oath of One or more credible Witness or Witnesses [*as the case may be*] by virtue of an Act made in the Third Year of the Reign of his Majesty King George the Fourth, intituled *An Act to prevent the cruel and improper Treatment of Cattle,* [*specifying the Offence, and Time and Place where the same was committed, as the case may be*]. Given under my Hand and Seal, the Day and Year above written."

[Justices to order Compensation to Persons vexatiously complained against. How enforced.]

V. And be it further enacted, That if on hearing any such Complaint as is herein-before mentioned, the Justice of the Peace or other Magistrate who shall hear the same shall be of opinion that such Complaint was frivolous or vexatious, then and in every such Case it shall be lawful for such Justice of the Peace or other Magistrate to order, adjudge and direct the Person or Persons making such Complaint, to pay to the Party complained of, any Sum of Money not exceeding the Sum of Twenty Shillings, as Compensation for the Trouble and Expence to which such Party may have been put by such Complaint; such Order or Adjudgment to be final between the said Parties, and the Sum thereby ordered or adjudged to be paid and levied in manner as is hereinbefore provided for enforcing Payment of the Sums of Money to be forfeited by the Persons convicted of the Offence hereinbefore mentioned.

[Limitation of Actions. Where Tried. Treble Costs.]

VI. And be it further enacted by the Authority aforesaid, That if any Action or Suit shall be brought or commenced against any Person or persons, for any thing done in pursuance of this Act, it shall be brought or commenced within Six Calendar Months next after every such Cause of Action shall have accrued, and not afterwards, and shall be brought, laid and tried in the County, City or Place in which such Offence shall have been committed, and not elsewhere; and the Defendant or Defendants in such Action or Suit may plead the General Issue, and give this Act and the special Matter in Evidence at any Trial or Trials to be had thereon, and that the same was done in pursuance and by authority of this Act; and if the same shall appear to have been so done, or if any such Action or Suit shall not be commenced within the Time before limited, or shall be laid or brought in any other County, City or Place than where the Offence shall have been committed, then and in any such Case the Jury or Juries shall find for the Defendant or Defendants; or if the Plaintiff or Plaintiffs shall become nonsuit, or shall discontinue his Action or Actions, or if Judgment shall be given for the Defendant or Defendants therein, then and in any of the Cases aforesaid such Defendant or Defendants shall have Treble Costs, and shall have such Remedy for recovering the same as any Defendant or Defendants hath or may have for his, her or their costs in any other Cases by Law.

A Collection of the Public General Statutes, passed in the Third Year of the Reign of His Majesty, King George the Fourth: Being the Third Session of the Seventh Parliament of the United Kingdom of Great Britain and Ireland. London: 1822, pp. 703–707.

Animals still need your help! Please consider making a donation of money or your time to the animal protection organization of your choice.

The Humane Society of the United States (HSUS): http://www.hsus
.org/
People for the Ethical Treatment of Animals (PETA): http://www.peta
.org/
The American Society for the Prevention of Cruelty to Animals (ASPCA):
http://www.aspca.org
The Royal Society for the Prevention of Cruelty to Animals (RSPCA):
http://www.rspca.org.uk/
Farm Sanctuary: http://www.farmsanctuary.org/
Fund for Animals: http://www.fundforanimals.org/
World Wildlife Fund (WWF): http://www.worldwildlife.org

There are many more, including many state and local organizations, that may be found by searching online for "animal rescue" or "animal protection."

A NOTE TO THE READER

MY WRITING OF this book was made possible by the groundbreaking work of earlier scholars, as well as others who are actively writing today. Two earlier books in particular were invaluable. Dix Harwood's 1928 study, *Love for Animals and How It Developed in Great Britain,* is thorough, learned, and particularly impressive in its detailed account of the literary record. Sir Keith Thomas's 1983 book, *Man and the Natural World: Changing Attitudes in England, 1500–1800,* is an extraordinarily comprehensive historical survey that contains a thorough account of intellectual developments while also being wonderfully rich in anecdotal material. My book is greatly indebted to both of these. A list of recent writers whose work has been important to me must first include Rod Preece, author and editor of several important studies in the history of animals and animal rights. In particular, I have made use of his impassioned and impressively learned 2005 book, *Brute Souls, Happy Beasts and Evolution* (which was published and came to my attention after I was already well under way on this book). The detail he amasses to make his argument that concern for animals has been present throughout the course of Western society, that it did not suddenly appear after 1800 (as some animal rights activists have assumed), has been useful in helping me refine my own approach. Our emphases differ—he stresses the fact that compassion for animals has always been represented by some writers throughout the history of ideas, and I stress the majority attitudes toward animals, their actual treatment, and the changes that led to political action—but I think we agree that the status of animals in past historical periods was complex and often contradictory, and that the idea of compassion for beasts did not suddenly arise from nowhere two centuries ago.

Animal studies has become a burgeoning field in recent years, encompassing historians, philosophers, theologians, literary scholars, classicists, sociologists, biologists, poets, journalists, novelists, and others. There are many scholars and writers whose work guided me as I ventured into this territory; those whose books and articles have been most directly relevant to this book appear in the bibliography. Among them I would like particularly to acknowledge the work of Harriet Ritvo, Hilda Kean, James Turner, David Perkins, and Erica Fudge. The primary focus of Ritvo, Kean, and Turner falls after my own historical period, and that of Fudge before it, but all of them have made significant contributions to my own understanding of the historical intersections between humans and non-human animals. Norm Phelps's *The Longest Struggle,* which came to my attention after I had completed work on this book, also usefully devotes several chapters to the early history of advocacy for animals.

I would also like to acknowledge the invaluable contribution made by the Edwin Mellen Press, whose Mellen Animal Rights Library series has made many earlier writings about animals available in modern, well-edited editions with detailed, useful introductions. There are also innumerable online sources of varying degrees of credibility and usefulness, but some, such as the Animal Rights Library (http://www.animal-rights-library.com/) and Animal Rights History (http://www.animal rightshistory.org/), provide helpful starting points for those who might want to investigate further historical attitudes toward animals.

A NOTE ON REFERENCES

Quotations from the Hebrew Bible and the New Testament are from the King James Version. I have consulted most of the rarer, more obscure printed pamphlets and books I cite in my notes and bibliography in hard copy at the British Library in London (primarily) and at specialist libraries such as the Huntington Library and my own university's Mandeville Special Collections Library. More and more of this kind of material is becoming available online, however, in easily accessed form via Google Books, and via more restricted sites such as Early English Books Online (EEBO) and Eighteenth Century Collections Online (ECCO). Material directly pertinent to the RSPCA, such as their record books and relevant printed material, I have consulted in the society's archives, located at the RSPCA Headquarters in Horsham, West Sussex.

Eighteenth- and nineteenth-century newspapers, magazines, and journals have been consulted in a combination of media: online; on microfilm produced by the British Library and the Library of Congress, available at my home library at the University of California, San Diego, and at the British Library; and sometimes in print form at these libraries. I have used the following internet sites for periodicals and other reference works.

The Times of London after 1801 has usually been accessed online via Chadwyck-Healey's Historical Newspapers site: http://historynews .chadwyck.com/noframes/home/home.cgi.

For the *Gentleman's Magazine,* vols. 1–20 (1731–50), the *Annual Register,* 1758–78, and the *Philosophical Transactions of the Royal Society,* 1757–77, I have generally used the Internet Library of Early Journals, http://www.bodley.ox.ac.uk/ilej/. For later issues of the *Philosophical Transactions of the Royal Society,* 1776–1886, I have consulted the Royal Society Web site: http://www.journals.royalsoc.ac.uk/content/120135/ ?sortorder=asc&p=b8fa084f65ac48d28ab7151ed3b25578&o=0.

Other periodicals consulted on microfilm:

Busy Body
Courier
London Magazine
Mercurius Publicus
Monthly Magazine
Morning Chronicle
Morning Herald
New Monthly Magazine

Sporting Magazine
Weekly Register

I have drawn my accounts of proceedings in the British Houses of Parliament from the reports of debates in the *Times* and the *Courier,* and from the following official sources, accessed in print at the British Library and sometimes via microfiche.

Journal of the House of Commons
Journal of the House of Lords
The Parliamentary Debates from the year 1803 to the Present Time. 1st series, 1803–1820. London: Hansard, et al., 1812 and following.
The Parliamentary Debates. 2nd series, 1820–1829. London: T. C. Hansard, 1820–1829.
The Parliamentary History of England, from the earliest period to the year 1803. 1743–1803. London: T. C. Hansard, 1812–1820.

I have consulted *The House of Commons Parliamentary Papers* from 1801 online: http://parlipapers.chadwyck.com/home.do.

For the sake of clarity and accessibility to a general readership, I have modernized most spelling and punctuation in the material I have quoted. I have followed this practice in contexts where modernized spelling, italicization, capitalization, and punctuation do not make a substantive difference in the meaning of the words. For instance, in Chapter One I have modernized spellings such as Samuel Pepys's "romantick" and "antick," and John Evelyn's "crawll, roare & make their severall cries"; in Chapter Three, I have modernized Lady Wentworth's idiosyncratic spelling. But in quotations from poetry and other "literary" genres, I preserve the original forms, as I also do when the point I am making refers to the typography itself, as in some of the newspaper advertisements I quote.

NOTES

INTRODUCTION: SAVED

3   *Large categories of animals*: Methods of raising food animals are still egregiously inhumane, and, although we have a Humane Slaughter Act, it does not cover all farmed animals and is often poorly enforced. However, there is now more attention being paid to the great cruelties perpetrated within our industrial agricultural system. For instance, Temple Grandin's innovative designs for more humane slaughterhouses are being more widely adopted within the meat industry.

9   *But in earlier times*: Siebert, "Elephant Crackup?"

9   *"the first national law"*: Ryder, *Animal Revolution*, 82. Martin's Act was not the first law protecting animals ever to exist in the English-speaking world: for instance, at least two seventeenth-century statues had been instituted, one in Ireland against tying a horse to a plow by its tail and pulling the wool off sheep, and one in the American colonies against treating animals cruelly (Ryder, 49). But the legislative sweep and status of Martin's Act was unprecedented.

10 *"By Jaysus"*: Hall, 1:229. Hall misremembered this meeting as having occurred before the passage of Martin's Act instead of two years later, so he remembered Martin as referring to his act of 1822. In fact, Martin was actually referring to subsequent attempts to get additional legislation passed. Hall, a Victorian, also renders the first part of Martin's exclamation as "By J———." I have taken the liberty of filling in the blank.

13 *"whether we walk upon two legs or four"*: Primatt, *Dissertation*, 18.

CHAPTER ONE: OF DUCHESSES AND DUCKS

17 *Cavendish, who fascinated him*: Unless otherwise stated, information regarding Margaret Cavendish in London is taken from the following sources: Pepys, 8:140–244; Evelyn, *Diary*, 3:482–83, and Ballad, 131–32; Mary Evelyn, "Letter to Ralph Bohun," in Bowerbank and Mendelson, 91–93; Whitaker, 288–302, 354–55.

18   *"yet may their perceptions and observations"*: Cavendish, *Philosophical Letters,* 114.

18   *"in the seventeenth century"*: Thomas, 128.

19   *Cavendish's writing was as wildly original*: Bowerbank and Mendelson, 29.

20   *"a very weak argument"*: Cavendish, *Philosophical Letters,* 41, 113.

20   *No woman was allowed*: "Women Scientists and the Royal Society," http://www
.royalsoc.ac.uk/publication.asp?id=1010.

21   *"I endeavour"*: Bowerbank and Mendelson, 245.

21   *akin to the warrior queen Zenobia*: Darley, 211.

21   *"so like a Cavelier"*: Evelyn, Ballad, 131.

23   *Once man had penetrated*: Bacon, *Da Sapientia Veterum,* 747; *Advancement of Learning,*
Aphorism 14, 245. Bacon's own translation from Proverbs here emphasizes mercy
to a greater degree than does the King James version: see Stuart, 12–14. For Bacon's
language of rape and slavery, see Merchant (70–72), discussing particularly Bacon's
The Masculine Birth of Time, The Refutation of Philosophies, and *De Augmentis.*

23   *"The veneration wherewith men"*: Quoted in Porter, "Environment and Enlightenment," 25.

24   *"one of the most curious monuments"*: Lovejoy, 186.

24   *"the ignorance of men"*: Cavendish, *Philosophical Letters,* 41.

24   *"[Man] is so Proud"*: Bowerbank and Mendelson, 258.

26   *"their Motions as natural"*: Evelyn, *Diary,* 4:24; see Altick's discussion of automa-
tons, 56–65.

26   *Having created a sensation*: Strandh, 176–79; Hankins and Silverman, 182–84. See
also Riskin, passim.

28   *Animals are essentially biological*: Descartes, 1:139–41.

28   *A dog may jump away*: Descartes's emphasis, explains Steiner, "is not so much
that animals are incapable of feeling pain as that they lack any kind of awareness; in the final analysis, animals are incapable of feeling precisely *because* they
lack consciousness." Steiner, *Anthropocentrism,* 290. My discussion of Descartes
is indebted to Steiner; P. Harrison, 479–83; and Thomas, 33–35.

29   *"I cannot share the opinion"*: Descartes, 3:302.

29   *"mutual obligation"*: Montaigne, 318, 329–31.

29   *Montaigne had his followers*: P. Harrison, 470–71, 481–82.

30   *"I observe no mind"*: Descartes, 3:303, 2:248.

30   *If beasts could actually feel*: Thomas, 33; Harwood, 97–104.

30   *Voltaire's liberal ideas*: Voltaire, 112–14.

30   *The enormously influential John Locke*: Locke, *Human Understanding,* 160.

30   *Eustace Budgell mockingly imagined*: Addison and Steele, *Guardian* 24 (8 Apr.
1713): 110.

31   *Anatomists dissecting animals*: Mandeville, 198. See also Garrett, viii–x.

31   *The qualities they express*: Cited in P. Harrison, 476.

32   *"as he is good for any thing"*: Cavendish, *Philosophical Letters,* 113–14, 41, 147.

32   *Descartes himself commented*: Thomas, 34–35. L. Rosenfield and Harwood,
(99–107), find evidence that the Cartesian beast-machine idea did enjoy influence in England, if in altered forms; Shugg and J. Turner think that it was not

particularly influential, while Thomas cites some prominent examples of individuals holding this belief, but says it was a minority opinion, 35. Preece, *Brute Souls,* believes it had relatively little influence in Britain.

32　*Although the question of animal rationality:* Ryder cites the example of the Indian Buddhist ruler Asoka (c. 260 B.C.E.), who banned hunting, and ancient Greek and Roman laws against killing an ox and cruelty to birds, 21, 50. Plutarch cited in Pope, "Against Barbarity," 235.

33　*Aristotle believed that humans: De Anima (On the Soul),* 2:2, 3; *Politics* 1:8; Augustine, *City of God,* I:20; Aquinas, *Summa Theologica,* 1, Questions 64.1, 65.3; *Summa Contra Gentiles,* chapters III, II2; Steiner, "Descartes," 272–73.

33　*"are foundational for the entire":* Steiner, "Descartes," 272–73.

33　*"For Paul, the ox":* Grant, 7–9.

34　*But other powerful and influential traditions:* Rod Preece's learned and impassioned book, *Brute Souls, Happy Beasts and Evolution,* reacts against earlier histories that have not acknowledged the complexity and multiplicity of attitudes toward animals during Western history. Not all early Christians saw "dominion" as absolute, by any means, though very influential voices did stress animals' God-given purpose of being useful to humans. Preece points out that "dominion" over animals was given to Adam prior to Noah being given animals as food, so arguably Adam's dominion did not extend as far as eating them. This historical sequence often was elided, however, in subsequent Christian interpretations of "dominion" within a post-Flood world. Furthermore, the fact that there were individual dissenters does not contradict the idea that the most pervasive beliefs, among both the elite and the common folk, were strongly anthropocentric. Philosophical debates among the educated elite often had little to do with the attitudes and practices of the vast majority of people in earlier times, as far as we can determine them.

34　*One tradition, which persisted:* See P. Harrison, 464.

35　*Such positions were in some ways:* Passmore, 12.

36　*Although recent scholarship:* Steiner, *Anthropocentrism,* 124–26.

36　*One early thirteenth-century:* Barber, 160; see also P. Harrison, 465–66.

36　*The assumption that animals:* Harwood, 12–16.

37　*Humans in a state of nature:* Hobbes, *Questions Concerning Liberty, Necessity and Chance,* No. 14, cited in Thomas, 171.

37　*Some dissenters from extreme anthropocentrism:* See Stuart, 102–5.

38　*To Cavendish, man becomes downright:* Cavendish, *Philosophical Letters,* 517–19.

38　*"principally designed for the being":* Bentley, 241.

38　*"breathtakingly anthropocentric":* Thomas, 18.

CHAPTER TWO: RUDE AND NASTY PLEASURES

40　*If the dogs tried to attack:* Details from Houghton, no. 108 (24 Aug. 1694), 1:289–91.

40　*"a very rude and nasty pleasure":* Pepys, 8:245–46.

41 *Particularly brave and tenacious*: *Daily Post*, 3 Aug. 1730; Misson, 24–27.

41 *"most heartily weary"*: Evelyn, *Diary*, 3:549.

41 *"this truly English sport"*: Von Uffenbach, 60.

42 *So entertaining did the earl*: E. Barry, 9–10. Most of this history was also told in a petition submitted by certain residents of Stamford against the bullbaiting bill of 1802: *Journal of the House of Commons*, 55:496.

42 *Ancient statutes in many towns*: Griffin, 59–64.

42 *The Spanish visitor Don Manuel*: Espriella, 3:191–92.

42 *"any thing that looks like fighting"*: Misson, 304.

42 *"I wish I knew"*: Steele, *Tatler* no. 134 (16 Feb. 1710).

43 *"temper that is become"*: Pope, "Against Barbarity," 233.

43 *Though the sport's heyday*: Hackwood, 226–88, esp. 231; Hug, *passim*.

43 *Bulls sometimes had their horns cut*: Bear parade quoted in Pinks, 162; bear attack in the *Grub Street Journal*, 19 Mar. 1730; names, Hug, n.p.

44 *In London there were ponds*: Badger baiting, Drabble, 931; duck baiting, Cameron, 131, and Pinks, 143.

44 *"the old East India Company lost by ten votes"*: Evelyn, *Diary*, 5:317.

44 *the baiting of an "East India Tyger"*: *Post Man*, 28 Feb.–2 Mar. 1699, rpt. 4–7, 9–11 Mar.

44 *At Bartholomew Fair*: Bartholomew Fair, *Post Man*, 6–9 Sept. 1701. Evelyn, *Diary*, 5:317; tiger in the *Post Man*: baiting, 28 Feb.–2 Mar. 1699, rpt. 4–7, 9–11 Mar.

45 *Though the popularity*: The major exception to the waning was the West Midlands, where authorities' attempts to ban these blood sports in the 1820s and 1830s were met with popular resistance. See Griffin, 223–49.

45 *"a true-born Old Englishman"*: Boswell, *London Journal*, 86–87.

46 *The cocks, which probably had been bred*: Cameron, 135.

46 *The din was horrific*: Von Uffenbach, 49.

46 *"There is a celestial spirit"*: Sherwood, *Letter to a Friend in Paris*, quoted in Pinks, 163–64.

46 *A 1723 manual for cock-keepers*: Quoted in Henderson, 239.

47 *"one of the great English diversions"*: Misson, 39.

48 *"pretty much fatigued"*: Boswell, 87.

48 *A cock was tethered*: Malcolmson, 119.

48 *"Mayest thou be punished"*: quoted in Hackwood, 290. In January 1737, the *Gentleman's Magazine* ran an article saying that cockthrowing was anti-French in origin, since the Latin for cock (*gallus*) also signified a Frenchman (*Gaul*), 6–8.

48 *Cockthrowing was the first*: Griffin notes that public attention to cockthrowing as manifested in certain periodicals was for the most part not attached to criticism of other forms of cruelty toward animals and pretty much died out after the early 1760s (122–24).

48 *The* Tatler *published*: *Tatler* no. 134 (16 Feb. 1710).

48 *In 1749, the* Gentleman's Magazine: *Gentleman's Magazine*, Apr. 1749, 148–49.

49 *The match ended when*: Drabble, 932–33.

49 *The long-established tradition*: Barnette, 175.

50 *"Throwing at cocks"*: *Weekly Register*, 13 May 1732.

50   "lord of a manor": Hay, 189–90.

50   Parliament passed the notorious Black Act: Thompson, 21–22.

51   The preservers of game: Romilly, 3:283–84.

51   The preservation of foxes: Thomas, 164.

51   "ravishingly delightful": Markham quoted in Thomas, 145.

51   Some feared that the good: See Perkins, 65.

52   "the groans of a dying beast": Bowerbank and Mendelson, 60.

52   in her extraordinary poem: "Hunting of the Stag," Cavendish, Poems and Fancies, n.p.; "Hunting of the Hare," Bowerbank and Mendelson, 255–58. In the latter poem, Cavendish is elaborating upon several stanzas in Shakespeare's erotic poem Venus and Adonis. But whereas Shakespeare's sympathetic portrayal of "poor Wat" occurs in five stanzas of a much longer poem, as Venus tries to convince Adonis to hunt the timid hare rather than the fierce boar (an animal that she fears, correctly, will kill him), Cavendish is concerned about the plight of the hare himself.

53   While a few localities managed: Some parishes issued bans against the blood sport of "throwing at cocks" as early as the mid-eighteenth century; the London neighborhood of Marylebone outlawed animal baiting prior to 1822.

CHAPTER THREE: PETS AND THE CITY

55   Lady Wentworth filled her letters: Lady Wentworth's letters are published in Cartwright, 40–307. Her spelling is highly irregular, which was not unusual in her day, especially among women, even aristocratic ones. I have normalized it for sake of clarity.

58   "birds, rabbits, hounds, and such": Quoted in Harwood, 23–24. However modest their convent lives were, most people joining religious orders of the day would have come from privileged backgrounds.

58   "By 1700 all the symptoms": Thomas, 117. This discussion of pet keeping is greatly indebted to Thomas, 100–120; Perkins also helpfully discusses attitudes toward pets, particularly in the poetry of the eighteenth century and the Romantic period, 44–63.

58   "infinitely more amusing": Morgan, 2:39.

59   Thomas succinctly itemizes: Thomas, 113–16.

60   Charles I's queen, Henrietta: Gibson, 11–13.

60   In one late-seventeenth-century comic play: Shadwell, The Lancashire Witches (1682), Act III.

60   the increasing popularity of cats: Thomas, 110.

61   Completing her family circle were: Frith, 37–40, 61. It is uncertain how much of her published life story was actually written or dictated by Frith herself.

62   Sir Isaac Newton, who first: See Ryder, 43.

63   "I am a little and he the most sorry": Pepys's pets: lion cub, 1:15, n. 2; cat, 3:173; monkey, 2:17; blackbird, 4:150, 152; canary, 6:8; eagle, 5:352; incontinent dog, 1:46, 54, 284–85; lost dog, 4:99; father's dog, 5:192.

63   Moralists particularly railed: Thomas, 40.

64 *"And to prevent any Farther Trouble"*: 1 July 1746.

65 *Hogarth, who was widely known*: In another self-portrait, *Painting the Comic Muse,* Hogarth did not include his pug, at least in the final version. Recent X-ray examination has shown an earlier state of the painting, however, in which his dog *does* appear quite prominently in the foreground—pissing on a pile of old master paintings (Gibson, 16). My discussion of pets in portraiture is based upon Gibson's study.

65 *An ad for a little spaniel*: Post Man, 4–6 Sept. 1701.

66 *"Will they never leave"*: Mercurius Publicus, 28 June–5 July 1660.

67 *"where the neighbors were almost poisoned"*: Morning Herald, 28 Jan. 1801. Quoted in Wilson, 138–39.

68 *"Tiny poet, great dog"*: Mack, 676.

68 *Horace Walpole doted upon*: To Richard West, 11 Nov. 1739, in Walpole, 28. On other dog: Hill, passim. My thanks also to Nicki Faircloth of Strawberry Hill, Landon, for her information about Walpole's pets.

68 *Cats had to overcome*: Busy Body no. 12, 1759. Thomas, 109–10.

69 *When she died*: Cited in Rogers, 88–89.

69 *He rejected the slurs*: Lawrence, *Philosophical and Practical Treatise,* 1:194–95.

70 *To the author of the memoir*: Woffington, 20–21.

71 *"And then in a sort of kindly"*: Boswell, *Life of Johnson,* 1073.

71 *Cats generally were not*: One notable exception to this dating is the portrait of Henry Wriothesley, the third earl of Southampton, whose portrait painted in 1603, while he was being held prisoner in the Tower, features a handsome cat in the background (Gibson, 12). On family groups with cats, see Gibson, 15, 38–39.

72 *To paint the human Kitty*: Gibson, 44–45.

73 *In one of these prints*: See Gatrell, 334–39.

74 *"at least one hare"*: Quoted and discussed in Perkins, 44–48.

74 *"It encouraged the middle classes"*: Thomas, 119.

CHAPTER FOUR: DANCING DOGS AND HORSES OF KNOWLEDGE

76 *"They were gallantly clad"*: Evelyn, Diary, 3:356.

77 *One attraction was a Giant Hog*: Altick, 39.

78 *"goose with four feet"*: Pepys, 4:298.

78 *"Apes" (chimps and macaques) and tigers . . . had been arriving*: Altick, 37.

78 *A 1713 poem*: Bartholomew Faire Scrapbook.

78 *"hog in armour"*: Grub-Street Journal, 16 Apr. 1730.

78 *Henri Misson was intrigued*: Misson, 280–81.

78 *visit to the Belle Savage Inn*: Evelyn, 4:389–91.

78 *famous rhinoceros, named Clara*: Ridley, 202–7.

79 *West Indies crocodile*: Evelyn, Diary, 3:93.

79 *In the thirteenth century*: See Harwood, 17–22.

80   *"stare in your face"*: London Spy 13 (1699).

80   *He did not mention whether this dog*: Von Uffenbach, 38–39.

80   *"their dresses, as well as their dances"*: See Rosenthal, 79.

81   *"Sir, a woman's preaching"*: Boswell, *Life of Johnson*, 290.

81   *The cruelty of this was overt*: London Stage 4:1, 357.

81   *Robert Hooke saw at Bartholomew Fair*: Hooke quoted in Altick, 36.

81   *A juggler named Breslaw*: On the performing marmoset, hare, and birds, see Strutt, 198–200.

82   *monkey on a tightrope*: Public Advertiser, 27 Oct. 1766 and into Nov.

82   *Von Uffenbach, roaming along Fleet Street*: Von Uffenbach, 174.

82   *"Man Teger"*: Altick, 38.

83   *"strange, but such dirty sport"*: Pepys, 4:298.

84   *"talks many things"*: Pepys, 5:132.

84   *In order to make this point*: Locke, from *Essay Concerning Human Understanding*, bk. 2, ch. 27: "Of Identity and Diversity" (http://oregonstate.edu/instruct/phl302/texts/locke/locke1/Book2c.html#Chapter%20XXVII). For a useful discussion of the implications of Locke's species blurring as an example of the "leap of affinity" that here produces "the conjunction of nonhuman and non-European," see L. Brown, 245–49.

84   *remarkable horse Morocco*: Toole-Stott, 130; Jay, 105.

85   *"a dog that seemed to do"*: Evelyn, *Diary*, 4:359.

85   *"to act much worse than the other day"*: Pepys, 9:297–301.

85   *"Little Military Learned Horse"*: Learned horses and Astley in Highfill et al., 1:182–84, 146–51.

85   *no learned animal in the eighteenth century*: On learned pigs, see Bondeson, 19–35, and Jay, 9–27.

86   *Sylas Neville, a mid-century diarist*: Neville, 3 May 1785, quoted in Highfill, et al., 9:183–84.

86   *The historian Joseph Strutt*: Strutt, 200.

86   *"than ever was Sir Isaac Newton"*: quoted in Altick, 40.

87   *Samuel Johnson's old friend*: Boswell, *Life of Johnson*, 1200–1201.

88   *Another showman had taught*: Parl. Hist. 36 (1801–1803): 842.

88   *"the inspired learning"*: Voice of Humanity 1, no. 1 (Feb. 1830); 54.

CHAPTER FIVE: ANIMAL CRIMES

90   *talked-about trials of the year*: Proceedings of Old Bailey, 11 July 1677, trial of Mary Hicks (t16770711-1; u16770711-1); 26 Apr. 1704, trial of Mary Price (t17040426-42).

91   *Edward Payson Evans's fascinating book*: References to Evans as following: punishment, 138; pigs as murderers, 158; Falaise trial, 140; Jews, 152–53; Chassenée, 18; animals in prison, 142–43; Franconia hangman, 146–47; sow and piglets, 153–54; Ferron trial, 150–51. See also Bondeson, 131–60; Chambers, 17 Jan., 1:126–29; Harwood, 7–11; and Preece, 241–42.

93   *In Britain, bestiality became*: Thomas, 39. The law briefly lapsed between 1553 and 1562–63.

93   *The stated penalty*: Coke quoted in Callaghan, para. 9; buried alive: *Fleta, seu Commentarius Juris Anglicani* (London: 1735), cited in Bailey, 145. Bailey notes that this penalty was probably not actually applied in the medieval period.

94   *"worthy of a shameful death"*: Gerald of Wales, 75–76.

94   *"turns man into a very beast"*: Capel quoted in Thomas, 39.

94   *"Buggery with beasts is"*: Gouge and Barker (1624) quoted in Callaghan, para. 6.

95   *"I love my little dog"*: Hildrop, 23.

95   *"Dear delicate Madam"*: T. Brown, 82–85; Pope, St. 3, l. 158, St. 1, L. 16; Tate, Act I, sc. ii.

95   *The execution of convicted animals*: Cf. Berman, passim.

95   *Evans assumes that this was because*: Evans, xxvi.

96   *"among primitive peoples"*: Harwood, 9.

99   *"men and beasts inhabited the same"*: Thomas, 98.

99   *"break her of that bad custom"*: quoted in Thomas, 97.

99   *In* The Merchant of Venice: Act 4, sc. i.

99   *The practice of hanging*: Berman, 326, n. 61.

99   *"I had the greyhound hanged"*: Woodforde, 457.

100   *"called this criminal to justice"*: Complete Newgate Calendar, 2:218–19.

100   *This was reported to his master*: Parl. Hist., 32:995–96.

100   *King James I ordered the baiting*: Thomas, 98.

101   *Evelyn believed that*: Evelyn, *Diary*, 3:491–92.

101   *"my 2 pigs were tolerably sober"*: Woodforde, 141.

102   *"will, without doubt, be called"*: De Saussure, 70.

102   *"a flatterer is called a spaniel"*: Espriella, 3:316.

102   *"you dog, you"*: The Craftsman printed a letter that mockingly surveyed the various permutations of "dog" used as a metaphor for humans, culminating in praise for the "true-bred English bulldogs" (no. 167, 13 Sept. 1729).

103   *"their independence and power"*: Ritro, *Animal Estate*, 1–2. In *Brute Souls*, Preece also remarks that the trials had demonstrated "a certain type of respect" for animals, although based on a lack of accurate understanding of animal nature (242).

CHAPTER SIX: PARLIAMENTS OF MONSTERS

107   *The several versions of Mary's story*: On Mary Toft: *Wonder of Wonders*, passim; St. André, passim; Todd, 1–37.

109   *"vents, voiding excrement"*: Evelyn, *Diary*, 3:93.

109   *"damn'd Trumpeter calling"*: T. Brown, 46.

109   *"a most strange and monstrous Living Milk Cow"*: quoted in Mullen and Reid, 118; see also Lyson and *Collection of Advertisements*.

109   *"A Surprising and wonderful Young Mermaid"*: quoted in Mullen and Reid, 118; see also Lyson and *Collection of Advertisements*.

110   *But once she was pregnant*: For a very interesting discussion of the debates between "ovists" and "animalculists," and the effects of maternal imagination, see Huet, 36–78. Her book in general has been of great help in my discussion of monstrosity.

110   *These powerful influences*: Ritvo, *Platypus*, discusses more incidents of monsters and various forms of apparent hybrids, particularly the attempts to explain and classify these phenomena (131–87).

111   *It died soon after its birth*: *Annual Register* 1759, 2:378–81. The article describing this case also reports one M. Eller's arguments against the workings of maternal imagination. Monsters, Eller argued, cannot be produced by imagination because imagination works only on the nerves, and there is no connection between the mother's nerves and those of the fetus. Ellis conjectured that the dog had eaten a turkey egg and that the molecules of the egg forced the molecules responsible for her puppy's head out of place and replaced them with turkey molecules. His view was ridiculed by the article's author, who wrote: "It is as well known as any fact can be, that there is very often a striking correspondence between some mark or defect in the infant, and some strong imagination or passion of the mother." He suggested sarcastically that dogs might be put to work breeding fowls of all kinds.

112   *"so much like a man"*: Pepys, 2:160.

112   *Edward Tyson dissected a creature*: Tyson, 2.

112   *John Floyer reported*: *Philosophical Transactions* 21 (1699): 431, 434.

112   *Tannakin Skinker*: On Skinker and other pig-shaped women, see Jay, 27–36.

113   *"there is hardly a company"*: *Times*, 16–17 Feb. 1815.

113   *In the later nineteenth century*: Chambers, 23 Aug., 2:255–57.

114   *Its head was covered*: *Voice of Humanity* 1, no. 1 (1830): 54.

114   *"Wherever we look"*: Thomas, 38.

115   *such monsters were genuine hybrids*: On the Feejee and other mermaids, see Bondeson, 36–63. The idea of the hybrid itself did not vanish with scientific debunking, nor did the anxiety caused by the possibility of some types of cross-species mixing. Donkeys and horses had long been bred to produce mules, and people knew that dogs and wolves could produce offspring. Less benign ideas of interbreeding, particularly the belief that apes and some human races could mate and produce offspring, remained viable, and, if anything, gained greater credence toward the end of the eighteenth century and in the nineteenth, as we shall see, in the contexts of new systems of classification of animals and humans, the emergence of evolutionary theory, explorations of racial difference, the establishment of racial hierarchies, and fears of miscegenation.

117   *"In attempting to shore up"*: Thomas, 40–41.

117   *"His hair was matted and bristling"*: De Saussure, 92–93.

118   *a creature from "Mount Tibet"*: Altick, 38.

118   *"Vast chain of being"*: Pope, "Essay on Man," I, l. 237.

118   *the vertical chain*: My discussion of the great chain of being is based principally upon Lovejoy, esp. 183–207.

119   *"follow all the links of this chain"*: Sprat, 110.

119   *"Every part of matter is peopled"*: Addison, *Spectator,* no. 519, 4:346.

119   *"vindicate the ways of God"*: "Essay on Man," quotations from *Poems*: I, l. 16; I, l. 294; 3, ll. 24–25; 3, ll. 43–48; I, ll. 223–24; I, l. 184.

120   *Furthermore, in Pope's satirical poems*: See Doody, 12–13.

121   *The idea of the great chain*: Rod Preece's *Brute Souls* contains a very interesting chapter on the great chain of being as a pre-Darwinian model of the continuity of creation that anticipates in important ways the theory of evolution (294–330).

121   *"There are some brutes"*: Locke, *Essay*, 3.6.12.

122   *"the very process of pushing"*: Turner, 8. See his discussion of race hierarchies and animals, 7–8; and Ritvo's *Platypus*, esp. 122–30: her book is a fascinating history of the ideology behind the classification of humans and animals.

123   *Such enlightened thinking*: Moore, 12.

123   *"the sense of the separation"*: Lovejoy, 231.

123   *"The question is not"*: Bentham, 283.

CHAPTER SEVEN: STAGES OF CRUELTY

129   *"in hopes of preventing"*: Hogarth, quoted in Paulson, 1:211. Steintrager points out the inherent contradiction in this polemic, however: that those whose treatment of animals was most in need of reform would be more likely to respond to the threat of the reprisals the series depicts than to respond to, or even understand, its call for pity and compassion for beasts (57–58). My discussion of *The Four Stages of Cruelty* is especially indebted to Paulson, 1:211–15, and Steintrager, 37–59.

131   *"It is hard"*: *Gentleman's Magazine,* 1789, 15–17.

133   *In combination with the pervasive idea*: J. Turner comments that because the concept of "cruelty" implies a desire to inflict pain, it presupposes the empathetic ability to appreciate that animals suffer, something he says people appear to have lacked before the eighteenth century (2). Hogarth certainly depicts intentional infliction of pain, though he saw cruelty in human *indifference* to animal suffering as well. From the animals' perspective, of course, the human intention behind their suffering was meaningless.

133   *One man who had torn*: Descriptions of such abuses recur constantly in the eighteenth and nineteenth centuries. These examples are taken from Perkins, 14, 16; *Parl. Deb,* 2nd ser., vol. 12, col. 1160; Plumptre, 136–39; Pain, 45–47; Thomas, 93–94; and Young, 128–29.

134   *Sheep had their wool pulled*: Tying horses' tails to plows and pulling the wool off sheep were outlawed in the early seventeenth century, but both practices continued nonetheless. They were particularly associated with Ireland.

134   *"feed in pain"*: Thomas, 94.

135   *If someone succeeded*: E. Barry, 10, citing *Blount's Antiquities.*

135   *Percival Stockdale, who wrote*: Stockdale, 15.

135   *John Lawrence, a sportsman*: Lawrence, *Philosophical and Practical Treatise*, 2:550–52.

135   *"The Great Cat Massacre"*: Darnton, 92–96.

137   *The Roman poet Ovid*: Metamorphoses, Bk. 15: http://etext.lib.virginia.edu/latin/ovid/trans/Metamorph15.htm.

139   *Butchers were neither exempt*: Stevenson, 236–37. At a time in which many offenses, such as pickpocketing, could carry a capital sentence, the jurors' compassion was often a petty criminal's only defense against the hangman.

141   *He eventually died*: Register Book of the Royal Society, Copy 2: 1666–1667, 290–92, 315–16. This volume contains numerous reports of transfusions between animals of the same and different species. Transfusions could also be performed on humans: the society once employed a human subject who received a dose of lamb's blood, apparently with no ill effect, though the more frequent human transfusions performed in Paris resulted in a fatality and thus brought an end to human transfusions in England.

142   *"This was an experiment"*: Guerrini, "Ethics," 400. Evelyn, *Diary*, 3:497–98; accounts of his participation in experiments using poison on animals: 3:289, 290, 403, 406.

143   *Elsewhere he expressed concern*: Boyle and Hooke quoted and discussed in Guerrini, "Ethics," 396–401.

143   *"he commits most of these barbarities"*: Spence, 1:118.

144   *"the painful physical experiments"*: Kant in Maehle and Trohler, 37.

144   *"It is time that"*: Johnson, *Idler* no. 17, 5 Aug. 1758.

145   *Yet other MPs defended*: *Parl. Deb*, 2nd ser., 12, cols. 657–61.

145   *"happy because I believe"*: quoted in Uglow, *Hogarth*, 500.

CHAPTER EIGHT: THE MEANEST WORM IS OUR SISTER

147   *"according to his friend Dr. Johnson"*: Boswell, *Life of Johnson*, 250; on Smart's life and incarceration, see also Williamson, passim.

147   *"most famous cat"*: Curry, 18.

148   *For he knows that God*: Smart, Fragment B, part 4.

151   *So how could we so wantonly destroy*: Dean, 2:49–50; T. Young, 193–94.

151   *"Such images of stewardship"*: Porter, 25–26.

152   *We should bear in mind*: Perkins, 32.

153   *When Adam and Eve fell*: Hildrop, Letter II, 10–11.

153   *"Brutes have souls"*: Hildrop, Letter II, 38.

153   *"injuries of the Fall"*: Dean, 1:105–6.

153   *clear that animals have souls*: Dean, vol. 2, passim.

154   *"Something better remains"*: Wesley, quoted in Kean, 19–20, and in A. Brown, 9.

154   *He died the year after*: Ryder, "Primatt."

155   *"cruelty of men to brutes"*: Primatt, 35–42.

155   *In it, he argued that since animals*: Pope, "Against Barbarity," 233.

155   *His citations from the Hebrew Bible*: Ryder, *Animal Revolution*, 62–63.

155   *Primatt was one of the first*: Perkins (41) finds the first actual mention of animal rights in the work of the Nonconformist vegetarian Thomas Tryon.

156   *"Did not the same Hand"*: Clemency, 7–10.

157   *Similar arguments were made*: T. Young, 187–92, 7–8.

158   *The philosopher David Hume argued*: Hume, *Enquiries*, 300.

158   *The natural historian Erasmus Darwin*: Darwin cited in Perkins, 24.

158   *Bentham's utilitarian philosophy*: Bentham, 283.

159   *"were early taught diligence"*: Locke, *Some Thoughts Concerning Education*, sec. 116.

160   *Though many reformers were certainly conscious*: Wollstonecraft and Baille cited in Perkins, 21.

161   *These girls feel the lesson*: My discussion of Wright's painting owes much to Kean, 15–17; on the Lunar Society, see Uglow, *Lunar Men*. Thanks also to Steve Ilott for help in reading this painting.

162   *"To make a comparison"*: Primatt, 75.

163   *But it sold fewer than*: Granger, 8, 10, 13, 15–17. Granger preached his sermon on 18 Oct. 1772 and published it the same year.

163   *As James Turner has observed*: J. Turner, 14.

CHAPTER NINE: THROW DOWN THE BUTCHER'S KNIFE

164   *At the time of his nervous*: Cheyne gives an account of his life in his *English Malady*, 325–70; my discussion of Cheyne is based upon this work, as well as Stuart, 163–80; Spencer, 217–19; and Mullett's introduction to Cheyne's *Letters*, 7–28. See also Guerrini, "Diet," passim.

165   *England's most famous vegetarian*: The *Oxford English Dictionary* lists the first occurrence of the word "vegetarian" in 1839, though Stuart says it was already in some use by this time. "Fruitarian" is given as originating in 1893, while "vegan" dates from the attempt in 1944 to distinguish a vegetable and fruit diet completely free of animal products from the other two terms.

165   *"When mighty Roast Beef"*: These lyrics were written by Henry Fielding for his play *The Covent Garden Opera* in 1731, but the song soon became detached from the play. The verses go on to humorously deplore the "Frenchification" of the English diet: "But since we have learnt / From all-vapouring France / To eat their ragouts / As well as to dance, / We're fed up with nothing / But vain complaisance / Oh the Roast Beef of Old England / And old English Roast Beef." And so forth.

166   *"the enormous immorality"*: Bolingbroke, quoted in Stuart, 163.

166   *"Who damns our trash"*: E. Young, "Epistles to Mr. Pope: Epistle II. From Oxford," ll. 217–20.

166   *That this logic could extend*: Acetaria, quoted in Stuart, 83.

167 *"vomit now and then"*: Cheyne, *Letters to Richardson*, 12 Sept. and 26 Oct. 1739, 57–58.

167 *Interest in a vegetable diet*: Stuart on Tyron, 60–88; on Evelyn, 1–38, 60–88.

168 *For fear of being labeled a fanatic*: Stuart, 134–36, 176–80.

169 *"What beast of prey"*: "On the Vegetable System of Diet," 340; see also Shelley's "A Vindication of a Natural Diet," in *Complete Works*.

169 *Pythagoras, who abstained from eating animal flesh*: The views of the historical, sixth-century BCE Pythagoras are, as modern scholars have shown, extremely difficult to define: later thinkers seem to have all too readily endowed the founder of their tradition with their own, much later views, obscuring what little traces of his own opinions there might have been. But it is clear that the tradition of Pythagoreanism was closely linked to the doctrine of metempsychosis. Thanks also to Edward Lee for his help with my discussion of Pythagoras.

170 *"stopped a man beating a dog"*: Discussed and quoted in Steiner, *Anthropocentrism*, 47–49.

171 *as Montaigne coolly pointed out*: Montaigne, "Of Cannibals." On cannibalism and its exaggerated reports in the modern West, see Ritvo, *Platypus*, 209–12.

172 *If souls live by turns*: Yang, 14; for his discussion of the Cambridge Platonists' views of metempsychosis, see 15–19.

172 *Moved by the ladies' example*: J. Z. Holwell (1779), quoted in Yang, 28. My account of Holwell is also indebted to Stuart's chapter on him, 275–94.

173 *Speaking as women*: My account of the "female Pythagoreans" that follows is strongly indebted to Doody's very helpful discussion; Doody also extends her argument to other women poets whom I do not discuss here. For a discussion of women's sentimental writing about animals as a figurative way of mounting a feminist critique of patriarchy, see Barker-Benfield, 235–37.

173 *"witty invention"*: Dean, 2:viii-x.

175 *In 1779, a young Scots poet*: Unless otherwise noted, my discussion of Oswald's biography is drawn from Erdman, passim; Garrett, xxiv–xxv, and Stuart; 295–312.

176 *"imitated the Gentoos"*: Quoted in Erdman, 32.

177 *Oswald, an atheist, rejected*: *Letters from France in 1802*, quoted in Erdman, 7–8.

177 *"the barbarous governments"*: Oswald, i–ii.

178 *"Were we forced"*: Oswald, 30–32. It is perhaps an indication of the nature of his audience, largely urban and upper- and middle-class, that Oswald uses such a sweeping "we," since certainly in his day there were significant numbers of people who personally killed the pigs or geese they ate. But they would be largely rural folk, those prosperous enough to eat meat on occasion but not to employ someone else to butcher it.

179 *The well-known Platonist*: Taylor's parody, published in 1792, was specifically directed at Wollstonecraft's *Vindication of the Rights of Men* (1790) and her famous *Vindication of the Rights of Woman* (1792).

180 *"I have often endeavoured"*: Quoted in Erdman, 7.

180 *Oswald joined the crowd*: Erdman, 90–91, 245–46.

180 *"conducive to peace"*: Quoted in Spencer, 50.

182 *Richard Martin of Connemara*: My account of Richard Martin's life throughout this book is based on descriptions written by those who knew him, on his appearances in newspapers and parliamentary records, on his letters in the British Library, and on the accounts of twentieth-century biographers. Of the latter, Lynam's book is by far the most thorough and well researched, although its complete lack of scholarly documentation is a serious and frustrating limitation. The absence of a well-documented biography of Martin makes Lynam's the most authoritative, however. I have also drawn upon the two shorter biographies of Martin, by Phillips and by Pain, and on Ryder's *Oxford Dictionary of National Biography* entry, "Martin, Richard."

184 *During this trial*: Martin repeatedly insulted Fitzgerald during the trial, hoping that this would prompt Fitzgerald to retaliate personally and thus give Martin an excuse to challenge him. Fitzgerald eventually complied, striking Martin with his cane at the theater and then fleeing. Still, he managed to evade Martin's challenge for three years. This anecdote was told by Martin himself, quoted by Barrington (3:136–47), and reprinted in *The Monthly Review* 2 (1832): 513–18. C. S. Hall later visited the saw pit in which the duel took place. An earlier account of the duel, *Memoirs of the Late George R. Fitzgerald and P. R. M'Donnel*, published in 1786 by "a Gentleman of the County Mayo," does not mention the shooting of Prime Serjeant, though it does describe Fitzgerald shooting other dogs as an "amusement." The cause of the duel given in this account was Fitzgerald's retaliation for Martin's courtroom insults.

184 *His reputation as a fearless*: William Jerdan was one of those to whom Martin showed off his dueling scars (Jerdan, 317).

184 *Though tormented by guilt*: Martin's biographers Lynam and Phillips both assume, perhaps wishfully, that this sad event made Martin swear off dueling forever. Kelly, however, cites evidence that Martin continued to duel subsequently.

184 *"Why the survivor, to be sure"*: The "survivor" anecdote has been often told, probably inaccurately, as spoken to Martin's friend the prince regent. The version I cite here was published in the *Dublin Journal* and reprinted in the *Times*, 9 October, 1824. According to Lynam, the occasion was the election of 1812, which Martin lost. For the Sheridan anecdote, see Jeffares. On dueling and Martin, see Barrington, 3:289–91; on dueling in general, and Martin's duel with Fitzgerald in particular, see Lynam, 36–59; MacCarthy, 113–30; and Kelly, 55–56, 150–57.

185 *"Sir, an ox cannot"*: Ryder, "Martin, Richard."

187 *"His observation was acute"*: Jerdan, 320.

188 *"were worse used than Negroes"*: Quoted in Phillips, 19.

188 *Bridget and her sisters*: Lynam, 8.

189 *"familiarized to spectacles of distress"*: Parr, 15.

191 *"his sterling qualities"*: Jerdan, 312.

193 *"I believe Dick Martin"*: Hall, 229–30.

193 *a kind and benevolent landlord*: Jerdan, 318.

194 *"No one need be afeared"*: Hall, 230–31.

194 *"renowned for hospitality"*: Burke, 1:322.

CHAPTER ELEVEN: TAKING THE BULL BY THE HORNS

201 *Sir William rose in the Commons*: Account of the debate in *Parl. Hist*, 35:202–14—the pagination of this volume is defective—and the London *Times*, 19 Apr. 1800. See also Kenyon-Jones, 79–87.

202 *Hill was particularly known*: On Hill, see Sydney, passim.

202 *No one raised any opposition*: A third MP is recorded as having spoken that day: William Baker, MP for Hertfordshire, agreed that bullbaiting was indeed an inhuman sport that "occasioned many mischiefs," but, he added, cockfighting was just as objectionable, and he hoped that the honorable gentlemen would consider banning it, too. *Journal of the House of Commons* 55:362, 371, 396.

202 *Windham was considered*: On Windham, see D. Wilkinson, and Rosebery's introduction to *The Windham Papers*.

203 *hunting was becoming more widespread*: Perkins, xiv, 64–88.

204 *the strategy of the abolitionists*: Some abolitionists, including William Wilberforce, were initially loath to attack slavery itself, hoping that if the trade were abolished, slavery would eventually die out on its own.

205 *A young man, Canning*: Hall, 1:156.

205 *"My lords, I have done"*: Jeffares, passim.

206 *An honorable friend of his*: It is unclear to whom Sheridan was referring, but he may have meant Thomas Erskine, who in 1800 was a member of the Commons, had long talked about proposing such a bill, and in 1809 did bring before the House of Lords the first animal welfare bill that would have covered horses.

207 *"misery so diverting"*: Lamb, 32–33.

207 *the bill lost by only two votes*: One supporter was a "Mr. Martin." In some histories he is mistaken for Richard Martin, who did not join the British Parliament until the following year; in fact, this was James Martin, MP for Tewkesbury, member of a prominent banking family. The actual vote was on a motion by Windham to delay further consideration of the bill for five months—that is, effectually to kill it—and Windham's motion received the majority of votes.

207 *The* Times . . . *crowed its approval*: *Times*, 25 Apr. 1800.

207 *"For dogs and hares"*: Cited in Henderson, 324. Henderson identifies this as referring to the defeat of Dent's 1802 bill, but it clearly refers to Pulteney's bill of 1800.

208 *He wrote in his diary*: Wilberforce, *Life*, 2:366.

208 *the Nightingale of the House of Commons*: Lean, 15.

209 *"he grew, and grew"*: Quoted in Wilberforce, *Life*, 1:27.

209 *"so disappointed and grieved"*: Wilberforce, *Life*, 2:340.

209 "Good causes": Pollack, 139.

210 "with the disease of a beast": Cobbett quoted in Pollack, 178.

210 "God Almighty has set": Wilberforce quoted in Furneaux, 57.

210 He suffered chronic stomach pain: Pollack, 78–81.

211 "argued it like a parish officer": Wilberforce, Life, 2:365–66.

211 both his and Hill's arguments: See Kean, 31–32.

211 "he had no idea": Wilberforce, Life, 2:366.

212 a drunken man was killed: Times, 17 Sept. 1801.

213 "feebly supporting himself": The Bury Post for Tuesday, 17 Nov., quoted in the Times, 24 Nov. 1801. Richmond identifies the day of the baiting as 5 Nov. (26), hence Guy Fawkes Day. The local authorities would soon succeed in suppressing this tradition; see Griffin, 232–33. Stockdale repeats this story but places the events in Bury, Lancashire, vii.

213 The horse authority John Lawrence: Lawrence, Philosophical and Practical Treatise, 1:132. The Times reported a comparable cruelty committed by two drovers against a cow: 26 July 1814.

213 "Good God!": Quoted in E. Barry, 6–7.

213 The following spring: Account of the debates taken from Parl. Hist., 36:829–54, and the Times between late April and early June 1802.

213 its sponsor was John Dent: Sheridan, General Leland, Lord Granville, and Leveson Gower joined Dent in preparing the bill. Journal of the House of Commons, 57:400. Other references in this volume: 409, 416, 496, 498, and "Petitions," 59.

214 The bill eventually passed: For the debate on 24 May 1796, see Parl. Hist., 32:994–1006; on Dent, see Fisher, passim.

215 the sorts of women: Supporting petitions from towns in Stafford similarly blamed industrial workers in the collieries, lime works, and iron works, who were "notorious for their depravity; and drunkenness, idleness, gaming, swearing, and every other species of disorder and riot." Journal of the House of Commons, 57:344, 348. Petitions came from Darlaston, Dudley, Titpton, Sedgley, Walfall, Wolverhampton, and Wednesbury in Stafford, a county in the newly industrializing Midlands; and from Wellington and Wenlock in the county of Salop. Two petitions supporting the bill also came from Stamford (416). Only the petitions from Salop specifically mentioned cruelty as one of their principal objections.

215 "foolish speech": Wilberforce, Life, 3:48.

215 "butcher's meat": George Canning to William Windham, 23 May 1802, in Windham, 2:188–90.

216 they were both extremist groups: Lumping together Jacobins, atheists, and Methodists as "fruit of the same tree" was a common attack by conservative opponents, as Kean remarks (24).

217 "a stupid dread of innovation": Romilly, 2:247–48.

218 Evangelicals were prone: See Bradley, esp. 94–118, and F. Brown, esp. 393–486.

219 no day of rest at all: Pollack, 59–60.

219 Thomas Macaulay famously quipped: Macaulay, 77.

219 *"chaining and staking down"*: Lawrence, *Philosophical and Practical Treatise,* 186.

220 *The bill was defeated again*: Emma Griffin points out that attempts to regulate or ban bullbaiting were ultimately less of a factor in its demise than the slow attrition of interest in the sport—though it does seem likely that changing public opinion, expressed in such contexts as sermons and growing personal disapproval of the practice, must have had an impact too, apart from the actual efficacy of editorializing in the press and passing of legislation. See Stockdale, vi.

220 *"All hopes of success"*: The *Times,* 22 April 1800.

221 *Richard Martin . . . was in Galway at the time*: This debate took place on 24 May 1802. Two letters written by Martin addressed from Galway dated 24 May and 6 June 1802 are in the British Library: Hardwicke Papers, vol. 386, Add. 35734, ff. 267, 330.

222 *Sanctioned by Windham and Parliament*: Times, 8 June 1802. Placard quoted in Perkins, 17; I have modernized its spelling.

CHAPTER TWELVE: THE UNFORTUNATE TOURIST'S DOG

223 *story of the faithful dog*: The story of Gough and his dog has been retold in the present day: see *The Guardian,* 15 March 2003, reporting on a show on the topic at the Wordsworth Trust in Grasmere. My account here is based principally upon Rawnsley.

224 *"How long didst thou think"*: Scott, "Helvellyn," printed in Rawnsley, 2nd ed.

224 *Greyfriars Bobby, who guarded his master's grave*: Bobby died in 1872.

226 *the implicit quid pro quo*: Humans were known to break this compact, however, and not just "savages" in other parts of the world. Dogs and especially cats were known to be eaten by some poorer Britons at this time and after, shocking as the breaking of this taboo was to most people. Britons did not generally eat horses, either, although this was, and is, common in western Europe. See Ritvo, *Platypus,* 208–9.

227 *Sarah Trimmer wrote many children's books*: For an especially detailed discussion of Trimmer's writings, see Ferguson, 7–26; also Ritvo, *Animal Estate,* 132.

228 *"The Bleat, the Bark"*: "Auguries of Innocence."

228 *"they pity and they eat"*: Goldsmith, *Citizen of the World,* 15, 38.

229 *"The day may come"*: Bentham, 283.

229 *Many who argued for animal protection*: For a valuable discussion of the uses, and limits, of the idea of sympathy when translated from abolition to animal protection, see Ellis, "Suffering Things," esp. 102–9. For this connection between imagining slaves and imagining animals, see also Brown, 262–63, and Spiegel, passim.

230 *Stockdale made the specific connection*: Stockdale, 9–13.

231 *Erskine was a high-spirited man*: The account of Erskine's life is based upon Lemmings and Stryker.

232 *Erskine was defending a man*: Stryker, 369.

232 "Trial by Jury": Erskine, Speeches, xix.

232 "spoke like other persons": Morgan, 118–19.

233 "a bill he was to bring": Romilly, 3:233–35; Stryker, 100.

234 "the sufferings of animals": Parl. Deb., 14, cols. 851–53.

234 Erskine finally introduced his bill: The account that follows of the debates that took place between 15 May and 2 June 1809 is based on Parl. Deb., 14:553–71, 804–8, 851–53. Kenyon-Jones gives a helpful account of them (88–94).

237 "Of the necessity of such": Times, 30 May 1809.

237 This bill attempted once again: Parl. Deb., 14:990, 1029–40. This text of Hansard is defective, with extra pages intervening. Windham's speech is also extensively recounted in the Times, 14 June 1809.

239 "horrors of the middle passage": Lawrence, Practical and Philosophical Treatise, 2:531.

240 As one admirer remarked: Earl of Rosebery, introduction to Windham Papers, v.

240 "a mere enjoyment of torture": Examiner, 24 June 1810, in Biographical Tracts 1810–1909, British Library 10600 h 13.

241 "one of the most pressing grievances": Report of the Society for Preventing Wanton Cruelty to Brute Animals, passim.

242 A bill to prevent: Parl. Debates, 34, cols. 1040–41.

243 His focus had not been: Erskine, Armata, 2:26–36.

244 he challenged the winner to a duel: Lynam, 172–76; Thorne, 4:565. The duel was not fought, but this election was apparently the occasion upon which Martin made his notorious joke that the man to win would be the survivor. Fortunately for him, he was wrong.

CHAPTER THIRTEEN: HUMANITY DICK

246 "any horse, cow, ox, heifer": "Bill to Prevent Cruel and Improper Treatment of Cattle," House of Commons Parliamentary Papers, 541, 18 May 1821.

247 "was gifted with an abundant fund": Jerdan, 320.

247 In the Commons: This debate on 1 June was covered in the Times, 2 June 1821, and Parl. Debs., 2nd ser. 5, cols. 1098–99. See also Wilson, 356–57, for a brief account of Martin's parliamentary animal protection activities and their reception. The Times in particular reported members laughing during debates on many kinds of bills.

250 At last, at the end of a month: Times, 30 June 1821. For the bill's amended form, see House of Commons Parliamentary Papers, 665, 15 June 1821.

250 Perhaps he looked so weary: See Lemmings.

251 their abuse . . . took untraditional, urbanized forms: Turner discusses the new phenomenon of "cruelty in a factory age," 15–38. Kean (30–31) emphasizes the importance of the sight of cruelty to urban animals as a factor promoting change, and notes that animals, like people, had become modern urban creatures, not just nostalgic relics of a lost rural tradition. See also Perkins, 13–14.

253 "when they were informed": Times, 8 Aug. 1820 and 7 Feb. 1821.

254 *In one famous instance*: Martin's visit to the *Morning Post* was recounted by both Hall (230) and Jerdan (318).

254 *"blundered into reform"*: Hall, 230.

254 *"sheer madcap"*: Jerdan, 312.

256 *No dog seemed to stand a chance*: Egan, 176–79.

257 *"only to the lowest and vilest"*: Martin's speech was reported in the *Times*, 17 May 1822. A few days earlier, he had introduced a petition from stagecoach owners complaining about the abuse of their horse by their drivers. The *Times* reported some laughs when Martin described the horse's nasty injuries: the next day Martin asserted that the laughter had been misrepresented and wanted to bring the writer to the bar of the House. Another member calmed him down, saying that the reporter may have "mistaken their merriment" (*Times*, 10–11 May 1822). There are so many instances of laughter reported at accounts of animal (and human) abuse in the *Times* (and in other papers, such as the *Courier*, which was sympathetic to Martin), however, that it seems likely that some members, at least, found the abuse amusing. The paper never specifies how many members engaged in the laughter.

258 *Among his other preparations*: *Times*, 17 May 1822. The *Times* covered the debates on the bill throughout May and June.

258 *A later account described*: *Voice of Humanity* 1, no. 1 (1830): 26. Besides "this den of infamy, vice, and cruelty" a few hundred yards from the Houses of Parliament, there were other pits in 1830. The article names five others in various locations around London (27).

258 *"Whereas it is expedient"*: An Act to prevent the cruel and improper Treatment of Cattle. 3 George IV, 22 July, 1822. This is the final, amended form of the act. This account of the debates on 24 May and 7 June 1822 is taken from *Parl. Deb.* 2nd ser., vol. 7, cols. 758–59, 873–74, and from the *Times*, 25 May 1822.

259 *The bill passed by a substantial voice-vote*: Although the galleries were cleared for a division—the process by which the members group themselves for a head count, used whenever the outcome is not clear (or whenever the members need to be held accountable)—in this case the bill passed handily, without need for the procedure. *Times*, 8 June 1822.

259 *he expressed his satisfaction*: *Times*, 11 June 1822.

259 *The bill passed easily*: *Journal of the House of Lords*, 17 and 18 July 1822; *Times*, 18 July 1822.

259 *"Lord Erskine tried to deliver"*: Quoted in Fairholme and Paine, 27.

259 *So Martin, who had assisted attempted prosecutions*: He had assisted in the unsuccessful prosecution of two men for abusing a horse on 16 June 1821, for instance (Fairholme and Paine, 28). In a letter to an unnamed correspondent now in the British Library, Martin told him which court he needed to contact—in this case, Southwark—and promised to attend himself (Add. 52484., F. 173., 6 Sept. 1825).

262 *"seeming very well pleased"*: *Times*, 3 Sept. 1823.

264 *"If I had a donkey"*: Ashton, *Modern Street Ballads*, 94–95.

CHAPTER FOURTEEN: FOR THE LOVE OF ANIMALS

266 *Once again the magistrates*: *Times*, 8 May 1823.

266 *"wantonly and cruelly beat"*: See Fairholme and Paine, 36, for example.

266 *"most fallacious"*: Wilberforce, 5:214.

266 *When, shortly thereafter, he introduced*: *Commons Journals*, 78 (18 June–7 July 1823).

267 *Bills he introduced to ban*: Ibid., 78–79 (1823–1824).

267 *a series of letters*: *Monthly Magazine* 50–52 (1820–21).

267 *Clericus, it has been plausibly suggested*: Fairholme and Paine, 24.

268 *Nothing more came of this group*: Ibid., 52.

268 *"I have nothing at all to do with it"*: *Courier*, 1 July 1825.

268 *A green plaque now marks*: At 77/78 St. Martin's Lane, WC2. Thanks to Chris Reed, archivist of the RSPCA, for information about this plaque.

269 *Several present, in addition to Broome*: J. Turner, 40.

269 *he published that same year his book*: Gompertz, 2–10, 15–21, 40.

270 *They discussed the impact*: details of the first meeting of the SPCA can be found in the RSPCA Minute Book, 16 June 1824; *Courier*, 17 June 1824; *Times*, 17 June 1824; and Fairholme and Paine, 55–58.

270 *"make 'em do it"*: Hall, 1:229.

271 *Following the lead of Broome*: On Broome, see Kramer, passim.

271 *the law was nonetheless making a significant difference*: Parl. Deb., 2nd ser., 12, cols. 660–61. This optimistic assessment was apparently true, relatively speaking, but as accounts by the SPCA and other animal protection organizations in the 1830s made clear, the abuses there remained horrific.

271 *he rose to introduce bill after bill*: The parliamentary debates in 1825–26 quoted in this chapter, unless otherwise noted, are taken from *Parl. Deb.*, 2nd ser., 12, cols. 657–661, 1002–13, 1160–62; 13, cols. 418–19, 1252–54; 14, cols. 647–57, 1391–92; 15, cols. 530–31.

273 *"certain odd gesticulations"*: *Times*, 21 Apr. 1826.

273 *"were thrown out actually before"*: SPCA Minute Books. Also quoted in Fairholme and Paine, 38.

273 *"Only conceive how Mr. Martin"*: *Times*, 9 Oct. 1824.

275 *a highly publicized lawsuit*: The *Chronicle's* allusion to *Blackwood's* line about murder was, "We dare not quote what follows about *murdering*." *Morning Chronicle*, 5 Sept, 1825; *Courier*, 6 Sept. 1825; letter to Ayles, British Library, Add. Ms. 52339, f. 126, 6 Sept. 1825; Guildhall hearing of 7 Sept. in the *Courier*, 8 Sept. 1825. During the court case in late September, Martin's fear for his life was ridiculed by the defense counsel; the case was eventually settled. Martin did not bring proceedings against *Blackwood's* because its proprietor, Baillie Blackwood, apologized, saying that the attack had run without his knowledge, and in October ran an article celebrating Martin's work. This piece was printed in both the *Courier* and the *Morning Chronicle*—though the latter professed to believe that it had been written by Martin himself. See Lynam (248–57) for a full account of this contretemps.

276 *he became its casualty*: Lynam, 262–71.

276 *"that dark and dismal day"*: Palette, v–vi.

276 *including a number of women*: Female participation in the SPCA in particular and the animal protection movement in general became quite extensive and important as the nineteenth century progressed, and many more women writers took up the cause of animals. See Ferguson for an insightful account of the work of several of these nineteenth-century women.

277 *They founded another organization*: Li gives a substantive account of these developments among animal protection organizations in the nineteenth century, and the following account is indebted to her work.

277 *So, from an early point*: Li quite rightly observes that it is important to remember that the early efforts on behalf of animals were the competing and/or complementary work of several societies that existed at the time, not just the SPCA—a fact that has often been underplayed in histories of the movement.

277 *Subsequently, the membership voted*: The Minute Book shows that on 26 May 1832 the merger was discussed and rejected at an SPCA meeting. This account of Gompertz's split from the SPCA is based on Li and on J. Turner, 40–45.

278 *"to give their good money"*: Quoted in Li.

278 *"Mr. Martin still lives"*: Quoted in Thorne, 4:565.

278 *"the late eccentric member"*: Times, 10 Jan. 1834.

279 *Parliament finally passed*: Times, 8 Oct. 1835, referring to the previous session. The year before, some progress had been made when clauses had been added to a preexisting act regulating the driving of animals in the street that banned animal fighting within five miles of Temple Bar.

279 *"He was the most determined enemy"*: Jerdan, 320.

279 *The organization pragmatically sought*: J. Turner (56–59) points out that the animal protection movement would allow respectable Victorians to address some of the conditions of the new industrial age that made them uneasy without threatening the social order that also made them prosperous. He also points out that, practically speaking, the RSPCA's respectable middle-class orientation was arguably the best strategy for actually alleviating cruelty to animals.

CONCLUSION: THE LEGACY OF ANIMAL PROTECTION

283 *have lately pointed out*: Michael Pollan's blog at the *New York Times* addresses many of these issues very helpfully: http://pollan.blogs.nytimes.com/.

BIBLIOGRAPHY

Addison, Joseph, and Richard Steele. *The Guardian*. Ed. by John Calhoun Stephens. Lexington: University Press of Kentucky, 1982.

———. *The Spectator*. Ed. by Donald F. Bond. 5 vols. Oxford: Clarendon Press, 1965.

———. *The Tatler*. Ed. by Donald F. Bond. 3 vols. New York: Oxford University Press, 1987.

Allin, Michael. *Zarafa*. New York: Dell Publishing, 1998.

Aquinas, Thomas. *Basic Writings of Saint Thomas Aquinas*. Ed. by Anton Pegis. 2 vols. Indianapolis: Hackett Publishing, 1997.

Altick, Richard D. *The Shows of London*. Cambridge, Mass.: Harvard University Press, 1978.

Anecdotes of Impudence. London: 1827.

Aristotle. *De Anima, Books II and III*. Trans. by D. W. Hamlyn. Oxford: Clarendon Press, 1993.

Arlott, John, and Arthur Daley. *Pageantry of Sport*. New York: Hawthorne Books, 1968.

Ashton, John. *Modern Street Ballads*. London: 1888.

———. *Social Life in the Reign of Queen Anne*. New York: Scribners, 1925.

Augustine. *The City of God Against the Pagans*. Trans. and ed. by R. W. Dyson. Cambridge, U.K.: Cambridge University Press, 1998.

Avery, Emmet L., Arthur H. Scouten, William Van Lennep, and George Winchester Stone, Jr., eds. *The London Stage, 1660–1800*. Vol. 4. Carbondale: Southern Illinois University Press, 1968.

Ayton, Richard. *Essays and Sketches of Character*. London: 1825.

Bacon, Francis. *The Advancement of Learning and Novum Organum*. Ed. by James Creighton. New York: Colonial Press, 1900.

———. *Da Sapientia Veterum*. In James Spedding, Robert Leslie Ellis, and Douglas Denon Heath, eds. *The Works of Francis Bacon*. Vol. 6. London: Longman, 1858.

Bailey, Derrick Sherwin. *Homosexuality and the Western Christian Tradition*. London: Longmans, Green, 1955. http://www.fordham.edu/halsall/pwh/englaw.html.

Baker, Thomas. *The Fine Lady's Airs*. London: 1708. http://lion.chadwyck.com/toc.do

?action=ew&divLevel=o&mapping=toc&area=Drama&id=Zooo055175&forward
=tocMarc&DurUrl=Yes.

Barber, Richard. *Bestiary.* Rochester, N.Y.: Boydell Press, 1992.

Barclay, John. *An Inquiry into the Opinions, Ancient and Modern, concerning Life and Orga-nization.* Edinburgh: 1822.

Barker-Benfield, G. J. *The Culture of Sensibility: Sex and Society in Eighteenth-Century Britain.* Chicago: University of Chicago Press, 1992.

Barnette, Martha. *Dog Days and Dandelions.* New York: St. Martin's Press, 2003.

Barrington, Jonah. *Personal Sketches of His Own Times (1827–32).* Chicago: Belford, Clarke, 1882.

Barry, David, M.D. *Experimental Researches on the Influence Exercised by Atmospheric Pres-sure upon the Progression of the Blood in the Veins, upon that function called Absorption, and upon the Prevention and Cure of the Symptoms Caused by the Bites of Rabid or Ven-omous Animals.* London: 1826.

Barry, Edward. *Bull Baiting! A Sermon on Barbarity to God's Dumb Creation.* Reading, U.K.: 1802.

"Bartholomew Faire." Scrapbook of Clippings, British Library. BL 74/C.70.h.6.(2).

Battigelli, Anna. *Margaret Cavendish and the Exiles of the Mind.* Lexington, Ky.: Univer-sity Press of Kentucky, 1998.

Beckoff, Marc, ed. *Encyclopedia of Animal Rights and Animal Welfare.* Westport, Conn.: Greenwood Press, 1998.

Beers, Diane L. *For the Prevention of Cruelty: The History and Legacy of Animal Rights Ac-tivism in the United States.* Athens, Ohio: Swallow Press, 2006.

Belozerskaya, Marina. *The Medici Giraffe and Other Tales of Exotic Animals and Power.* New York: Little, Brown, 2006.

Bentham, Jeremy. *Introduction to the Principles of Morals and Legislation.* Ed. by J. H. Burns and H.L.A. Hart. Oxford: Clarendon Press, 1996.

Bentley, Richard. *The Folly and Unreasonableness of Atheism.* 4th ed. London: 1699.

Berman, Paul Schiff. "Rats, Pigs, and Statues on Trial: The Creation of Cultural Nar-ratives in the Prosecution of Animals and Inanimate Objects." *New York University Law Review* 69, no. 2 (May 1994): 288–326.

Berry, James. *Tales of the West of Ireland.* Dublin: Dolmen Press, 1975.

Bingley, William. *Animal Biography, or Popular Zoology.* 3 vols. 4th ed. London: 1813.

The Black Book; or, Corruption Unmask'd. 3rd ed. London: 1826.

Blake, William. *The Complete Poetry and Prose of William Blake.* Ed. by David V. Erd-man. Berkeley, Calif.: University of California Press, 1982.

Bondeson, Jan. *The Feejee Mermaid and Other Essays in Natural and Unnatural History.* Ithaca: Cornell University Press, 1999.

Boswell, James. *Boswell's London Journal, 1762–1763.* Ed. by Frederick A. Pottle. New York: McGraw-Hill, 1950.

———. *The Life of Samuel Johnson.* New York: Everyman, 1992.

Bougeant, Guillaume Hyacinthe. *A Philosophical Amusement upon the Language of Beasts.* 1739. In Aaron Garrett, ed., *Animal Rights and Souls in the Eighteenth Century.* Vol. 1. Bristol, U.K.: Thoemmes Press, 2000.

Boulton, William B. *The Amusements of Old London.* 2 vols. London: John C. Nimmo, 1901.

Bowerbank, Sylvia. *Speaking for Nature: Women and Ecologies of Early Modern England.* Baltimore: Johns Hopkins University Press, 2004.

———, and Sara Mendelson, eds. *Paper Bodies: A Margaret Cavendish Reader.* Ontario, Canada: Broadview Press, 2000.

Bradley, Ian. *The Call to Seriousness: The Evangelical Impact on the Victorians.* London: Jonathan Cape, 1976.

Broome, Arthur. *SPCA Prospectus.* London: 1824.

Brown, Antony. *Who Cares for Animals?* London: Heinemann, 1974.

Brown, Ford K. *Fathers of the Victorians: The Age of Wilberforce.* Cambridge, U.K.: Cambridge University Press, 1961.

Brown, Laura. *Fables of Modernity: Literature and Culture in the English Eighteenth Century.* Ithaca: Cornell University Press, 2001.

Brown, Thomas. *Amusements Serious and Comical.* London, 1700. Literature Online, http://gateway.proquest.com/openurl?ctx_ver=Z39.882003&xri:pqil:res_ver=0.2 &res_id=xri:lion-us&rft_id=xri:lion:ft:pr:Z000026106:0.

Buffon, George Louis Leclerc. *Natural History.* Trans. by William Smellie. London, 1781. http://faculty.njcu.edu/fmoran/buffonhome.htm.

Burke, Bernard. *Vicissitudes of Families.* 2 vols. London: Longmans, Green, Reader and Dyer, 1869.

Callaghan, Dympna. "(Un)natural Loving: Swine, Pets, and Flowers in Venus and Adonis." *Early Modern Culture,* 2003. http://emc.eserver.org/1-3/callaghan.html.

Cameron, David Kerr. *London's Pleasures: From Restoration to Regency.* Thrupp, U.K.: Sutton Publishing, 2001.

Carpenter, Andrew, ed. *Verse in English from Eighteenth-Century Ireland.* Cork, Ireland: Cork University Press, 1998.

Carritt, E. F. *A Calendar of British Taste from 1600 to 1800.* London: Routledge & Kegan Paul, 1948.

Carter, H. E. "Veterinary History and the RSPCA: The First Fifty Years." *Veterinary History* 6, no. 2 (1989–90): 62–71.

Cartwright, James J., ed. *The Wentworth Papers, 1705–1739.* London: Wyman & Sons, 1883.

Cavendish, Margaret. *Philosophical and Physical Opinions.* London: 1663.

———. *Philosophical Letters; or, Modest Reflections upon some Opinions in Natural Philosophy, Maintained by several Famous and Learned Authors of this Age, Expressed by way of Letters.* London: 1664.

———. *Poems and Fancies.* London: 1653.

Cecil, David. *The Stricken Deer; or, The Life of Cowper.* London: Constable and Company, 1929.

Chalmers, Alexander, ed. *The British Essayists; with Prefaces, Historical and Biographical.* London: 1808.

Chambers, Robert, ed. *The Book of Days: A Miscellany of Popular Antiquities. 1862–64.* 2 vols. Facsimile ed. Detroit: Gale Research, 1967.

Chapuis, Alfred, and Edouard Gélis, *Le monde des automates*. 2 vols. Paris: 1928.

Cheyne, George. *The English Malady*. Ed. by Roy Porter. London: Routledge, 1991.

———. *The Letters of Doctor George Cheyne to Samuel Richardson (1733–1743)*. Ed. by Charles F. Mullett. Columbia, Mo.: University of Missouri Press, 1943.

Clarke, Paul A. B., and Andrew Linzey, eds. *Political Theory and Animal Rights*. London: Pluto Press, 1990.

Clemency to Brutes: The substance of two Sermons preached on a Shrove-Sunday, with a particular View to dissuade from that species of Cruelty annually practiced in England, The Throwing at Cocks. London: 1761.

Coleman, Sydney H. *Humane Society Leaders in America*. Albany, N.Y.: American Humane Association, 1924.

"A Collection of Advertisements, etc. relating to Bartholomew Fair." Scrapbook. British Library, c. 70. H. 6 (2).

The Complete Newgate Calendar. London: Navarre Society, 1926. http://tarlton.law.utexas.edu/lpop/etext/completenewgate.htm.

Cope, Harriet. *A Monody to the Memory of Thomas Lord Erskine*. London: 1824.

Coventry, Francis. *Pompey the Little; or, The Life and Adventures of a Lap-Dog*. Ed. by Robert Adams Day. London: Oxford University Press, 1974.

Cowie, Leonard W. "Parr, Samuel (1747–1825)," *Oxford Dictionary of National Biography*, Oxford University Press, 2004. http://www.oxforddnb.com/view/article/21402.

Cowper, William. *The Poems of William Cowper*. Ed. by John D. Baird and Charles Ryskamp. 3 vols. Oxford: Clarendon Press, 1980–1995.

Cowper, William. *The Task*. London: 1787.

Curry, Neil. *Christopher Smart*. Tavistock, U.K.: Northcote House, 2005.

Daly, Macdonald. "Vivisection in Eighteenth-Century Britain." *British Journal of Eighteenth-Century Studies* 12, no. 1 (1989): 57–67.

Darley, Gillian. *John Evelyn: Living for Ingenuity*. New Haven: Yale University Press, 2006.

Darnton, Robert. *The Great Cat Massacre and Other Episodes in French Cultural History*. New York: Vintage Books, 1985.

Darwin, Erasmus. *The Essential Writings of Erasmus Darwin*. Ed. by Desmond King-Hole. London: MacGibbon and Kee, 1968.

Dean, Richard. *An Essay on the Future Life of Brutes*. 1768. In Aaron Garrett, ed., *Animal Rights and Souls in the Eighteenth Century*. Vol. 2. Bristol, U.K.: Thoemmes Press, 2000.

Dembeck, Hermann. *Animals and Men*. Trans. by Richard and Clara Winston. Garden City, N.Y.: Natural History Press, 1965.

De Saussure, César. *A Foreign View of England in 1725–1729*. Trans. and ed. by Madame Van Muyden. London: Caliban Books, 1995.

Descartes, René. *The Philosophical Writings of Descartes*. 3 vols. Trans. and ed. by John Cottingham, Robert Stoothoff, Dugald Murdoch, and Anthony Kenny. Cambridge, U.K.: Cambridge University Press, 1991.

The Devil among the fancy; or, The pugilistic courts in uproar: to which is added, a whimsical dialogue between Dickey Martin, M.P. and Charley Eastup . . . on the subject of bears, badgers, bull-dogs, and the famous monkey, Jacco Maccacco; showing the comparative humanity of the sports pursued in high and low life. London: 1822.

Donald, Diana. "'Beastly Sights': The Treatment of Animals as a Moral Theme in Representations of London c. 1820–1850." *Art History* 22, no. 4 (1999): 514–44.

———. *Picturing Animals in Britian, 1750–1850.* New Haven: Yale University Press for Paul Mellon Centre for Studies in British Art, 2008.

Doody, Margaret. "Sensuousness in the Poetry of Eighteenth-Century Women Poets." In Isobel Armstrong and Virginia Blain, eds., *Women's Poetry in the Enlightenment: The Making of a Canon, 1730–1820.* London: Macmillan, 1999.

Douthwaite, Julia V. "Rewriting the Savage: The Extraordinary Fictions of the 'Wild Girl of Champagne.'" *Eighteenth-Century Studies* 28, no. 2 (1994–95): 163–192.

Drabble, Phil. "Staffords and Baiting Sports." In Brian Vesey-Fitzgerald, ed., *The Book of the Dog.* London: Nicholson & Watson, 1948.

Edgeworth, Maria. *The Life and Letters of Maria Edgeworth.* Vol. 2. Project Gutenberg. http://www.gutenberg.org/catalog/world/readfile?fk_files=16912&pageno=1.

Egan, Pierce. *Life in London.* 1821. Reprint London: Methuen, 1904.

Ellis, Markman. *The Politics of Sensibility.* Cambridge, U.K.: Cambridge University Press, 1996.

———. "Suffering Things: Lapdogs, Slaves, and Counter-Sensibility." In Mark Blackwell, ed., *The Secret Life of Things: Animals, Objects, and It-Narratives in Eighteenth-Century England.* Lewisburg, Penn.: Bucknell University Press, 2007.

Erdman, David V. *Commerce des Lumières: John Oswald and the British in Paris, 1790–1793.* Columbia, Mo.: University of Missouri Press, 1986.

Erskine, Thomas. *Armata.* 2nd ed. 2 vols. London: 1817.

———. *Cruelty to Animals. The Speech of Lord Erskine, in the House of Peers, on the second Reading of the Bill for Preventing Malicious and Wanton Cruelty to Animals.* Edinburgh: 1809.

———. *The Poetical Works of the Right Honourable Thomas, Lord Erskine.* London: 1823.

———. *The Speech of Lord Erskine in the House of Peers.* Ed. by Arthur Broome. London: Society for the Prevention of Cruelty to Animals, 1824.

———. *Speeches of Thomas Lord Erskine.* Ed. by Edward Walford. 2 vols. London: 1870.

Espriella, Don Manuel Alvarez. *Letters from England.* Trans. by Robert Southey. 3 vols. London: 1814.

Evans, E. P. *The Criminal Prosecution and Capital Punishment of Animals.* 1906. Reprint London: Faber & Faber, 1987.

Evelyn, John. Ballad: "I'll tell thee, Jo." London: National Archives. PRO State Papers 29/450/102, fo. 164.

———. *The Diary of John Evelyn.* 5 vols. Ed. by E. S. de Beer. Oxford: Clarendon Press, 1955.

Fairholme, Edward G., and Wellesley Pain. *A Century of Work for Animals: The History of the RSPCA, 1824–1924.* London: John Murray, 1924.

Ferguson, Moira. *Animal Advocacy and Englishwomen, 1780–1900: Patriots, Nation and Empire.* Ann Arbor: University of Michigan Press, 1998.

Fildes, Valerie A. *Wet Nursing: A History from Antiquity to the Present*. New York: Basil Blackwell, 1988.

Fisher, D. R. "Dent, John (b. in or after 1761, d. 1826)." *Oxford Dictionary of National Biography*, Oxford University Press, 2004. http://www.oxforddnb.com/view/article/65137.

Fitter, R.S.R. *London's Natural History*. 1945. Reprint London: Bloomsbury, 1990.

Floyer, John, and Edward Tyson. "A Relation of Two Monstrous Pigs, with the Resemblance of Humane Faces, and Two Young Turkeys Joined by the Breast." *Philosophical Transactions of the Royal Society* 21 (1699): 431–35.

Franklin, Julian H. *Animal Rights and Moral Philosophy*. New York: Columbia University Press, 2005.

Frith, Mary. *The Life and Death of Mal Cutpurse*. In Janet Todd and Elizabeth Spearing, eds., *Counterfeit Ladies*. New York: New York University Press, 1994.

Fudge, Erica. *Animal*. London: Reaktion Books, 2002.

———. *Brutal Reasoning: Animals, Rationality and Humanity in Early Modern England*. Ithaca: Cornell University Press, 2006.

———. *Perceiving Animals: Humans and Beasts in Early Modern Culture*. London: Macmillan, 2000.

———, Ruth Gilbert, and Susan Wiseman, eds. *At the Borders of the Human: Beasts, Bodies and Natural Philosophy in the Early Modern Period*. London: Macmillan, 1999.

Furneaux, Robin. *William Wilberforce*. London: Hamish Hamilton, 1974.

Garrett, Aaron. Introduction to *Animal Rights and Souls in the Eighteenth Century*. Vol. 1, vii–xxvi. Bristol, U.K.: Thoemmes Press, 2000.

Gattrell, Vic. *City of Laughter: Sex and Satire in Eighteenth-Century London*. New York: Walker, 2007.

Gay, John. *Poetry and Prose*. Ed. by Vinton A. Dearling. Oxford: Clarendon Press, 1974.

George, Wilma, and Brunsdon Yapp. *The Naming of the Beasts: Natural History in the Medieval Bestiary*. London: Duckworth, 1991.

Gerald of Wales. *The History and Topography of Ireland*. Trans. by John J. O'Meara. New York: Penguin, 1982.

Gibson, Robin. *The Face in the Corner: Animals in Portraits from the Collections of the National Portrait Gallery*. London: National Portrait Gallery, 1998.

Glacken, Clarence J. *Traces on the Rhodian Shore: Nature and Culture in Western Thought from Ancient Times to the End of the Eighteenth Century*. Berkeley, Calif.: University of California Press, 1967.

Goldsmith, Oliver. *The Citizen of the World*. London: Everyman's Library, 1970.

———. *An History of the Earth and Animated Nature*. 8 vols. London: 1774.

Gompertz, Lewis. *Moral Inquiries on the Situation of Man and of Brutes*. London: 1824.

———. *Objects and Address of the Society for the Prevention of Cruelty to Animals: Established in June, 1824*. London: 1829.

Gordon, Pryse Lockhart. *Personal Memoirs; or, Reminiscences of Men and Manners at Home and Abroad*. 2 vols. London: 1830.

Grandin, Temple, and Catherine Johnson. *Animals in Translation: Using the Mysteries of Autism to Decode Animal Behavior*. New York: Scribner, 2005.

Granger, James. *An Apology for the Brute Creation; or, Abuse of Animals Censured.* London: 1772.

Grant, Robert. *Early Christians and Animals.* London: Routledge, 1999.

Gregory, William. "An Account of a Monstrous Foetus, Resembling a Hooded Monkey." *Philosophical Transactions of the Royal Society* 41 (1739–1741): 764–67.

Griffin, Emma. *England's Revelry: A History of Popular Sports and Pastimes, 1660–1830.* Oxford: Oxford University Press, 2005.

The Grub Street Journal, 1731–33. Ed. by Bertrand A. Goldgar. 4 vols. London: Pickering and Chatto, 2002.

Guerrini, Anita. "A Diet for a Sensitive Soul: Vegetarianism in Eighteenth-Century Britain." *Eighteenth-Century Life* 23, no. 2 (May 1999): 34–42.

———. "The Ethics of Animal Experimentation in Seventeenth-Century England." *Journal of the History of Ideas* 50, no. 3 (July–Sept. 1989): 391–407.

———. *Experimenting with Humans and Animals: From Galen to Animal Rights.* Baltimore: Johns Hopkins University Press, 2003.

Hackwood, Frederick W. *Old English Sports.* London: T. Fisher Unwin, 1907.

Hall, Samuel Carter. *Retrospect of a Long Life: From 1815 to 1883.* London: 1883.

Hankins, Thomas J., and Robert J. Silverman. *Instruments and the Imagination.* Princeton, N.J.: Princeton University Press, 1995.

Haraway, Donna. *The Companion Species Manifesto: Dogs, People, and Significant Otherness.* Chicago: Prickly Paradigm, 2003.

———. *Primate Visions: Gender, Race, and Nature in the World of Modern Science.* New York: Routledge, 1989.

Harrison, Brian. "Animals and the State in Nineteenth-Century England." *The English Historical Review* 88, no. 349 (Oct. 1973): 786–820.

Harrison, Peter. "The Virtues of Animals in Seventeenth-Century Thought." *Journal of the History of Ideas* 59, no. 3 (1998): 463–84.

Harwood, Dix. *Love for Animals and How It Developed in Great Britain.* Ed. by Rod Preece and David Fraser. Lewiston, N.Y.: Edwin Mellen Press, 2002.

Hay, Douglas. "Poaching and the Game Laws on Cannock Chase." In Douglas Hay, Peter Linebaugh, John D. Rule, E. P. Thompson, and Cal Winslow, eds., *Albion's Fatal Tree: Crime and Society in Eighteenth-Century England.* New York: Pantheon, 1985.

John, Lord Hervey. *Lord Hervey and His Friends, 1726–38.* Ed. by the Earl of Ilchester. London: John Murray, 1950.

Heyrick, Elizabeth. *Cursory Remarks on the Evil Tendency of Unrestrained Cruelty; particularly on that practiced in Smithfield Market.* London: 1823.

Highfill, Philip H., Jr., Kalman A. Burnim, and Edward A. Langhans, eds. *A Biographical Dictionary of Actors, Actresses, Musicians, Dancers, Managers and Other Stage Personnel in London, 1660–1800.* 10 vols. Carbondale, Ill.: Southern Illinois University Press, 1973–1993.

Hill, Peter. "One Man and His Dogs." Twickenham Society, *Eel Pie* 5 (Nov. 2003).

Hildrop, John. *Free Thoughts upon the Brute Creation.* 1743. In Aaron Garrett, ed., *Animal Rights and Souls in the Eighteenth Century.* Vol. 1. Bristol, U.K.: Thoemmes Press, 2000.

Hochschild, Adam. *Bury the Chains: Prophets and Rebels in the Fight to Free an Empire's Slaves.* Boston: Houghton Mifflin, 2005.

Hogarth, William. *A Dissertation on Mr. Hogarth's Six Prints.* London: 1751.

Hollands, Clive. "Animal Rights in the Political Arena." In Peter Singer, ed. *In Defense of Animals.* New York: Basil Blackwell, 1985.

Hood, Thomas. "Ode To Richard Martin, Esq., M.P. for Galway." In *The Poetical Works of Thomas Hood*, 284–86. http://www.gutenberg.org/catalog/world/readfile?fk_files=179433&pageno=284.

Houghton, John. *A Collection for the Improvement of Husbandry and Trade. 1682–1703.* 3 vols. London: 1727.

Hubbard, Clifford L. B. "The Dog in Trade." In Brian Vesey-Fitzgerald, ed., *The Book of the Dog.* London: Nicholson & Watson, 1948.

Huet, Marie-Hélène. *Monstrous Imagination.* Cambridge, Mass.: Harvard University Press, 1993.

Hug, Tobias. " 'You Should Go to *Hockley in the Hole,* and to *Marybone,* Child, to Learn Valour': On the Social Logic of Animal Baiting in Early Modern London." *Renaissance Journal* 2, no. 1 (2004). www2.warwick.ac.uk/fac/arts/ren/publications/journal/nine/hug.doc.

Hume, David. *Enquiries Concerning Human Understanding and Concerning the Principles of Morals.* Ed. by L. A. Selby-Bigge. Oxford: Clarendon Press, 1975.

———. *A Treatise of Human Nature.* Vol. 1. London: J. M. Dent and Sons, 1911.

Jaeger, Muriel. *Before Victoria.* London: Chatto & Windus, 1956.

Jay, Ricky. *Learned Pigs and Fireproof Women.* New York: Warner Books, 1987.

Jeffares, A. Norman. "Sheridan, Richard Brinsley (1751–1816)." *Oxford Dictionary of National Biography.* Oxford: Oxford University Press, 2004. http://www.oxforddnb.com/view/article/25367.

Jerdan, William. *Men I Have Known.* London: 1866.

Julia and the Pet-Lamb; or, Good Temper and Compassion Rewarded. London: 1813.

Kean, Hilda. *Animal Rights: Political and Social Change in Britain Since 1800.* London: Reaktion Books, 1998.

Kelly, James. *"That Damn'd Thing Called Honour": Duelling in Ireland, 1570–1860.* Cork, Ireland: Cork University Press, 1995.

Kenny, Kevin, ed. *Ireland and the British Empire.* Oxford: Oxford University Press, 2004.

Kenyon-Jones, Christine. *Kindred Brutes: Animals in Romantic-Period Writing.* Aldershot, U.K.: Ashgate Press, 2001.

Kete, Kathleen. *The Beast in the Boudoir: Petkeeping in Nineteenth-Century Paris.* Berkeley, Calif.: University of California Press, 1994.

Kingsolver, Barbara, Camille Kingsolver, and Steven L. Hopp. *Animal, Vegetable, Miracle: A Year of Food Life.* New York: HarperCollins, 2007.

Kramer, Molly Baer. "Broome, Arthur MacLoughlin [Arthur Eugenius] (1779–1837)." *Oxford Dictionary of National Biography.* Oxford: Oxford University Press, 2004. http://www.oxforddnb.com/view/article/38498.

Kuzniar, Alice A. *Melancholia's Dog.* Chicago: University of Chicago Press, 2006.

Lamb, John. [Attributed] *A Letter to the Right Hon. William Windham, on his opposition to Lord Erskine's Bill, for the Prevention of Cruelty to Animals.* London: 1810.

Lawrence, John. *The Horse in All His Varieties and Uses.* London: 1829.

———. *Philosophical and Practical Treatise on Horses, and on the Moral Duties of Man towards the Brute Creation.* 2 vols. 3rd ed. London: 1810.

Lean, Garth. *God's Politician: William Wilberforce's Struggle.* London: Darton, Longman and Todd, 1980.

Lee, Rawdon B. *A History and Description of the Modern Dogs of Great Britain and Ireland: Non-sporting Division.* London: Horace Cox, 1894.

Lemmings, David. "Erskine, Thomas, first Baron Erskine (1750–1823)." *Oxford Dictionary of National Biography.* Oxford: Oxford University Press, 2004. http://www.oxforddnb.com/view/article/8873.

Li, Chien-hui, "A Union of Christianity, Humanity, and Philanthropy: The Christian Tradition and the Prevention of Cruelty to Animals in Nineteenth-Century England." *Society & Animals: Journal of Human-Animal Studies* 8, no. 3 (2000). http://www.psyeta.org/sa/sa8.3/chien.shtml.

The Life and Adventures of Toby, the Sapient Pig: with his opinions on Men and Manners. Written by Himself. London: [1805].

Lippincott, Louise, and Andreas Blühm. *Fierce Friends: Artists and Animals, 1750–1900.* London: Merrell Publishers, 2005.

Locke, John. *Essay Concerning Human Understanding.* Ed. by Peter Nidditch. Oxford: Clarendon Press, 1975.

———. *Some Thoughts Concerning Education.* Ed. by John W. Yolto and Jean Yolto. Oxford: Clarendon Press, 1989.

Lonsdale, Roger, ed. *Eighteenth-Century Women Poets.* Oxford: Oxford University Press, 1989.

Lovejoy, Arthur O. *The Great Chain of Being: A Study in the History of an Idea.* Cambridge, Mass.: Harvard University Press, 1936.

Lynam, Shevawn. *Humanity Dick Martin: "King of Connemara," 1754–1834.* Lilliput Press, 1989.

Lyson, Daniel. "Collectanea." Scrapbook, British Library c. 103. k. 11.

MacCarthy, Mary. *Fighting Fitzgerald and Other Papers.* New York: Putnam, 1931.

Macaulay, Thomas Babington. *The History of England.* Vol. 1. London: Longmans, Green, 1867.

Mack, Maynard. *Alexander Pope: A Life.* New York: Norton, 1985.

Maehle, Andreas-Holger, and Ulrich Tröhler, "Animal Experimentation from Antiquity to the End of the Eighteenth Century: Attitudes and Arguments." In Nicolaas A. Rupke, ed., *Vivisection in Historical Perspective.* London: Routledge, 1990.

Malcolmson, Robert W. *Popular Recreations in English Society, 1700–1850.* Cambridge, U.K.: Cambridge University Press, 1973.

Mandeville, Bernard. *The Fable of the Bees.* London: Penguin Books, 1989.

Mason, Jennifer. *Civilized Creatures: Urban Animals, Sentimental Culture, and American Literature, 1850–1900.* Baltimore: Johns Hopkins University Press, 2005.

Masson, Jeffrey Moussaieff. *The Pig Who Sang to the Moon*. New York: Vintage, 2005.

———, and Susan McCarthy. *When Elephants Weep: The Emotional Lives of Animals*. New York: Dell, 1995.

McCreery, Cindy. *The Satirical Gaze: Prints of Women in Late Eighteenth-Century England*. Oxford: Clarendon Press, 2004.

McKay, W. R., ed. *Observations, Rules and Orders of the House of Commons*. London: Her Majesty's Stationery Office, 1989.

Memoirs of the Celebrated Mrs. Woffington. 2nd ed. London: 1760.

Memoirs of the late George R. Fitzgerald and P. R. M'Donnel . . . by a Gentleman of the Co. Mayo. Dublin: 1786.

Merchant, Carolyn. *The Death of Nature: Women, Ecology and the Scientific Revolution*. New York: Harper & Row, 1980.

Mettrie, Julian Offray de La. *Man a Machine and Man a Plant*. Trans. Richard A. Watson and Maya Rybalka. Indianapolis: Hackett, 1994.

Misson, Henri. *M. Misson's Memoirs and Observations in His Travels over England*. Translated by John Ozell. London: 1719.

Monboddo, Lord (James Burnett). *Orangutans and the Origins of Human Nature*. In Aaron Garrett, ed., *Animal Rights and Souls in the Eighteenth Century*. Vol. 6. Bristol, U.K.: Thoemmes Press, 2000.

Montaigne, Michel de. "Of Cruelty" and "Apology for Raymond Sebond." In *The Complete Works of Montaigne*. Trans. by Donald M. Frame. Palo Alto: Stanford University Press, 1958.

Moore, Thomas. *The Sin and Folly of Cruelty to Brute Animals*. Birmingham: 1810.

Morgan, Lady (Sydney Owenson). *Book of the Boudoir*. 2 vols. London: 1829.

Morley, Henry. *Memoirs of Bartholomew Fair*. London: George Routledge and Sons, 1892.

Moss, Arthur. *Valiant Crusade: The History of the R.S.P.C.A.* London: Cassell, 1961.

Mullan, John, and Christopher Reid, eds. *Eighteenth-Century Popular Culture: A Selection*. Oxford: Oxford University Press, 2000.

The New Parliament. An Appendix to the Black Book. 3rd ed. London: 1826.

Nicholson, George. *On the Primeval Diet of Man: Vegetarianism and Human Conduct Towards Animals*. Ed. by Rod Preece. Lewiston, N.Y.: Edwin Mellen Press, 1999.

Nicolson, Marjorie, and G. S. Rousseau. *"This Long Disease, My Life": Alexander Pope and the Sciences*. Princeton, N.J.: Princeton University Press, 1968.

Nussbaum, Felicity A. *The Limits of the Human: Fictions of Anomaly, Race and Gender in the Long Eighteenth Century*. Cambridge, U.K.: Cambridge University Press, 2003.

On Cruelty to Beasts. Liverpool: n.d.

Oswald, John. *The Cry of Nature; or, An Appeal to Mercy and to Justice, on behalf of the Persecuted Animals*. 1791. In Aaron Garrett, ed., *Animal Rights and Souls in the Eighteenth Century*. Vol. 4. Bristol, U.K.: Thoemmes Press, 2000.

Pacificus, Philo. *The Friend of Peace*. Vol. 4. Cambridge, U.K.: 1827.

Pain, Wellesley. *Richard Martin*. London: Leonard Parsons, 1925.

Palette, Peregrine. *Crayons from the Commons; or, Members in Relievo*. London: 1831.

Palmeri, Frank, ed. *Humans and Other Animals in Eighteenth-Century British Culture.* Burlington, Vt.: Ashgate, 2006.

Parr, Samuel. *Discourse on Education and on the Plans Pursued in Charity Schools.* London: 1786.

Parissien, Steven. *George IV: Inspiration of the Regency.* New York: St. Martin's Press, 2001.

Passmore, John. *Man's Responsibility for Nature.* New York: Scribners, 1974.

Paulson, Ronald, ed. *Hogarth's Graphic Works.* 2 vols. New Haven: Yale University Press, 1970.

Pepys, Samuel. *The Diary of Samuel Pepys: A New and Complete Transcription.* 10 vols. Ed. by Robert Latham and William Matthews. Berkeley, Calif.: University of California Press, 1970–1983.

Percival, Thomas. *Father's Instructions, Consisting of Moral Tales, Fables and Reflections.* London: 1776.

Perkin, Harold. *The Origins of Modern English Society, 1780–1880.* London: Routledge and Kegan Paul, 1969.

Perkins, David. *Romanticism and Animal Rights.* Cambridge, Mass.: Cambridge University Press, 2003.

Phelps, Norm. *The Longest Struggle: Animal Advocacy from Pythagoras to PETA.* New York: Lantern Books, 2007.

Phillips, Peter. *Humanity Dick: The Eccentric Member for Galway.* Tunbridge Wells, U.K.: Parapress, 2003.

Pickering, Samuel F., Jr. *John Locke and Children's Books in Eighteenth-Century England.* Knoxville: Tennessee University Press, 1981.

———. *Moral Instruction for Children, 1749–1820.* Athens, Ga.: University of Georgia Press, 1993.

The Pigs Petition Against Bartholomew-Fair; With Their Humble Thanks to those Unworthy Preservers of So Much Innocent Blood. 1712. In John Mullan and Christopher Reid, eds., *Eighteenth-Century Popular Culture: A Selection.* Oxford: Oxford University Press, 2000.

Pinks, William J. *The History of Clerkenwell.* Ed. by Edward J. Wood. London: 1865.

Plumptre, James, and Thomas Lantaffe. *The Experienced Butcher.* London: 1816.

Pollack, John. *Wilberforce.* Tring, U.K.: Lion Publishing, 1977.

Pollan, Michael. *The Omnivore's Dilemma.* New York: Penguin, 2006.

Pope, Alexander. "Against Barbarity to Animals." In John Calhoun Stephens, ed., *The Guardian.* No. 61, 233–37. Lexington: University Press of Kentucky, 1982.

———. *The Poems of Alexander Pope.* Ed. by John Butt. New Haven: Yale University Press, 1963.

Porter, Roy. "The Environment and the Enlightenment: The English Experience." In Lorraine Daston and Gianna Pomata, eds. *The Faces of Nature in Enlightenment Europe.* Berlin: Berliner Wisssenschafts-Verlag, 2003.

Porter, Roy. "The People's Health in Georgian England." In Tim Harris, ed., *Popular Culture in England, c. 1500–1850.* New York: St. Martin's Press, 1995.

Pratt, Samuel Jackson. *Pity's Gift: A Collection of Interesting Tales, to Excite the Compassion of Youth for the Animal Creation.* London: 1798.

———. *The Triumph of Benevolence*. London: 1786.

Preece, Rod. *Awe for the Tiger, Love for the Lamb: A Chronicle of Sensibility to Animals.* Vancouver, B.C.: University of British Columbia Press, 2002.

———. *Brute Souls, Happy Beasts and Evolution: The Historical Status of Animals.* Vancouver, B.C.: University of British Columbia Press, 2005.

Preston, Claire. *Bee*. London: Reaktion Books, 2006.

Primatt, Humphrey. *A Dissertation on the Duty of Mercy and Sin of Cruelty to Brute Animals.* 1776. In Aaron Garrett, ed., *Animal Rights and Souls in the Eighteenth Century.* Vol. 3. Bristol, U.K.: Thoemmes Press, 2000.

———. *The Duty of Mercy and the Sin of Cruelty to Brute Animals.* Ed. by Arthur Broome. London: 1822.

The Proceedings of the Old Bailey, 1674–1834. http://www.oldbaileyonline.org/. Prospectus, Royal Society for the Prevention of Cruelty to Animals. London: 1824.

Rawnsley, Rev. H. D. *The Story of Gough and His Dog on Hellvellyn.* Carlisle, U.K.: 1892.

Regenstein, Lewis G. *Replenish the Earth: A History of Organized Religion's Treatment of Animals and Nature.* New York: Crossroad, 1991.

Register Book of the Royal Society. Copy II: 1666–1667. Available in the Scientific Archives of the Royal Society, London.

Report of the Society for Preventing Wanton Cruelty to Brute Animals. Instituted at Liverpool, October 25, 1809. Liverpool: 1809.

Richmond, Leigh. *A Sermon on the Sin of Cruelty towards the Brute Creation.* Bath, U.K., 1802.

Ridley, Glynis. *Clara's Grand Tour: Travels with a Rhinoceros in Eighteenth-Century Europe.* New York: Atlantic Monthly Press, 2004.

Riskin, Jessica. "The Defecating Duck; or, The Ambiguous Origins of Artificial Life." *Critical Inquiry* 29, no. 4 (2003): 599–633.

Ritvo, Harriet. *The Animal Estate: The English and Other Creatures in the Victorian Age.* Cambridge, Mass.: Harvard University Press, 1987.

———. *The Platypus and the Mermaid and Other Figments of the Classifying Imagination.* Cambridge, Mass.: Harvard University Press, 1997.

Robbins, Louise E. *Elephant Slaves and Pampered Parrots: Exotic Animals in Eighteenth-Century Paris.* Baltimore: Johns Hopkins University Press, 2002.

Roberts, M.J.D. *Making English Morals: Voluntary Association and Moral Reform in England, 1787–1886.* Cambridge, U.K.: Cambridge University Press, 2004.

Rogers, Katharine M. *Cat*. London: Reaktion Books, 2006.

———. *The Cat and the Human Imagination: Feline Images from Bast to Garfield.* Ann Arbor: University of Michigan Press, 2000.

———. *First Friend: A History of Dogs and Humans.* New York: St. Martin's Press, 2005.

Rollin, Bernard E. *The Unheeded Cry: Animal Consciousness, Animal Pain and Science.* Oxford: Oxford University Press, 1989.

Romilly, Samuel. *Memoirs of the Life of Sir Samuel Romilly, Written by Himself.* 3 vols. London: John Murray, 1840.

Rosenfeld, Sybil. *The Theatre of the London Fairs in the 18th Century.* Cambridge, U.K.: Cambridge University Press, 1960.

Rosenfield, Leonora. *From Beast-Machine to Man-Machine.* New York: Oxford University Press, 1941.

Rousseau, George Sebastian. "The Consumption of Meat in an Age of Materialism: Materialism, Vitalism, and some Enlightenment Debates over National Stereotypes." In Robert C. Leitz III and Kevin Cope, eds., *Imagining the Sciences: Expressions of New Knowledge in the "Long" Eighteenth Century.* New York: AMS Press, 2004.

Rowe, M. J., and W. H. McBryde. "Pulteney, Sir William, fifth baronet (1729–1805)." *Oxford Dictionary of National Biography.* Oxford: Oxford University Press, 2004. http://www.oxforddnb.com/view/article/56208.

Ryder, Richard D. *Animal Revolution: Changing Attitudes Towards Speciesism.* 2nd ed. Oxford: Berg, 2000.

———. "Martin, Richard (1754–1834)." *Oxford Dictionary of National Biography,* Oxford: Oxford University Press, 2004. http://www.oxforddnb.com/view/article/18207.

———. "Primatt, Humphrey (bap. 1735, d. 1776/7)." *Oxford Dictionary of National Biography.* Oxford: Oxford University Press, 2004. http://www.oxforddnb.com/view/article/47020.

Sabloff, Annabelle. *Reordering the Natural World: Humans and Animals in the City.* Toronto: University of Toronto Press, 2001.

Schlosser, Eric. *Fast Food Nation.* New York: HarperCollins, 2002.

Scully, Matthew. *Dominion: The Power of Man, the Suffering of Animals, and the Call to Mercy.* New York: St. Martin's, 2001.

Siebert, Charles. "An Elephant Crackup?" *The New York Times Magazine,* 8 Oct. 2006. http://www.nytimes.com/2006/10/08/magazine/08elephant.html.

Shell, Marc. "The Family Pet." *Representations* 15 (1986): 121–53.

Shelley, Percy Bysshe. *The Complete Works of Percy Bysshe Shelley.* Roger Ingpen and Walter E. Peck, eds. Vol 6. New York: Gordian Press, 1965.

Shesgreen, Sean, ed. *The Criers and Hawkers of London: Engravings and Drawings by Marcellus Laroon.* Stanford, Calif.: Stanford University Press, 1990.

Shugg, Wallace. "The Cartesian Beast-Machine in English Literature (1663–1750)." *Journal of the History of Ideas* 29, no. 2 (1968): 279–92.

———. "Humanitarian Attitudes in the Early Animal Experiments of the Royal Society." *Annals of Science* 24, no. 3 (1968): 228–38.

The Sin of Cruelty. London: Religious Tract Society, no. 51, n.d.

Singer, Peter. *Animal Liberation.* 2nd ed. London: Jonathan Cape, 1990.

———, and Jim Mason. *The Way We Eat: Why Our Food Choices Matter.* Emmaus, Penn.: Rodale, 2006.

A Sketch of the Character of the Late Lord Erskine. London: 1823.

Society for the Prevention of Cruelty to Animals Minute Book, 1824–1832. Available at the Royal Society for the Prevention of Cruelty to Animals Headquarters, Horsham, West Sussex.

Society for the Prevention of Cruelty to Animals Prospectus. London: 1824.

Spence, Joseph. *Observations, Anecdotes, and Characters of Books and Men.* Ed. by James Osborn. 2 vols. Oxford: Clarendon Press, 1966.

Spencer, Colin. *The Heretic's Feast: A History of Vegetarianism*. Hanover, N.H.: University Press of New England, 1993.

Spiegel, Marjorie. *The Dreaded Comparison: Human and Animal Slavery*. New York: Mirror Books, 1998.

Sprat, Thomas. *The History of the Royal-Society of London*. London: 1667.

St. André, Nathaniel. *A Short Narrative of an Extraordinary Delivery of Rabbets, Perform'd by Mr. John Howard Surgeon at Guilford, published by M. St. André Surgeon and Anatomist to his Majesty*. London: 1727.

Steiner, Gary. *Anthropocentrism and Its Discontents*. Pittsburgh: University of Pittsburgh Press, 2005.

———. "Descartes on the Moral Status of Animals." *Archiv für Geschichte der Philosophie* 80, no. 3 (1998): 268–91.

Steintrager, James A. *Cruel Delight: Enlightenment Culture and the Inhuman*. Bloomington: Indiana University Press, 2004.

Stevenson, Lloyd G. "On the Supposed Exclusion of Surgeons and Butchers from Jury Duty." *Journal of the History of Medicine and Allied Sciences* 9 (April 1954): 235–38.

Stockdale, Percival. *A Remonstrance against Inhumanity to Animals, and particularly against the savage practice of Bull-Baiting*. Alnwick, U.K.: 1802.

The Story of the Learned Pig. By an Officer of the Royal Navy. London: 1786.

Strandh, Sigvard. *A History of the Machine*. Trans. by Ann Henning. New York: A & W Publishers, 1979.

Strutt, Joseph. *The Sports and Pastimes of the People of England*. Ed. by Charles Cox. Detroit: Singing Tree Press, 1968.

Stryker, Lloyd Paul. *For the Defense: Thomas Erskine*. New York: Doubleday, 1947.

Stuart, Tristram. *The Bloodless Revolution: Radical Vegetarians and the Discovery of India*. London: HarperCollins, 2006.

Swift, Jonathan. *Gulliver's Travels*. Oxford: Oxford University Press, 2005.

Sydney, W. C. "Hill, Sir Richard, second baronet (1733–1808)," rev. S. J. Skedd. *Oxford Dictionary of National Biography*. Oxford: Oxford University Press, 2004. http://www.oxforddnb.com/view/article/13290.

Taylor, Eric. *The House of Commons at Work*. London: Macmillan, 1979.

Taylor, Thomas. *A Vindication of the Rights of Brutes* (1927). Gainesville, Fla.: Scholars' Facsimiles & Reprints, 1966.

Thomas, Elizabeth Marshall. *The Hidden Life of Dogs*. New York: Houghton Mifflin, 1993.

———. *The Tribe of Tiger*. New York: Simon & Schuster, 1994.

Thompson, E. P. *Whigs and Hunters: The Origin of the Black Act*. New York: Pantheon, 1975.

Thorne, R. G., ed. *The History of Parliament: The House of Commons*. 5 vols. London: Secker and Warburg, 1986.

Thomas, Keith. *Man and the Natural World: Changing Attitudes in England, 1500–1800*. Oxford: Oxford University Press, 1983.

Todd, Dennis. *Imagining Monsters: Miscreations of Self in Eighteenth-Century England*. Chicago: University of Chicago Press, 1995.

Toogood, John. *The Book of Nature: A Discourse on Some of Those Instances of the Power, Wisdom, and Goodness of God, which are within the reach of common observation.* 4th ed. Boston: 1802.

Trimmer, Sarah. *Fabulous Histories.* London: 1786.

———. *The History of the Robins.* London: 1821.

Turner, E. S. *All Heaven in a Rage.* London: Michael Joseph, 1964.

Turner, James. *Reckoning with the Beast.* Baltimore: Johns Hopkins University Press, 1980.

Tyson, Edward. *The Anatomy of a Pygmy Compared with that of a Monkey, an Ape, and a Man.* 2nd ed. London: 1751.

Uffenbach, Zacharias Conrad von. *London in 1710: From the Travels of Zacharias Conrad von Uffenbach.* Trans. and ed. by W. H. Quarrell and Margaret Mare. London: Faber & Faber, 1934.

Uglow, Jenny. *Hogarth: A Life and a World.* London: Faber & Faber, 1997.

———. *The Lunar Men: The Friends Who Made the Future.* London: Faber & Faber, 2002.

The Voice of Humanity. London: 1830–32.

The Voice of Humanity: Observations on a Few of the Instances of Cruelty to Animals, against which no legislative provision is made. London: 1827.

Voltaire. *Philosophical Dictionary.* Trans. by Peter Gay. New York: Basic Books, 1962.

Wakefield, Dick. *Anna Laetitia Barbauld.* London: Centaur Press, 2001.

Walpole, Horace. *The Letters of Horace Walpole.* Vol. 1. Ed. by Peter Cunningham. Edinburgh: 1906.

Ward, Edward. *The London Spy.* Ed. by Kenneth Fenwick. London: Folio Society, 1955.

Whitaker, Katie. *Mad Madge: The Extraordinary Life of Margaret Cavendish, Duchess of Newcastle, the First Woman to Live by Her Pen.* New York: Basic Books, 2002.

White, Gilbert. *The Natural History and Antiquities of Selborne.* London: The Ray Society, 1993.

Wilberforce, Robert Isaac, and Samuel Wilberforce. *The Life of William Wilberforce.* 5 vols. London: John Murray, 1838.

———, eds. *The Correspondence of William Wilberforce.* 2 vols. London: 1840.

Wilkinson, David. "Windham, William (1750–1810)." *Oxford Dictionary of National Biography.* Oxford: Oxford University Press, 2004. http://www.oxforddnb.com/view/article/29725.

Wilkinson, Lise. *Animals and Disease: An Introduction to the History of Comparative Medicine.* Cambridge, U.K.: Cambridge University Press, 1992.

Williamson, Karina. "Smart, Christopher (1722–1771)." *Oxford Dictionary of National Biography.* Oxford: Oxford University Press, 2004. http://www.oxforddnb.com/view/article/25739.

———, ed. *Jubilate Agno. The Poetical Works of Christopher Smart.* Vol. 1. Oxford: Clarendon Press, 1980.

Wilson, Ben. *The Making of Victorian Values: Decency and Dissent in Britain, 1789–1837.* New York: Penguin Press, 2007.

Windham, William. *The Windham Papers.* 2 vols. London: Herbert Jenkins, 1913.

Wise, Steven M. *Rattling the Cage: Towards Legal Rights for Animals.* Cambridge, Mass.: Perseus Books, 2000.

Wolf, Lucien. "Gompertz, Lewis (1783/4–1861)," rev. Ben Marsden. *Oxford Dictionary of National Biography.* Oxford: Oxford University Press, 2004. http://www.oxforddnb.com/view/article/10934.

Wolfe, Cary, ed. *Zoontologies: The Question of the Animal.* Minneapolis: University of Minnesota Press, 2003.

The Wonder of Wonders; or, A True and Perfect Narrative of a Woman near Guildford in Surrey, who was Delivered lately of Seventeen Rabbits, and Three Legs of a Tabby Cat, &c. Ipswich, U.K.: 1726.

Woodforde, James. *The Diary of a Country Parson, 1758–1802.* Ed. by John Beresford. Oxford: Oxford University Press, 1935.

Wordsworth, William. *Poems.* Ed. by John Hayden. New Haven: Yale University Press, 1981.

Youatt, William. *The Obligation and Extent of Humanity to Brutes* (1839). Lewiston, N.Y.: Edwin Mellen Press, 2003.

Young, Edward. *The Complete Works.* 1854. http://lion.chadwyck.com/toc.do?action=new&divLevel=0&mapping=toc&area=Poetry&id=Z000545535&forward=tocMarc&DurUrl=Yes.

Young, Thomas. *An Essay on Humanity to Animals.* 1798. In Aaron Garrett, ed., *Animal Rights and Souls in the Eighteenth Century.* Vol. 5. Bristol, U.K.: Thoemmes Press, 2000.

ACKNOWLEDGMENTS

IN WRITING *For the Love of Animals,* I have once again benefited from the assistance, the support, and, best of all, the friendship of a group of people who have come to occupy a special place in my life. My first thanks go to my wonderful agent, Amy Rennert, for her advice and encouragement, and especially for the warm friendship she and her partner, Louise Kollenbaum, have extended to me. It is a friendship I treasure: they are two of my favorite people, with whom I have had many good times, in Los Angeles and San Francisco, New York and London, and I look forward to many, many more to come.

I also owe Amy a debt of gratitude for bringing me into the fold of Henry Holt. There I met Kenn Russell, Holt's executive managing editor, who has given me invaluable advice on many occasions throughout the entire process of writing, and whom I love as a dear friend, sharing recipes, theater gossip, reading recommendations, and the pleasures of New York and London. I also want to extend particular thanks to my editor, Helen Atsma, who came into this project at a late stage and, faced with the unenviable task of replacing a beloved predecessor, did so with warmth, humor, enthusiasm, dedication, and impeccable editorial judgment. This book is much the better for her work on it, and it has been a great pleasure working with her.

It has been another great pleasure to work once more with Supurna Banerjee, who is as lovely as ever, and the soul of graceful efficiency. And I have been delighted to work again with Jolanta Benal, copy editor extraordinaire, humbling as it was to look at my manuscript after she finished with it; as a dog trainer who lives in a house full of pets, Jolanta is my ideal reader in every sense. My thanks go also to Matthew Enderlin, both for his helpful advice on images and for the pleasures of his friendship, company, and excellent cooking, and to Holt's art director, Lisa Fyfe, for the truly wonderful cover design. (One of my friends declared herself "in love with that dog," and so am I!) I would also like to thank John Sterling for his consistent interest in, and support of, this project.

Finally, I want to convey my thanks to my original editor, George Hodgman, who, despite having moved recently to another publishing house, remains engaged with this book in ways both helpful and hilarious. Over the course of two books, I have learned much from him—some of which actually has to do with book writing. Most important, George remains a deeply cherished friend.

I would like to express my gratitude, once again, to our dear friends in London: first, Dana Kubick and Mark Leffler, and Avril and John Marcus, for their hospitality, companionship, and generosity in taking us on all those lovely excursions to National Trust houses and country pubs. I am grateful to Dana, as well, for reading draft chapters of the work in progress, and her constant encouragement. I am also grateful for the advice, encouragement, and friendship of Joss Bennathan, Annie Tunnicliffe, Sudha Berry, Nicki Faircloth (who gave me useful information about Horace Walpole's pets), and her husband, Duncan. Most of this book has been researched and much of it written in the beautiful and welcoming Islington home of Sir Eric and Lady Ash—Eric and Clare—who have made us feel, often quite literally, that their house is our house, too. I also want to thank Eric, former treasurer of the Royal Society, for introducing me to the society's library and archives.

My research for this book was conducted primarily in and near London. I would like to thank the staff of the archives of the Royal Society for the Prevention of Cruelty to Animals, located in Horsham, West Sussex: particularly Christopher Reed, who has patiently and helpfully answered my questions, and Pat Squire, who warmly welcomed me when I did research there. Thanks also to Becky Murray of the RSPCA photo library. Thanks are due to the staffs of the British Library in London, particularly the Rare Books and the Manuscripts reading rooms; the National Archives at Kew; the London Metropolitan Archives; the Royal Society Library; the Guildhall Library; the National Gallery; and the National Portrait Gallery. In the United States, I'd like to thank the staffs of the Huntington Library, the UCLA Libraries, and the St. Louis Art Museum. A huge debt of gratitude is owed to the staff of the Geisel Library on my home campus, the University of California, San Diego, especially the Inter-library Loan and Circulation staffs, without whose work I could not have written this book.

Particular thanks go to my friend Rob Melton, our theatergoing companion and Geisel Library's Literature and Theatre bibliographer, who has helped often with books and information; and to Lynda Claassen, head of the Mandeville Special Collections Library at UCSD, for her invaluable assistance with illustrations. Many other friends have played valuable roles, direct and indirect, in making this book possible. I want to thank Michele Greenstein for her work on my Web site, and for the hospitality she and her husband, Jack Greenstein, have showed us on many occasions. Steve Ilott helped me with advice about particular images, kept me notified of relevant books in the arts, and has been a constant friend and encourager. Karen Hollis read early drafts and gave me very useful feedback. Heather Fowler generously and patiently has instructed me in the ways of MySpace and Facebook, for which I am deeply grateful. I would also like to thank Ann Laddon, Adrian Jaffer, Lori Chamberlain (and her dogs Franklin and Ruby, companions on our lagoon walks), Michael Davidson, Don Wayne, Susan Smith, Sheldon Nodelman, Louis Montrose, Robert Folkenflik, Shelley Streeby, Curtis Marez, Lucinda Rubio-Barrack, Camille Forbes, Deborah Morrow, Jennifer Janis, Dr. John Beccari and Dr. Justie Ryman. Lisa Stefanacci, proprietor of Book Works bookstore, generously hosted my launch party. My trips to London would not have been possible without the excellent cat care and reliable house-sitting of Karen Van Ness. I'd like to thank my colleagues in the Literature Department of UCSD for a supportive work environment, and want to extend a special thanks to my former and present graduate and undergraduate students of recent years, especially Ted McCombs, Emily Kugler, Jamie Rosenthal, Neal Ahuja, Amie Filkow, John Higgins, Jessica Audino, and the members of my LTEN/120 Class in winter 2008. Thanks also to Lillian Nedwick, who was a resourceful and energetic research assistant.

I appreciate the support I have received from members of my family: from my sisters, Susan Schenck, Mary Kay Eckhart, and Nancy Helphenstine, and my parents, George and Jane Shevelow, who encouraged us to fill our house with dogs, cats, hamsters, turtles, gerbils, guppies, and goldfish as we grew up. I'd like to thank my stepdaughter, Susanna Lee, her husband, Denis Crean, and their daughter, Charlotte; and Sandra Lee, Erik tenBroeke, Peter Kok, and Maya and Sara tenBroeke. Our cats Chloe, Graham, and Maxine were constant presences on my desk during the writing of this book, and certainly left their virtual (and sometimes literal) paw prints on it in many ways.

Final thanks go to two people who were crucial in innumerable ways to my writing this book. Milane Christiansen—fellow cat lover, mixer of the world's best gin and tonic, and fount of book-trade wisdom gleaned from her three decades as owner of the Book Works of Del Mar, California, a national treasure—has been so generous so often with her help, advice, and encouragement that I cannot begin to catalog her contributions. Her comments when reading the early chapters were critical in establishing the shape of this book, and I have relied on her expert advice and friendship every step of the way.

Once again, my last and greatest thanks go to my husband, Edward Lee, who has given his time, his assistance, and his moral, technical, and logistical help when it was most needed. He read the entire manuscript carefully and made invaluable suggestions about both form and content, and I benefited enormously from his professional knowledge of the ancient, medieval, and early modern philosophical traditions. More mundanely, but no less crucially, he also looked after the cats when I took research trips, and he staged a one-man cooking, cleaning, and dishwashing production that ran many weeks when I was spending long days in front of the word processor. This book could not have been written without his support and love, in which I am, as always, greatly blessed.

INDEX

Note: Page numbers in *italics* refer to illustrations

ABOUT THE AUTHOR

A SPECIALIST IN eighteenth-century British literature and culture, Kathryn Shevelow is an award-winning professor at the University of California at San Diego. She is the author of *Charlotte: Being a True Account of an Actress's Flamboyant Adventures in Eighteenth-Century London's Wild and Wicked Theatrical World* and *Women and Print Culture;* she lives in Solana Beach, California.